PARIS
BY THE NUMBERS

Ultra Travel Guide to Paris

"As Necessary As Your Passport"

Bonne Journée!
Kathleen Goodman
your Wellness Community
friend & French connection.

Paris By The Numbers

www.parisbythenumbers.com

Published by
KLG Marketing
10 N. Kingshighway Blvd., Suite 5-C
St. Louis, Missouri 63108 USA

Cover Photography by Hiroko Saita
Photography by Ed Goodman
Layout and Design by Greig Graphics
www.greigweb.com

Printed in the United States of America, Corley Printing Co.
ISBN 0-9748937-3-0
Library of Congress Control Number 2004090711
SAN 257-9928

Travelers using ***Paris By The Numbers*** are welcome to share your suggestions, comments and ideas for future editions by writing to the publisher. For bulk sales inquires, please contact KLG Marketing via **www.parisbythenumbers.com**

Here's What Readers Say

*"Paris is a city I love and **PBTN** is a great addition to my collection! I'll be taking it on my next trip to Paris!"*

Cheryl Matzker, O'Fallon, IL

"I have received your book and it looks splendid. I shall recommend it to all Paris aficionados here in Denmark."

Gitte Kjaerulff, Denmark

"I'm thrilled that this book exists! It's exactly what I've been looking for!"

Cam Wilder, Paris, 15th arrondissement

*"**PBTN** is impressively organized. Most other travel guides are either addictive or practical. This one is absolutely both!"*

Kevin Payne, Ft. Lauderdale, FL

"Your book should be called "secret addresses in Paris." It's amazingly simple and so helpful."

New York Resident

"Move over Michelin!"

St. Louis Post-Dispatch

"Your book made our first experience to Paris such a treat. Lots of great memories."

Ken & Chris, San Francisco, CA

*"**Paris By The Numbers** is a real gem. I'll be the first to buy the next edition!"*

Donald Dwight, Lyme, NH

Introduction: Paris

Bonjour and Hello!

Thank you for choosing ***Paris By The Numbers*** travel guide. Our guide takes advantage of the numbered arrondissement (ah-rahn-deez-uh-mohn) and easy geographic layout of Paris to guide you around Paris from experience to experience rather than to one place after another.

There is a class of tourists who never seem to see the things they're visiting. They prefer to look at directions to the next place rather than take in what's around them now.

No other travel guide offers this unique format that makes Paris more accessible and less intimidating. ***Paris By The Numbers*** remains the most current of all Paris guidebooks and none are edited and updated as regularly to insure that you get the most current information.

Paris By The Numbers is not fancy: it is practical, easy to use, and easy to carry – yet filled with more listings, useful telephone numbers and Metro stations. A friend in Paris calls it her "secret address book of Paris." Discover Paris the way Parisians do.

- **No more shuffling between chapters of a bulky guidebook.**
- **No need to stop at every intersection to double-check where you are and where to go next.**
- **You'll know shops, restaurants, art galleries, famous sights, and historic landmarks within blocks of anywhere you find yourself in Paris.**

Getting to know the 20 arrondissements of Paris (the numbers!) is easy. The arrondissements are arranged in a spiral beginning with "1e" at the Louvre museum and circling clockwise around the River Seine, ending at "20e." They are not confusing and are very similar to postal zip codes. You will find a "number" on street signs. You will be given a "number" when asking for directions. You will be asked for a "number" by the cab driver before he drives to your desired location.

"Just when I thought no guide book would ever offer a unique perspective, I discovered ***Paris By The Numbers...***" — Emily Costas, Bonjour Paris

It's **EASY!** All you need is your favorite street map of Paris and a copy of ***Paris By The Numbers.***

It's **FUN!** on the same page - or the same chapter, you get entertaining suggestions: a famous wine bar, the best place to kiss, a free concert in a beautiful church, a new designer boutique - either down the street or right next door!

Each arrondissement has its own chapter and includes: Famous Sights, Diversions, Superlatives, Shopping, Restaurants, and Nightlife. We divide restaurants into two categories: Plats du Jour - moderately priced restaurants, cafés, and bistros; and Gastronomique - expensive gourmet feasts produced by some of the finest chefs in the world. Everything you need to make this the best trip ever!

A HINT! Take the time to read ***Paris By The Numbers*** before your trip and make some notes (or highlight) special things you want to do. Plan a day filled with our "bests" from one or several arrondissements. Perhaps you'll pick a "number" and enjoy a day in the arrondissement of your choice. Read all about the neighborhood around your hotel so you'll feel more at home. And, make sure you read our Paris Essentials and Paris Travel Tips. Visit **www.parisbythenumbers.com**.

Once you arrive in Paris, you will quickly learn that Paris has so much to do and so much to see that ***Paris By The Numbers'*** 2,115 listings will not include every shop, every café, or every restaurant and club. We're selective and distinctive in our choices. Take your real walk around Paris with ***Paris By The Numbers*** and discover Paris the way Parisians do.

Bon Voyage!

Table of Contents

Paris Essentials

Charles de Gaulle (Roissy) Airport: Information: 01.48.62.22.80. Arrival at airport may require a bus shuttle from the plane to the terminal. You will then clear customs and collect your bags. All passengers will then leave from main exit which is clearly marked SORTIE. If you have a private car reserved, your driver will be standing here holding a sign with your name on it. If you do not see them, have patience due to traffic and flight delays. It is important to have contact information such as your hotel, telephone number, car service name and telephone, just in case driver does not show up. Private car service usually costs $100, plus tip. If desirable, you can reach Paris by train from CDG to central Paris (Gare du Nord, Châtelet, St-Michel) via RER line B train from Terminal 2. The train takes you to main RER and Metro Stations: Gare-du-Nord, Châtelet-Les-Halles, St-Michel, and Denfert-Rochereau. From Terminal 1 there is free shuttle bus ("navette" in French) to the SNCF train station in Terminal 2. Taxi service takes 40-60 minutes @ $50. Shuttle service is available for two or more at 01.42.35.10.11; 01.43.90.91.91 or 01.47.37.06.56.

CDG **Airport Hotels: Hilton** (01.49.19.77.77), Ibis (01.49.19.19.19), Novotel (01.49.19.27.27), Radisson (01.60.03.63.00) All offer shuttle service.

Orly Airport: Information: 01.49.75.15.15.
Orly has two terminals: Sud (South) for international flights and Ouest (West) for domestic flights. Free shuttle service connects the two terminals. Air France buses leave from Exit E out of Orly Ouest and Exit K Platform 5 for Orly Sud. 5:45a - 11p to Gare des Invalides for under $10 USD one-way.

TIP! Don't take meterless taxi from Orly Sud or Orly Ouest. Hire a metered cab from taxi stands. It is cheaper and safer.

TIP! It is a good idea to buy a copy of "Pariscope" (published weekly, Wednesdays) at the airport and read it while you are in the car heading into Paris. There is usually a lot of morning traffic and this is a fun way to find out the weekly events, music, and entertainment during your stay. You can also buy Metro passes at the airport, too.

CURRENCY: It is a good idea to bring some Euros with you. You will find ATM machines throughout Paris and they offer the most current exchange rate. Some credit card companies charge a fee for cash advances but still come out more favorable than bank rates. French BANKS are usually open 9a-5p.

TIP! The American Express Bureaux de Change is open from 6:30a – 11p daily. Located in terminals 1, 2A, 2B, 2C, 2D, 2F at CDG/Roissy and Orly Sud.

Departure VAT Tax Forms: Make sure envelopes have proper postage - some stores do not put stamps on envelopes. At CDG Terminal 2, go to Sortie (Gate) 5. You will find yellow post box at Gate 6. VAT Rebates are given when you spend MORE

THAN $175 AT THE SAME STORE ON SAME DAY. If you want to receive a cash refund for your VAT while still in Paris, get the paperwork from the store and go to the Madelios Department Store at 23 Bd. de la Madeleine (M: Madeleine) at the corner of Rue Duphot. Take the escalator to second floor (remember that the first floor is above the ground floor), Les Trois Quartiers, and walk about 30 feet. Go to Cash Refund Department on your right. They will exchange your paperwork for cash. Please remember that you still need to go to Customs at the airport and mail the forms.

TIP! If you purchase enough to qualify, ask if the shop has VAT forms. Some shops do not readily offer the forms and not all shops have them.

Office de Tourism: 08.92.68.30.00. €.34 per minute. www.parisinfo.com

Paris Tourist Offices: In 1e: 25 Rue Pyramides (M: Pyramides) Open Mon-Saturday, 9a-7p. In 9e: 11 Rue Scribe (M: Opéra) Mon-Saturday, 9a-6:30p. In 12e: 20 Blvd Diderot (M: Gare de Lyon) Mon-Saturday 8a-6p. In 18e: 72 Blvd Rochechouart (M: Anvers) Mon-Saturday 10a-6p.

US Embassy, 8e: 2 Ave Gabriel (M: Concorde) 01.43.12.22.22. and in 1e:2 Rue Saint Florentin. 08.10.26.46.26. M-F 9a-3p.

Lost Passport, the US Consulate will issue a three-month temporary replacement.

To find the closest hospital: 01.40.27.37.81.

SOS: 01.46.21.46.46. Calls accepted 3p-11p.

Medical Emergencies: (24 hours) 47.07.77.77 (In French).

Police: (Prefecture) 01.53.71.53.71.or 01.53.73.53.73.

PHARMACIES OPEN AT NIGHT:

4e. Chatelet Les Halles, 10 Blvd de Sebastopol. 42.72.03.23.

8e. Franklin-Roosevelt, 2 Rue Jean Mermoz. 43.59.86.55.
Galerie des Champs, 84 Ave des Champs Elysées. 45.62.02.41.

9e. Place Clichy, 6 Pl de Clichy. 48.74.65.18.

14e. Pharmacie des Arts, 106 Blvd du Montparnasse, 43.35.44.88.

18e. Barbès, 64 Blvd Barbès, 46.06.02.61.

TIP! Monoprix stores are located throughout Paris and carry toiletries, clothing, food, pastries and wine. The one located in the 8e. at 52 Ave Champs Elysées (M: Franklin D Roosevelt) 53.77.65.65. is open 24/7.

METRO: This is the BEST way to travel around Paris. One ticket costs €1.30. We RECOMMEND that you buy "un carnet" or pack of ten tickets for €10.50 at the booth in any station.

TIP! The CARTE l'ORANGE is the most economical because it is good for unlimited metro/bus usage for 7 days and sold Mon-Tues-Wed. It expires on Sundays, so if you arrive on a Saturday, buy tickets as-you-go and wait until Monday. You will get a small ticket, a card, and a plastic holder. Insert a small 1" photo (there are photo machines at some Metros and train stations that will take 4 photos so two people can share.) Fill out the back of the card, attach the photo to card, seal it in the plastic holder and write the number on ticket. SAVE the packet and card with photo for future trips to Paris. Navigo passes, which are cards that contain a scan-able chip are steadily replacing the Carte l'Orange.

While at the Metro station you might consider buying the **Paris Visité**. This is good for 1 or 3 consecutive days of unlimited travel on buses, RER, SNCF, and Metro Zones 1-3 and Zones 1-5 (including Versailles, Disneyland, both airports) and works just like the Carte l'Orange, but may be easier or less expensive depending upon day of arrival.

IMPORTANT METRO NOTES: SORTIE means Exit. INTERDIT means No Entrance. CORRESPONDENCE means it is a passageway that enables you to change trains without leaving the station. Some train doors do not open automatically, so you will need to pull on handles for entering/departing. IF YOUR TICKET DOES NOT VALIDATE, do not throw it away, but go to ticket window and ask the agent to double check.

Metro trains stop running at 12:30 am

METRO LINES:

01 Château Vincennes ... La Défense

02 Nation ... Porte Dauphine

03 Gallieni ... Porte de Levallois-Becon

3b Porte des Lilas ... Gambetta

04 Porte d'Orléans ... Porte de Clignancourt

05 Place d'Italie ... Bobigny

06 Nation ... Charles-de-Gaulle-Etoile

07 Marie d'Ivry ... La Courneuve

08 Balard ... Creteil-Prefecture

09 Porte de Sevrés ... Marie de Montreuil

10 Gare d'Austerlitz...Boulogne-Pont de Saint Cloud

11 Châtelet ... Marie des Lilas

12 Marie d'Issy ... Porte de la Chapelle

13 Saint-Denis ... Chatillon-Montrouge

14 Bibliothèque F. Mitterrand ... Madeleine

BUSES use same ticket as Metro and bus maps are free at Metro stations. Buses run from 6:30am to 8:30 pm and generally require one ticket.

RATP telephone is 08.92.68.77.14.

BALABUS only runs Sundays and national holidays from RATP Metro stations, 12:30p – 8:30p. They are a good, economical way to see Paris with stops along the way. They run from Gare de Lyon to Grand Arche de Defense on the Right Bank and then on to the Left Bank. You can use your Metro passes.

BATOBUS: 44.11.33.99. Seine Riverboats stop at Tour Eiffel, Musée d'Orsay, St-Germain-des-Prés, Notre-Dame, Hotel de Ville, Louvre, and Champs Elysées and can be a good substitute for Metro. They run April - October. Cost €3.50 per stop or day pass for €10.

TIP! Art Process Bus Tours: 47.00.90.85. Begin at Opera Bastille (12e) and run every 3rd Saturday. €50 Reservation required and includes lunch. In French with bilingual guide.

RAIL Information: 7a-10p every day (.34 charge) for SNCF schedules, fares, reservations. 08.92.35.35.35. RATP, Metro, Bus Information at same charge at 08.91.36.20.20. English.

TAXIS can be found at designated "streets/stations" and usually will not stop if hailed. BE SURE you have name, arrondissement number, and telephone number of your destination written down in case there is a translation problem. Taxis now charge minimum fares. By law, taxis do not allow person to sit in front seat.

BIKE TOURS. Fat Tire, 24 Rue Edgar Faure, 15e. (M: Dupleix) 01.56.58.10.54/www.fattirebiketoursparis.com In English. Day €24/Evening €28. No credit cards.Offers walking tours too. Another is Paris a Velo, 28 rue Baudin (M: Richard Lenoir) 01.48.87.60.01. Reservations usually required.

MOTORBIKE Taxis. City-bird, 08.26.10.01.00. will pick you up and take you where you want to go. They also offer motorbike tours.

SEINE RIVER CRUISES are fun. (At night you can peek inside the mansions along the Seine because of all the lights.) The barges are open for day, evening, lunch, and dinner cruises. Call for schedule and information:

Bateaux-Mouches, 8e (M: Alma-Marceau) 40.76.99.99.

Bateaux Parisiens, Left Bank, 7e, Port de la Bourdonnais (M: Bir Hakeim)

Bateau Parisiens, Right Bank, 5e, Quai Montebello Pier (M: St-Michel) 44.11.33.44.

Vedettes de Pont Neuf, 1e, Square du Vert-Galant (M: Pont Neuf) 46.33.98.38.

Vedettes de Paris, 7e, Port de Suffren (M: Bir Hakeim) 47.05.71.29.

Yachts de Paris, 4e, Port Henri IV (M: Quai de la Rapee)
Dinner cruises for private hire or individuals. 44.54.14.70.

Carte Musée (Paris Museum & Monument Pass) is a Museum Pass that saves time - NO WAITING IN LINES - and is a good investment if you plan to visit a lot of museums in 1/3/5 consecutive days. €18/€36/€54. Check out the list of more than 60 participating museums before you buy to make sure your selections are included. This handy pass is usually cheaper when you purchase upon arrival in Paris at main Metro stations, fnac shops, participating museums and Office de Tourisme.

Museum and City Passes are now available before you leave. Prices are guaranteed in US dollars, so check conversion rates to get the best deal. Paris Museum & Monument Pass (see above description) from $24. Paris Visité Pass includes bus and metro ticket, discount book and tourist map, all enclosed in its own wallet. Order at www.museumpass.com or www.ticketsto.com.

TIP! Museums are free on the first Sunday of each month. Admission price to most museums and monuments are lower on other Sundays. Most are closed on Mondays, except the Louvre, which is closed on Tuesdays.

IT IS **IMPORTANT** to note that "street numbers/addresses" are marked differently than in U.S. The streets in Paris that run North and South (perpendicular to the Seine) begin with "1" at the Seine and increase as the street continues away from the River. As you face away from the Seine, odd numbers are on the left side and even numbers are on the right. East and West streets (parallel to the Seine) increase from East to West. In a nutshell, you can find yourself confused when the even numbers go down on one side and the odd numbers go up on the same street!

MAIN Post Office: Paris-Louvre, 1e. 52 Rue du Louvre (M: Louvre) is open 24 hours. 40.28.76.00. Others are open Mon-Friday 8a-6p and Saturday 8a-12p.

TELEPHONES accept only telecartes, plastic phonecards, sold at post offices, newsstands. To call the US from France, dial 00-1-area code + phone number. SPRINT: 0.800.99.00.87. AT&T: 0.800.99.00.11 or 1-800-487-7646, Card#, area code + phone number. To call France from the U.S., dial 011-33+area code (i.e. Paris is 01, Nice is 04)+phone number.

THEATRE: Tickets can be purchases for HALF-PRICE at Kiosque Theatre, Pl de la Madeleine (8e) Cash Only. Tues-Sat. 12:30p - 7:45p and Sunday. 12:30p-3:45p.

TIP! Get tickets in advance for the Moulin Rouge show ($109-207) by phone, 33.01.53.09.82.82 or online at moulinrouge.fr. Book the Lido show ($97-255) by phone, 33.01.40.76.56.10 or online at lido.fr. The smaller Au Lapin Agile reserves by phone at 33.01.46.06.85.87 or au-lapin-agile.com

ORDERING FOOD: It's a good idea to tell the waiter how you prefer your food prepared - especially if you like medium-to-well done meat. French chefs think it's a sin to serve anything well-done so most restaurants will serve it on the rare side, unless you tell them otherwise.

Paris Essentials

TIP! Cafés often charge more for drinks served at a table than at the bar, and even a little more if served at a table on the terrace. Also, if you see tables covered with a tablecloth, that means they are reserved for customers who want a meal.

TIPPING: At restaurants and bars the prices legally include a service charge, (service compris) but it's good form to leave 2-3% extra. Taxis: consider leaving additional small amount, up to 15%. Housekeepers leave $2/day. Porters get $1/bag. Hairstylists: tip well.

FRANCE ISSUES SMOKING BAN

PARIS: Smoking will be banned in most public places beginning in February 2007, and in bars, restaurants, hotels and nightclubs 11 months later.

"We have decided to ban smoking in public places, from Feb. 1, 2007," Prime Minister Dominique de Villepin told RTL radio and LCI television. Nightclubs and bars that sell tobacco would have until Jan. 1, 2008, at the latest, to comply with the rules, he said.

Public places include railroad stations, museums, government offices and shops, but the ban will not extend to the streets or to hotel rooms.

Paris Travel Tips

MUST-SEES AND DO'S

Of course! Cathédrale de Notre Dame de Paris, 1e.
Of course! Louvre, 1e.
Musée de L'Orangerie, 1e.
Sainte-Chappelle, 1e.
Marché aux Fleurs, 1e.
Musée Picasso, 3e.
Of course! Marais district, 3e. and 4e.
Of course! Boulevard St-Germain-des-Prés, 5e. 6e. 7e.
Luxembourg Gardens, 6e.
Hotel des Invalides/Napoleon's Tomb, 7e.
Musée d'Orsay, 7e.
Musée Rodin, 7e.
Of course! Tour d'Eiffel, 7e.
Of course! Arc de Triomphe, 8e.
Musée Jacquemart-André, 8e.
Musée Marmottan, 16e.
Of course! Montmartre and Sacré Coeur, 18e.

TIP! French law still keeps most shops closed on **Sundays,** unless they are located in a district that is designated as "tourism" such as parts of the Marais. Sunday is the traditional day for Parisians to bargain at flea markets or to enjoy the activities of the marchés. Since most museums are open on Sundays, this is a very busy day and you should expect crowds. However, since most museums have boutiques and gift shops, this is a good day to find unique gifts and last-minute souvenirs.

MARCHÉS AND PUCÉS:

Paris is famous for its marchés and pucés. Pucés are flea markets and Paris boasts the largest in the world. **Pucés de Clignancourt aka Pucés de St. Ouen** is in 18e. and more than 2,500 antique dealers are represented in ten main markets.

Marchés feature "natural" products such as flowers, green grocers, sausages, seafood, cheeses, mushrooms – as well as "natural talents" in works of art, jewelry, sculptures. The latter are called **marchés des creation.** Due to the propensity of the French to cook with the freshest ingredients, almost every arrondissement has a marché, so it will be easy for you to shop the way Parisians do!

Paris Travel Tips

COVERED MARKETS

(good for rainy days!)

Tues-Saturday 8a-1p and 4p – 7:30p

Sunday 8a-1p

3e Marché des Enfants Touges, 39 Rue de Bretagne (M: St-Sébastien Froissant)

6e Marché de Saint-Germain, 4-8 Rue Lobineau (M: Mabillon)

8e Marché de l'Europe, 1 Rue Corvetto (M: Miromesnil)

10e Marché Saint-Quentin, 85 bis Blvd Magenta (M: Gare de l'Est)

Marché Saint-Martin, 31-33 Rue du Château d'Eau (M: Château d'Eau)

12e Marché Beauvau, Place d'Aligre (M: Ledru-Rollin)

16e Marché Passy, Place de Passy (M: La Muette)

Marché Saint-Didier, Angle des Rues Mesnil/Sain-Didier (M: Victor Hugo)

17e Marché Batignolles, 96 bis Rue Lemercier (M: Brochant)

Marché Ternes, 8 bis Rue Lebon (M: Ternes)

18e Marché La Chapelle, 10 Rue L'Olive (M: Marx Dormoy)

19e Marché Riquet, 42 Rue Riquet (M: Riquet)

Marché Secrétan, 33 Ave Secrétan (M: Bolivar)

OPEN-AIR MARKETS

Open-Air Markets are usually open from 7a – 2:30p and among Arrondissements they rotate days, i.e. Wed/Sat or Tues/Fri or Thu/Sat

Here are some of our favorites:

1e Marché Saint-Honore, Place du Marché St-Honore (M: Pyramides) Wed/Sat

5e Marché Maubert, Pl Maubert-Mutualité (M: Maubert-Mutualité) Tues/Thu/Sat

Marché Mouffetard, Place Monge (M: Pl Monge) Wed/Fri/Sun

7e Marché Saxe Breteuil, Ave de Saxe (M: Ségur) Thu/Sat

11e Marché Bastille, Richard Lenoir Market, Blvd Richard Lenoir (M:Bastille) Thu/Sun

Marché Charonne, Blvd de Charonne (M: Alexandre-Dumas) Wed/Sat

12e Marché Ledru-Rollin, Ave Ledru-Rollin (M: Dare de Lyon) Thu/Sat

13e Marché Auguste Blanqui/Gobelins, Blvd Auguste Blanqui (M: Place d'Italie) Tues/Fri/Sun

16e Marché Président Wilson, Ave du Président Wilson (M: Iéna) Wed/Sat

SPECIALTY MARKETS AND PUCÉS:

8e Marché Timbres (stamps) Champs Elysées (M: Champs-Elysées-Clemenceau) Thu/Sat/Sun

11e Marché de la Création - Bastille, Blvd Richard-Lenoir (M: Bastille) Enter Rue Amelot or St-Sabin. Sat. 9a-7:30p

14e Marché de la Creation – Edgar Quinet,Blvd Edgar Quinet (M: Edgar-Quinet) Sun. 9a-7:30p

Pucés de Vanves, Ave de la Porte de Vanves, G. Lafenestre, and Rue Marc Sangnier (M: Porte de Vanves) Sat/Sun 7a – 7:30p

18e Pucés de Clignancourt aka Pucés de St. Ouen. The world's largest flea market

20e Pucés de Montreuil, Ave de la Porte de Montreuil (M: Porte de Montreuil) Sat/Sun/Mon 7a – 7:30p

SOME PARKS & GARDENS:

(by numbered arrondissement)

Jardins des Halles, 1e (M: Les Halles)

Jardin du Palais-Royal, 1e (M: Palais-Royal)

Jardin des Tuileries, 1e (M: Concorde)

Jardin des Plantes, 5e (M: Gare d'Austerlitz)

Jardin du Luxembourg, 6e (M: Luxembourg)

Jardin du Champ-de-Mars, 7e (M: Tour Eiffel)

Parc de Monceau, 8e (M: Monceau)

Bois de Vincennes, 12e (M: Porte-Doree)

Parc Floral de Paris, 12e (M: Chateau-de-Vincennes)

La Promenade Plantee, 12e (M: Bastille)

Parc Montsouris, 14e (M: Cité-Université)

Parc Andre Citroen, 15e (M: Balard)

Bois de Boulogne, 16e (M: Porte-Maillot)

Parc de Bagatelle, 16e (M: Porte-Maillot) within Bois de Boulogne.

Jardins du Trocadero, 16e (M: Trocadero)

Parc des Buttes-Chaumont, 19e. (M: Buttes-Chaumont)

Parc de la Villette, 19e (M: Porte de la Villette)

Parc de Belleville, 20e (M: Couronnes)

Paris Travel Tips

SOME FOUNTAINS:

(by numbered arrondissement)
Châtelet Fountain, 1e. Pl du Châtelet, Two Sphinxes. 1808.
Fontaine de la Victoire, 1e. Pl du Châtelet.
Fontaine des Innocents, 1e. Square des Inocents. Renaissance, 1547.
Molière Fountain, 1e. Rue de Richelieu.
Fontaine de Stravinsky, 4e. Pl Igor Stravinsky.
Fontaine de Pot-de-Fer, 5e. Rue Mouffetard.
Medicis Fountain, 6e. Jardin du Luxembourg.
Observatory Fountain, 6e. Jardin du Luxembourg.
Four Seasons Fountain, 7e. 57 Rue de Grenelle. 1739.
Trocadero Fountains, 16e. Pl du Trocadero.

FREE OR ALMOST FREE:

1e.

Au Duc des Lombards, free entry to this music bar during Happy Hour, 6p.
Eglise St. Eustache, free concerts and 5:30p organ recitals on Sundays.
Jardin des Tuileries.
Louvre, first Sunday of every month. Always free for 18 years and under.

2e.

Musée du Parfum, free Mon-Sat.

3e.

Musée Picasso, first Sunday of every month. Always free for 18 years and under.

4e.

Centre Pompidou, first Sunday of every month. Always free for 18 years and under.
Collège de France, free lectures, open to all.
Eglise St-Merri, free classical music Sat 9p/Sunday 4p.
Maison de Victor Hugo, permanent collection is free, temporary exhibits vary in price.
Maison Européenne de la Photographie, Wednesday evenings from 5-8p.
Pavillon de l'Arsenal, free library, video room, and photo center devoted to Paris architecture and urbanism.
The Studio, watch the dancers.

5e.

Institut du Monde Arabe, free and one of the best views of Paris.

Jardin des Plantes

Jardin de Cluny, inside Musée du Moyen Age.

Marché Mouffetard, join the fun on Sunday mornings, singing and dancing.

6e.

Café de Flore, join in the free debates on first Wednesday of each month, 7p.

Café Laurent, free jazz, good cocktails.

Jardin du Luxembourg, absolutely wonderful.

Le Select Montparnesse holds philosophy sessions on Mondays, 7p.

Le Sénat, Palais du Luxembourg, is beautiful.

Les Marionnettes du Luxembourg, barely free puppet shows.

Musée Zadkine, permanent exhibitions are free.

7e.

Américan Church, free concerts, classical usually. Donations are welcome.

Deyrolle, just go upstairs to see wonderful stuffed animals.

8e.

Parc du Monceau.

9e.

Drouot auction house, view antiques and items before auctions:

Tues, Thurs, Saturday, 11a – 6p.

Eglise de la Trinité, Thursdays 12:45 – 1:30 p, free classical or sacred music.

Fragonard Musée du Parfum, free 9a-5p. Closed Sunday.

Galeries Lafayette, a free stunning view of the Opéra Garnier and Paris rooftops.

Musée de la Parfumerie, free Mon Saturday.

Paroisee de la Sainte-Trinite, free concerts on Thursdays, 12:45p.

Printemps Haussmann, a great free view of Pl Madeleine.

11e.

Marché de la Creation Bastille, Saturdays, 9:30a – 7p, an artists' market filled with painters, photographers, sculptors.

12e.

Opéra Bastille, €5 standing-room-only tix go on sale 45 minutes before show times.

Casse-Croute à la Bastille L'Opéra, free Thursday concerts and/or lectures, 1-2p.

Parc Floral de Paris

Viaduc des Arts

Paris Travel Tips

13e.

Conservatoire de Paris Maurice Ravel, free on first-come, first-seated basis.

14e.

Cimetière du Montparnasse, cemetery has "the Kiss'", Man Ray gravestones, among others.
L'Observatoire de Paris, free the first Saturday of every month, 2:30 p.
Puces de Vanves, a favorite flea market, Saturdays and Sundays.

15e.

Watch the puzzle-makers at Puzzle Michele Wilson.

16e.

Bois de Boulogne, a fabulous huge park.
Musée Guimet's Annex, free admission into this beautiful garden.
Outdoor market on Ave President Wilson, Wednesday and Saturday mornings.
Radio France, free concerts.

18e.

Basilique Sacré Coeur.
Cimitière de Montmartre, view the graves of Dumas, Degas, Foucault, Truffaut.
I Love You wall, see the words "I Love You" in every language in the world.
Place Emile-Goudreau, for a great view.

19e.

Conservatoire National Supérieur de Musique et de Danse de Paris, free concerts most of the time.
Parc de la Villette.

20e.

Cimetière du Père Lachaise, free.
Les Lucioles, receive a free drink when you read poetry on Tuesday evenings.
Marché de Belleville, Tuesdays and Fridays.

SOME TERRACES TO ENJOY:

Beauvilliers, 18e.
Café Beaubourg, 4e.
Café Les Deux Magots, 6e.
Café L'Homme, 16e.
Café Marly, 1e.
Chez Francis, 8e.
Cour Jardin, 8e. in the interior of the Plaza Athénée.
Maison de l'Amerique Latine, 7e.
Pré Catelan, 16e.
Terrasse Hotel, 18e.

TIP! Look for Marionnaud stores throughout Paris. They vary in size, selection, and variety of merchandise but usually have lower prices than department stores.

SOME ANTIQUE CENTERS:

Association Prestige Matignon: 1e. Art galleries along Avenue Matignon, Rue du Faubourg-St-Honore and Avenue DeClasse. You might begin at (M: St Philippe du Roule) and walk East and end up at Champs-Elysées or Palais de l'Elysées.

Louvre des Antiquaires, 1e. Large gathering of antique dealers all under one roof at 2 Pl de Palais-Royal (M: Palais-Royal) 01.42.97.27.00. Open Sun/Tues 11a - 7p.

Carre Rive Gauche: 6e and 7e. Located along Left Bank streets such as Quai Voltaire, Rue de L'Universite, Rue du Bac. The association is made up of over 100 antique dealers and art galleries. 01.42.60.70.10.

Village Suisse, 15e. 78 Ave de Suffren/54 Ave de la Motte Picquet (M: La Motte Picquet) 43.06.07.22. Over 100 dealers. Mon/Thu 10:30a - 7p.

Pucés de St. Ouen, 18e. A well-known flea market, also sometimes simply called "Clignancourt." It is composed of several sections known as "markets". 142 Rue des Rosiers (M: Porte de Clignancourt) Short walk from Metro. Saturdays-Sundays.

Paris Travel Tips

PASSAGES:

18th and 19th century covered shopping arcades. Some get really touristy, while others are quite charming.

TIP! They are great for rainy days in Paris!

1e.

Passages des Pavillons, 6 Rue de Beaujolais (M: Pyramides)

Galerie Vero-Dodat, 19 Rue Jean-Jacques Rousseau (M: Palais-Royal)

2e.

Passages du Caire, 2 Pl du Caire (M: Sentier)

Passages Choiseul, 44 Rue des Petits Champs (M: Quatre-Septembre) Ironwork entrance.

Galerie Colbert, 6 Rue des Petits Champs (M: Bourse)

Passages des Princes, 97 Rue de Richelieu (M: Richelieu-Drouot)

Passage des Panoramas, 10 Rue Saint-Marc and 11 Blvd Montmartre (M: Bourse)

Galerie Vivienne, 4 Rue des Petits Champs (M: Bourse) Glass-covered arcade in stylish neighborhood.

Passage du Grand-Cerf, 145 Rue Saint-Denis (M: Etienne Marcel) Trendy

9e.

Passage Jouffroy, 10 Blvd Montmartre (M: Richelieu Druout)

Passage Verdeau, 31 bis, Rue du Faubourg-Montmartre (M: Le Pelletier)

10e.

Passage de L'industrie, 42 Rue du Faubourg-Saint-Denis (M: Strasbourg-St-Denis)

WEATHER:

Everyone asks about the weather! We've been to Paris in February when the temperature was 70° and I remember an August visit when I shivered in the rain and cold temperatures hovering at 46°. One consistent fact is that Paris is a rainy city, so bring an umbrella – or be prepared to buy one. "April in Paris" is more than a song, it is one of the driest months, on average. In our opinion, no matter when you go the city will envelope you with its charm and will not dampen your spirit of adventure and romance.

Excursions Outside of Paris

You can get SNCF rail schedules at www.sncf.com to help plan many of these day trips. We also recommend verifying schedules when you arrive in Paris. Your hotel concierge can help you. Make sure you go to the train station and buy your tickets a few days in advance.

Chartres. Recommended in nice weather. The major attraction is the Cathédrale Notre-Dame, an impressive example of Gothic architecture and stained glass windows. Free. There's a wonderful view from the tower for €4. Enjoy walking the narrow streets of this Medieval town on the Eure River. Office of Tourisme fax is 02.37.21.51.91. Enjoy lunch at Les Picholines, 6 Rue du Cheval Blanc. 02.37.36.85.84.

Get there: Hourly trains depart Paris from Gare Montparnesse.

Disneyland Paris. Have fun at Disneyland Park with Adventureland and Frontierland, Walt Disney Studios. Enter the Studios via the Front Lot to see the production Animagique, a black light show of cult cartoon clips. Open 9a – 6p. 01.60.30.60.30. Advance reservations from the U.S. at 407-934-7639. You can buy all-in-one-day Park/RER-Disneyland tickets at train stations.

Get there: RER trains depart every 15 minutes from Gare de Lyon, Châtelet-Les-Halles, and Nation. It's a 40 minute ride to Marne-La-Vallée-Chessy, 100 yards away from the entrance to the park.

Giverny. Simply put: Monet's water lilies. A wonderful day trip, in nice weather, away from the bustle of Paris into the pretty pink home of Claude Monet. See the spectacular garden and the famous water-lily pond and Japanese bridge. You will not, however, see any original Monets hanging in his studio or house. 84 rue Claude-Monet. 02.32.51.28.21. 10 a – 6p. €5.50. Closed Monday. At 99 rue Claude-Monet, visit the spacious Musée d'Art Americain, 02.32.51.94.65. You will enjoy seeing a good collection of works by American Impressionists, as well as temporary exhibitions. In between, make reservations for lunch at Les Jardins de Giverny, 02.32.21.60.80. it's an easy walk to Monet's home from here.

Get there: Depart Gare St-Lazare and arrive in Vernon in 50 minutes. You can rent bikes, but we recommend taking a 5 km taxi ride. Arrive back in Vernon with time to walk around and sip pastis at one of the cafés before getting on the train back to Paris.

TIP! Check the train schedules before you buy tickets because the routes on some of the trains make more stops along the way so it takes a little longer. Also, make sure you pre-arrange a pickup time and place with your taxi driver because it can be very crowded around Monet's home and confusing at the end of the day and this special trip deserves no worries.

Excursions Outside of Paris

La Défense. Located at the end of the Metro Line 1. You will see a collection of sculptures by masters such as César, Calder, and Miró in between high-rise buildings. The juxtaposition of urban and the open-air museum is striking. La Défense offers stunning views of Paris. The Grand Arche is one of France's most popular tourist attractions. Also, be sure to visit the museum in the centre.

Pont de Sevres. The National Museum of Ceramics. 30 minutes from Paris by Metro. Walk across the bridge over the Seine to the museum. Open daily, except Tuesdays, 10a-5p. Admission is €3. The museum houses an extensive collection of porcelain, European ceramics, French faience and Middle Eastern ceramics dating back to 4th century BC.

Get there: Take the Metro Line 9.

Reims. It's pronounced "rance", rhymes with France and, yes, you will impress everyone –and receive a return smile, by pronouncing it correctly. Stroll a quaint city, visit Notre Dame Church, built in 1211, and sip champagnes. A wonderful day. Call ahead to make appointments: Krug, 03.26.84.44.20. Louis Roederer, 03.26.40.42.11. Veuve Clicquot, 03.56.89.54.41. Pommery, 03.26.61.62.63. Some have special times for English-speaking visitors.

Get there: Trains depart from Gare de l'Est and arrive at Reims station in 90 minutes.

Versailles. It's easy to spend the entire day at the Chateau, the Gardens, the Grand and Petit Trianon. The better the weather, the better your day in Versailles will be. The Grand Appartement of Louis XIV consists of six gilded salons. The Queen's Appartement is where you will see the famous Hall of Mirrors. Marie Antoinette's favorite place was the Petit Trianon and hamlet. 01.30.83.78.00. Admission €9. Closed Mondays. From April 1 – October 1st the gardens come alive with music, the Grandes Eaux Musicales, staged on Sat/Sun at 11:00a and 3:30 p and 5:15p. 01.30.83.78.88. Admission €7, not included in Carte Musée et Monuments. On Friday and Saturday nights in August and September, reservations are necessary for Les Fetes de Nuit at 9:30p for music, fountain and fireworks show. We almost enjoy the 2,000 acres of spectacular lawns, gardens, sculptures and fountains more than the Chateau on days when it's body-against-body inside. The gardens are open until sunset. Versailles Office de Tourisme, 2 bis Ave de Paris. 01.39.24.88.88 or 01.30.83.77.77. The Chateau is open Tuesday-Sundays from 9a-6p. Carte Musée holders enter via Porte B, others enter Porte A. There are lines everywhere. Toilets cost €.50. A beautiful refuge away from the crowds is La Flottille restaurant down the hill from the Chateau in the gardens. It has a wonderful terrace and cozy décor inside, a full bar and friendly staff. €11.50 for lunch suggestion du jour.

TIP! The most efficient way to visit Versailles is to buy the Passeport Versailles at any RER station. It includes RT train ride and you get easier access via Porte C to avoid most of the long lines. Also includes audio tour, entrance to the Gardens and Les Grandes Eaux.

Get there: RER-C from Paris, Left Bank St-Michel station, to Versailles-Rive-Gauche (this train goes on to Normandy) arrives in 30 minutes and is nearest to the Chateau. The SNCF departs from Gare St-Lazare in Paris and arrives at Versailles-Rive Droit which is 10-15 minute walk to the Chateau. This is ideal if you plan to visit the town first.

MORE THAN JUST A DAY TRIP:

Go to **Avignon, Marseille,** and **Nice** by TGV Mediterranée train service. You can travel to **Aix-en-Provence** in slightly less than 3 hours, for example. Great for longer visits when you can plan Paris-Provence-Riviera vacations or if you simply want to leave Paris for a couple of days' tour of Avignon.

Take the TGV to **Beaune** via Dijon, in 2½ hours. The train station is on the east side, just outside the city walls and is a little more than 10 minute walk. Taxis are easily available, too. Here is the beautiful capital of Burgundy with cobblestone streets, picturesque squares, unique shops and rich architecture. Find the tourist office at the city center, Hotel Dieu. And, of course, wine! Make sure to visit the Musée du vin de Bourgogne. Plan a half-day visit to the vineyards by horse-drawn carriage or rent bikes.

Visit the **Loire Valley.** The TGV high speed rail service to Tours, in the heart of the Loire Valley, takes about one hour. 2½ hours to Saumur (change trains at Angers), to Langeais (change in St-Pierre-des-Corps), or to Chinon (change in Tours) Trains depart from Montparnesse stations or take the direct train from CDG airport. You can rent bikes or cars in Tours and buses are readily available. A trip to Loire requires advance planning and careful selection of the chateaux and grounds and gardens you want to see. A few recommendations: Ussé, Azay le Rideau, Saumur, Angers, Chenonceaux and Ambroise. Most are open all year, but are closed between noon – 2 o'clock pm.

English-French Cheat Sheet

POLITENESS IS DE RIGEUR (NECESSARY)

As my husband says: "You get what you give" and when visiting a foreign country a smile and a little effort to try and speak the "native tongue" goes a long way. You may be surprised at how friendly the French people are! Many will smile back and speak English and those that are not fluent will smile back and try their best to help you. Always acknowledge and welcome the person you are speaking to first before asking a question or making a request. Speaking softly gets you much more than screaming or yelling.

Hello	bonjour
Goodbye	au revoir
Good evening	bon soir
Yes/No	oui/non
Forbidden	Interdit(e)
Please	s'il vous plait
Thank you	merci
Pardon	pardon
Excuse me	excusez-moi
How are you?	Comment allez-vous?
Very well, thank you.	Très bien, merci.
You're welcome.	De rien.
Okay.	D'accord.
Do you speak English?	Parlez-vous Anglais?
I do not speak French.	Je ne parle pas Francais.
I do not understand.	Je ne comprends pas.
I am sorry.	Je suis désolé.
Where is?	Ou est?

How much?	C'est combien?
How much is it?	Combien est-ce?
Expensive/ Inexpensive	cher/ pas cher
Big/small	grand/petit
Good/bad	bien/mauvais
Open/close	ouvert/fermé
Free	libre
When do you Open?/Close?	A quelle heure ouvrez-vous? fermé-vous?
Here/there	ici/là
Left/right	gauche/droit
At what time?	A quelle heure?
What time is it?	Quelle heure est-il?
Tomorrow	demain
Today	aujourdh'ui
To leave	partir
Do you have?	Avez-vous?
Right?	N'est-ce pas?
Of course!	Bien sur!
Help!	Au secours!

I am lost	Je me suis perdu.
Get out/Exit	Sortie/sortir
Menu	la carte
Breakfast	le petit-déjeuner
Lunch	déjeuner
Dinner	le diner
The bill	l'addition
I would like	J'aimerais
A drink	une boisson
A glass	un verre
Carbonated/still	gazeuse/non gazeuse
Tea	le thè
Water	d'eau
Milk	le lait
Coffee/black /milk	le café/café noir /café crème
Sugar	le sucre
Salt	du sel
Wine	vin
Red/White/Dry	rouge/blanc/sec
Wine list	la carte des vins
Beer	bière
Eggs	oeufs
Vegetables	legumes
Soup	potage
Cheese	fromage
Chicken	poulet
Ham	le jambon
Meat	la viande
Lamb	agneau
Fish	le poisson/ fruits de mer
Rare	saignant
Well done	bien cuit
That's all	C'est tout
A table for two please	Une table pour deux, s'il vous plait
I'm from the USA	Je viens des Etats-Unis.
I'm hungry.	J'ai faim.
I'm thirsty.	J'ai soif.
Do you take credit cards?	Acceptez-vous les cartes de credit?
I have a reservation.	J'ai une reservation.
I would like to buy postcards.	Je voudrais acheter des cartes postales.

Days of the week:

Monday	Lundi
Tuesday	Maredi
Wednesday	Mercredi
Thursday	Jeudl
Friday	Vendredi
Saturday	Samedi
Sunday	Dimanche

My Special Travel Notes

1e. Louvre, Ile de Cité

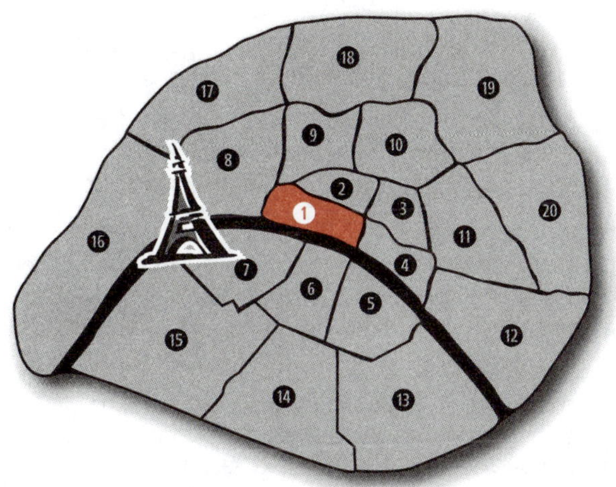

Make sure to go to **Musée de l'Orangerie,** our favorite museum in Paris.

Pamper yourself by booking a facial at **Nuxe Spa** and a haircut with John Nollet.

Spend an afternoon visiting Europe's biggest wine store, **Lavinia.**

We felt like royalty during our lunch at **Le Meurice,** where Chef Yannick Alleno presents a superb menu in an elegant dining room.

MAJOR METROS:

- LOUVRE RIVOLI
- CHÂTELET
- LES HALLES
- PALAIS-ROYAL
- TUILERIES

1e. Louvre, Ile de Cité

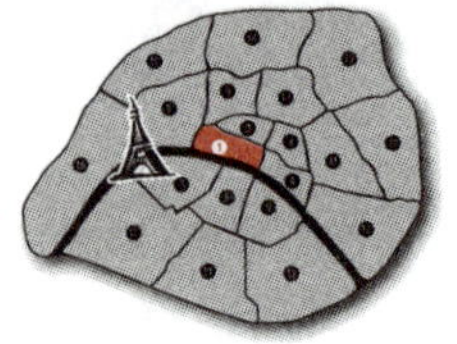

1

FAMOUS SIGHTS:

Conciergie, 1 Qaui de l'Horloge (M: St-Michel) 53.73.78.50. 10a-5p. This once served as a prison and torture chamber. See Marie-Antoinette's cell. Public clock, sculptures. Nearby is **Sainte-Chappelle,** 4 Blvd du Palais. (M: Cité) 53.73.78.50. 10a-5p. Admission €5.34 Enter through the Palais de Justice and view the stunning stained glass windows. Call for live concerts. We heard Vivaldi's Opéra Four Seasons and loved it. A FAVORITE.

Jeu de Paume, 1 Pl de la Concorde (M: Concorde) Noon -7p. Closed Mon. Access via northeast corner in **Tuileries.** Call for exhibition information. 47.03.12.50. Entrance €6. Also called the **Galerie Nationale du Photographie.**

Jardin des Tuileries, bordering **Pl de La Concorde** (M: Tuileries or Concorde) Spectacular garden with statues everywhere. 7:30a - 8:30p in spring and summer, otherwise 7:30a-7:30p. You will find the the **Octagonal Fountain** and Terraces. If you're hungry or want to rest, go to Café Renard, 42.96.50.56.

Musée du Louvre, To avoid the long line at the main entrance at the IM Pei Pyramid, enter Galerie du Carrousel, 99 Rue de Rivoli (M: Palais-Royal/Musée-du-Louvre). Another entrance is at the Ports des Lions. 40.20.51.51. Open daily 9a-6p./until 9:45p on Mon/Wed. Closed Tuesday. TIP: You can buy an English-language copy of "Destination Louvre" which is available in the children's museum shop in the Carrousel. The book's pages are color-coded to match the free museum guide and highlights the locations of the 12 best-known works of art on each of the 4 floors. Friday nights, open until 10p and if you are 26 or younger you may enter for free after 6pm on these Fridays. Reduced price on Sundays. Free the first Sunday of each month. Shops under the Louvre, **Louvre des Antiquaires,** are open every day. The **I M Pei glass pyramid** is a famous architectural sight and sits above the **Cour Napoleon.** You will find **Venus de Milo** on ground floor of Sully Wing, **Mona Lisa and Winged Victory** on first floor of Denon Wing.

Musée des Art Décoratifs, 107-111 Rue de Rivoli (M: Palais-Royal) This is considered part of the Louvre complex. 44.55.57.50. 150,000 objects from 1st through 21st century. Toy gallery features 12,000 toys. Make sure you visit the boutique, with an exclusive collection of art, fashion, and jewelry. Complex includes **Musée de la Mode et du Textile** exhibitions change (accessories, dresses, outfits, costumes, fabrics) and upstairs is the **Musée de la Publicité** advertising art and posters. €6. Closed Monday.

Musée de l' Orangerie de Tuileries, Pl de la Concorde.(M: Concord) 44.77.80.07. Southeast corner of Tuileries. The only museum in the world where you will see Monet's murals. Private collection of modern art from Cezanne, Renoir, Matisse, Modigliani. 12:30p – 7 p. Closed Tues. A FAVORITE.

Place du Châtelet, Between Quai de Gesvres and Ave Victoria. (M: Châtelet) See the **Châtelet Fountain** designed in 1808 and all its sphinxes.

DIVERSIONS:

Window shop, stroll, and sit in cafés in **Marché Montorgueil** along Rue Montorgueil (M: Etienne Marcel) Quartier Montorgueil's cobblestone street.

Aux Bains Montorgueil, 55 Rue Montorgueil (M: Sentier) 44.88.01.78. Boutique spa for women. Steam bath, black soap scrub, and massage for €88, includes tea and pastries for added pleasure.

Bike Rental: Roue Libre, 1 passage Mondetour (M: Les Halles) 08.10.44.15.34. Seven days, weekly.

Caudalie Spa, Hotel Meurice, 228 Rue de Rivoli. 44.58.10.28. Try the "Crushed Cabernet" 45-min. moisturizing scrub.

Colette's final residence is at #9 rue de Beaujolais (M: Palais-Royal) behind the Palais-Royal.

Day Spa, Espace Bien-Etre, Hotel Meurice, 228 Rue de Rivoli (M: Palais-Royal) 44.58.10.77. Marble oasis with treatments like the Sauvignon Massage @ $110.

Ecole Ritz Escoffier, 15 Pl Vendome (M: Tuileries) 43.16.30.50. These cooking courses fill up, so call ahead. Organized into themes. Cooking demonstrations are offered on Monday afternoons for €47.

Eglise Saint-Germain-L'Auxerrois, 2 Pl du Louvre (M: Louvre) Free church bell concerts. Wednesdays, 2:30p.

Eglise Saint-Roch, 296 Rue St-Honore (M: Pyramides) Enjoy free concerts mid-day on Tuesdays.

Forum Les Halles - Gardens, jazz clubs, cafés, shops. Underground you'll find a mall, swimming pool, cinemas. (M: Châtelet-Les-Halles).

Eglise St. Eustache, This church is on Place du Jour (M: Les Halles) 42.36.31.05 Well-known for 5:30 pm organ recitals on Sundays. Classical and baroque music. Free. Open from 9a-7p.

Galerie Vero Dodat, 19 Rue Jean Jacques Rousseau (M: Tuileries) Built in 1826, includes many shops selling old-fashioned toys, art, antiques in this passage with beautiful ceiling. 7a-10p. Closed Sat.

Gym and Health Club at Ritz Carlton, 15 Pl Vendome (M: Opéra) 43.16.30.60. Flexible memberships for non-guests. Facilities include Turkish baths, spa treatments, squash courts, jacuzzis, largest private pool in Paris.

Gymnase Club, 147 bis Rue St-Honore (M: Madeleine) 47.03.95.44. €23 for Day pass.

Hair Colorist to the stars - Christophe Robin, 7 Rue du Mont Thabor (M: Tuileries) Very expensive. 42.60.99.15.

Haircut - that perfect French bob - Lynne Bertin, 78 rue Jean Jacques-Rousseau (M: Les Halles) 42.36.04.59.

1e. Louvre, Ile de Cité

1

Hair: Rodolphe. 26-28 Rue Danielle Casanova (M: Pyramides) 42.61.46.59. Color specialist.

Institut Payot, 10 Rue Castiglione (M: Concorde) 42.60.32.87. Wonderful facials in beautiful setting.

Louvre des Antiquaires, 2 Pl du Palais-Royal. (M: Palais-Royal) 42.97.27.00. 250 Antique dealers in former department store, 3 floors. Tues-Sunday. from 11a-7p.

Marché aux Fleurs, Place Louis-Lépine (M: Cité) Flower market on Île de la Cité and has birds on Sundays. Located on Rue de la Cité between Rue de Lutèce and Quai de la Corse. A FAVORITE.

Midis du Louvre, Underground auditorium du Louvre hosts Noon-time music series by young musicians. (M: Palais-Royal).

Nuxe Spa, 32 Rue Montorgueil (M: Les Halles) 55.80.71.40 Quintessential spa experience. Laboratoire Nuxe face and body treatments. A FAVORITE. Book Hair stylist John Nollet at 55.80.71.50.

Palais Royal is bordered by streets Rue Montpensier, Rue Beaujolais and Rue de Valois. (M: Palais-Royal) You will find a courtyard with Daniel Buren's famous white and black columns to read, relax and people-watch. Excellent shopping opportunities in the shops at Galerie Montpensier and Gallerie De Valois. A FAVORITE.

Pavillon des Arts, Les Halles, 101 Rue Rambuteau (M: Châtelet-Les-Halles) 42.33.82.50. Closed Mondays. Call for exhibitions.

Pedicure at Hôtel Coste, 239 Rue Faubourg St-Honore (M: Tuileries) 42.44.50.00. Fax is 42.44.50.01 for advanced reservations, which are required most of the time.

Place Dauphine, (M: Pont Neuf) - Quai des Orfèvres. Peaceful square on Ile de la Cité.

Place du Palais-Royal, Pl Colette, Hôtel du Louvre, Comédie Française, Rue Rohan and Rue Richelieu (M: Palais-Royal). A FAVORITE area.

Place Vendôme - Rue de Castiglione intersects Rue St-Honore, Ritz Carlton, ritzy shops (M: Opéra).

Pont des Arts footbridge crosses the Seine. A FAVORITE with painters and lovers. (M: Pont Neuf).

Shiseido, Jardins du Palais-Royal, 142 Galerie de Valois (M: Palais-Royal) 49.27.09.09. Spa & perfumes.

Spa – La Bulle Kenzo, 1 Rue du Pont Neuf (M: Pont Neuf) 73.04.20.04. Fourth floor, modern, bright décor. Choose from "starting to smile" and "amnesia" massages among list. €80 one hour. Reserve in advance. 10a – 8p. Closed Sunday.

Spa at Ritz Carlton, Place Vendome. 43.16.30.30.

Square du Vert-Galant, reached by the stairs behind the king's statue on Pont Neuf. Great on sunny days. Take the Bateaux Vedettes Pont Neuf, 46.33.98.38 boat tours on the Seine (M: Pont Neuf).

The Squat, 39 Rue de Rivoli (M: Châtelet) City-supported renovated building housing new artists' contemporary art.

Théâtre du Châtelet, 2 Rue Edouard Colonne (M: Châtelet) has Sunday morning performances, 1st-come seats.

SUPERLATIVES:

Best Baguettes: Gosselin, 125 Rue St-Honore (M: Louvre-Rivoli) 45.08.03.59.

Best Boutique: Didier Ludot - see "Shops"

Best Bread: Julien, 75 Rue St-Honore (M: Louvre) 42.36.24.83. Sandwiches, too.

Best Café for coffee lovers: Café Verlet, 256 Rue St-Honore. (M: Tuileries) 42.60.67.39. Another location at 173 Rue St-Honore (M: Palais-Royal) 42.60.05.55.

Best Chocolate: Jean-Paul Hevin, 231 Rue St-Honore (M: Tuileries) 55.35.35.96.

Best Cosmetic Store: By Terry de Gunzberg, 21 Galerie Vero-Dodat (M: Palais-Royal) 44.76.00.76.

Best duty-free beauty products: Catherine, 7 Rue de Castiglione (M: Concorde) 42.61.02.89.

Best Japanese food: Kinugawa, 9 Rue du Mont Thabor (M: Tuileries) 42.60.65.07. Expensive sushi.

Best Onion soup: Au Pied de Cochon, 6 Rue Coquillere (M: Châtelet-Les Halles) 40.13.77.00. Dinner for two $68.

Best picnic fare: Flo Prestige, 42 Pl du Marché St-Honore (M: Pyramides) 42.61.45.46. Gourmet take-out deli with delectable and expensive selection of cheeses, charcuterie, salads, daily specials. Will deliver to your hotel. Daily, til 11pm.

Best Sherry/Dessert Wine bar: Juvéniles Wine Bar, 47 Rue de Richelieu (M: Palais-Royal) owned by Willi's. See "Restaurants."

Best Wine bar: Le Rubis, 10 Rue du Marché St-Honore (M: Tuileries) 42.61.03.34. Small and smoky. Moderate food prices.

Best Wine bar (tie): Willi's Wine Bar, 13 Rue des Petits-Champs (north exit of Jardins du Palais-Royal, turn left. (M: Bourse) 42.61.05.09. Stay to enjoy the food, too. Closed Sundays.

Biggest Wine shop in Europe: Lavinia, 3-5 Blvd de la Madeleine (M:Madeleine) 42.97.20.20 Has 5,500 different wines. A FAVORITE.

Fashionista Haven for Dining: Côstes, 239 Rue Faubourg St-Honore (M:Tuileries) 42.44.50.25. Inside the Hotel Côstes, this is the "place" to see and be seen. Eclectic menu, intimate.

First English Bookstore: Galignani, 224 Rue de Rivoli (M: Tuileries) 42.60.76.07. Open since 1802.

Good Burgers: Café Castiglione, 235 Rue St-Honore (M: Opéra) 42.60.68.22. The wait staff is friendly and they know a little English.

Great Cheeseburgers, Ferdi, 32 Rue Mont Thabor (M: Concorde) 42.60.82.52. Available only at lunch.

Great people-watching: Café Ruc, 159 Rue St-Honore (M: Palais-Royal) 42.60.97.54.

More great people-watching: Café La Coupe d'Or, 330 Rue St-Honore (M: Tuileries) 42.60.43.26. It's right across the street from Colette.

Hippest place for drinks after Louvre: Le Fumoir, 6 Rue Amiral de Coligny (M: Louvre-Rivoli) 42.92.00.24

Most beautiful church: Eglise St-Germain-L'Auxerrois, 2 Pl du Louvre (M: Louvre-Rivoli) 42.60.13.96.

Most elegant tea salon: Angélina, 226 Rue de Rivoli (M: Concorde) 42.60.82.00. Circa 1803. Marble tables, gilt décor. Breakfast, lunch, and afternoon tea. Some believe they serve the world's best hot chocolate.

Most exclusive flowers: By appointment only. **Luc Gaignard,** 13 Rue Bouloi (M: Louvre) 42.21.42.00.

Most terrific pâte/terrines: Le Dauphin, 167 Rue St-Honore (M: Palais-Royal) 42.60.40.11.

Snobbiest Night Spot: Cabaret, 2 Pl du Palais-Royal.(M: Palais-Royal) 58.62.56.25 Bar and restaurant, lunch and dinner. Very snobby so make sure they don't seat you downstairs when everyone else is upstairs and vice versa. aka **Le Cab.**

SHOPS :

Agatha, 5 Pl des Victoires (M: Etienne Marcel) 40.39.08.25. Jewelry boutique. Low prices on designer pieces. There are several Agatha stores in Paris.

Agnes B., 6 Rue du Jour (M: Etienne Marcel) 45.08.56.56. Chic Paris looks. 10a-7p.

Alexandra de Gastines, 10 Rue des Moulins (M: Pyramides) 40.23.90.10. Haute couture.

André Courrèges, 7 Rue Turbigo (M: Etienne Marcel). 53.67.30.00. Couture designs, plus Café Blanc for lunch.

Anna Joliet Boites à Musique, 9 Rue de Beaujolais, Jardins du Palais-Royal. (M: Palais-Royal) 42.96.55.13. Music boxes. Reasonably priced and good selection.

Appartement 217, 217 Rue St-Honore (M: Tuileries) 42.96.00.96. Former beauty director of Colette, Stephane Jaulin, directs this bio-spa with natural skin care line and soothing, absolutely decadent facials.

Arche, 11 Blvd de la Madeleine (M: Madeleine) 40.15.91.85. Shoes.

Artisan Parfumeur's Grand Boutique, 2 Rue de l'Amiral de Coligny (M: Louvre) 44.88.27.50 Boutique of scents and candles. Upstairs you'll find a counter where you can create your own fragrances.

Astier de Villatte, 173 Rue St-Honore (M: Louvre) 42.60.74.13. Designer specializing in home décor, tableware, ceramic vases, accessories, and fun objects.

Atelier du Bracelet Parisien, 7 Rue St-Hyacinth (M: Pyramides) 42.86.13.70. Custom watch-bands and leather goods.

Au Vase de Delft,19 Rue Cambon (M: Concorde) 42.60.92.49. Good selection of jewelry and antiques.

Baan phi sua, 46 Rue de Richelieu (M: Palais-Royal) 42.96.54.67. Décor, candles, Thailand.

Barbara Bui, 23 Rue Etienne Marcel (M: Etienne Marcel) Rock and roll urban designer. 40.26.43.65. Café is up the street, #27.

Boucheron, 26 Pl Vendôme (M: Opéra) 42.61.58.16. Luxury jewelry.

Boutique 20 Sur 20, 3 Rue Lavandières (M: Châtelet) 45.08.44.94. Vintage bakelite and costume jewelry.

By Terry de Gunzberg, 21 Galerie Vero-Dodat (M: Palais-Royal) 44.76.00.76. Cosmetics.

Cacharel, 5 Pl des Victoires (M: Bourse) 42.33.29.88. Designer clothes and new swimwear line.

Cadolle Hermine, 14 Rue Cambon (M: Concorde) 42.60.94.22. Poupie Cadolle sells deluxe lingerie, French beachwear and perfume. Creates items to order. Her great-great grandmother invented the brassiere in 1900.

Caractère, 384 Rue St-Honore (M: Concorde) 42.60.03.15. 1st French boutique for Italian ready-to-wear line.

Carrousel du Louvre - mall under Louvre - entrance at 99 Rue de Rivoli. Open 7 days/week. Make sure you compare prices among stores, since merchandise varies. Toilets cost 50 cents, unless you go right in after someone else before door closes.

Cartier, 23 Pl Vendome (M: Opéra) 44.55.32.20. Famous jewelry.

Casa Design, 16 Ave Victoria (M: Châtelet) 42.36.36.68. Home décor.

Castelbajac Concept Store, 31 Pl du Marché St-Honore (M: Tuileries) 42.60.41.55. Funky mix.

Catherine, 7 Rue de Castiglione (M: Concorde) 42.61.02.89. Good for duty-free products.

Chanel, 31 Rue Cambon (M: Concorde) 42.86.28.00. Haute couture designer.

1e. Louvre, Ile de Cité

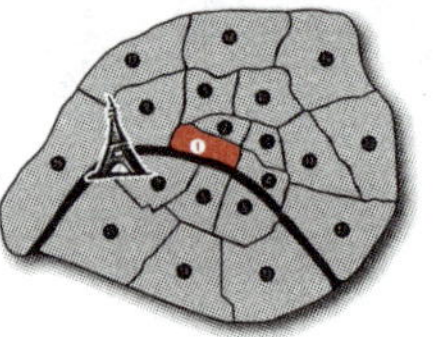

Chanel Boutique, 18 Pl. Vendome (M: Tuileries) 55.35.50.00. High fashion.

Chanel Joaillerie, 18 Pl Vendôme (M: Tuileries) 55.35.50.00 Jewelry store by Chanel designer.

Chantal Thomass, 211 Rue St-Honore (M: Tuileries) 42.60.40.56. Lingerie designer.

Charles Chocolatier, 15 Rue Montorgueil (M: Les Halles) 45.08.57.77.

Charvet, 8 Pl Vendôme (M: Tuileries) 42.60.30.70. Finest mens' tailored shirts and silk ties.

Chaumet, 12 Pl Vendôme (M: Opéra) 44.77.24.00 Luxury jewelry.

Christian Louboutin, 19 Rue Jean Jacques-Rousseau (M: Les Halles) 42.36.05.31. Designer shoes.

Claude Jeantet, 10 Rue Therèse (M: Pyramides) 42.86.01.36. Cardboard curiosities. Fun shop.

Colette, 213 Rue St-Honore (M: Tuileries) 55.35.33.90 Don't miss this boutique department store. Closed Sunday. A FAVORITE.

Cop Copine, 80 Rue Rambuteau (M: Les Halles) 40.28.03.72. Fashion friendly, hip boutique.

Cop Copine, 37 Etienne Marcel (M: Etienne Marcel) 53.00.94.84. Hip boutique with affordable collections. A FAVORITE.

Dary's, 362 Rue St-Honore (M: Tuileries) 42.60.95.23. Vintage jewelry, art deco, Dior brooches.

Dehillerin, 18-20 Rue Coquillière (M: Les Halles) 42.36.53.13. Specialty cookware. Founded in 1820. Everything for the kitchen. Bins of utensils. Closed Sunday. A FAVORITE.

Didier Ludot, 20-24 Galerie Montpensier (M: Palais-Royal) 42.96.06.56. Famous vintage store with Hermès, Prada. Chanel, others. Closed Sunday.

Didier Ludot, 125 Galerie de Valois (M: Palais-Royal) 40.15.01.04. Dedicated to black dresses.

Dior Joaillerie, 8 Pl Vendôme (M: Madeleine) 42.96.30.84. Haute jewelry designed by Victoire de Castellane.

Dolce&Gabanna, 244 Rue de Rivoli (M: Concorde) 42.86.00.44. Their "second line."

E. B Meyrowitz Opticians, 5 Rue Castiglione (M: Tuileries) 42.60.63.64. Exclusive Meyrowitz line of eyewear and fashionable designer frames.

Editions de Parfums, 21 Rue du Mont Thabor (M: Concorde) 42.22.77.22. Original scents. Perfumes from Frédéric Malle.

Eric Bergere, 16 Rue de la Soudière (M: Tuileries) 47.03.33.19. Boutique.

Etam, 67-73 Rue de Rivoli (M: Pont Neuf) 44.76.73.73. France's equivalent to H & M. Affordable, trendy.

Faerber, 14 Rue de Castiglione (M: Tuileries) 44.50.50.44. Haute jewelry by Ida Faerber.

Fifi Chachnil, 231 Rue St-Honore (M: Tuileries) 42.61.21.83. Lingerie + swimwear.

Foie Gras Luxe, 26 Rue Montmartre. (M: Les Halles) 42.33.28.15. Closed Sat/Sun

Franck Namani, 2 Rue de Castiglione (M: Tuileries) 49.27.05.53. Women's and men's casual collections on first floor and suits on second floor.

Fred, 7 Pl Vendôme (M: Tuileries) 42.86.60.60 Exquisite jewelry, diamonds.

Gabrielle Geppert, 31 Galerie Montpensier, Jardins du Palais-Royal (M: Palais-Royal) 42.61.53.52. Cute shop, vintage pieces.

Galerie Arcade Colette, Jardins du Palais-Royal, 155 Galerie de Valois, 17 Rue de Valois (M: Palais-Royal) 42.86.05.38. Collections vary. Open 2:30p-7p. Closed Sun/Mon

Galerie d'Art Joyce, 168 Galerie Valois (M: Palais-Royal) 40.15.03.72. Objets d'art and unique décor accessories.

Galerie Laguiole, 1 Pl St Opportun (M: Châtelet -Les-Halles) 40.28.09.42. Famous hand-made cutlery, wine-keys. Closed Sunday. They do not ship.

Galerie Vero Dodat, 19 Rue Jean Jacques Rousseau (M: Tuileries) Built in 1826, includes many shops selling old-fashioned toys, art, antiques in this passage with beautiful ceiling. 7a-10p. Closed Sat.

Galignani, 224 Rue de Rivoli (M: Tuileries) 42.60.76.07. Bookstore.Open since 1802.

Gargantua, 284 Rue St-Honore (M: Tuileries) 42.60.52.54. One-stop food shop for picnics in Tuileries.

Giorgio Armani, 6 Pl Vendome (M: Tuileries) 42.86.64.90. Haute couture.

Gosselin, 125 Rue St-Honore (M: Louvre-Rivoli) 45.08.03.59. Bakery, confectioner. Delicious.

Goyard, 233 Rue St-Honore (M: Tuileries) 42.60.57.04. Couture house founded in 1853 for fine luggage.

Habitat, 8 Rue du Pont Neuf (M: Pont Neuf) 53.00.99.88. Contemporary furniture design.

Heller Artisinat, 259 Rue St-Honore (M: Tuileries) 47.03.99.46. Jewelry.

Il pour l'homme, 209 Rue St-Honore (M: Tuileries) 42.60.43.56. Funky & stylish home decor.

Jack Gomme, 6 Rue Montmartre (M; Etienne Marcel) 40.41.10.24. Fine leather handbags and travel accessories.

Jack Henry, 1 Rue Montmartre (M: Les Halles) 42.21.46.01. Chic designs by Claudine Pierlot.

1e. Louvre, Ile de Cité

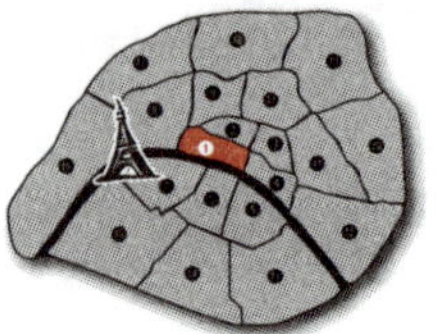

Jacques Le Corre, 193 Rue St-Honore (M: Tuileries) 42.96.97.40. Distinctive line of hats, bags, shoes.

JAR Jewelry, 7 Pl Vendôme (M: Tuileries) 42.96.33.66 One of the world's finest jewelers. By appointment only.

JAR Parfums, 14 Rue Castiglione (M: Tuileries) 40.20.47.20. Original perfumes and an original presentation of Golcondo (premier scent), along with Ferme Tes Yeux, Jardenia, Jarling. Over-the-top scents and cents.

Jean-Paul Hevin, 231 Rue St-Honore (M: Tuileries) 55.35.35.96. Famous chocolatier.

John Galliano, 384 Rue St-Honore (M: Madeleine) 55.35.40.40. Designer.

Joseph, 277 Rue St-Honore (M: Tuileries) 53.45.83.30. 2 floors + Joe's restaurant - a trendy salad and sushi bar.

Just Campagne, 342 Rue St-Honore (M: Tuileries) 40.15.02.13. Fine handcrafted leather and unique bags.

Kabuki, 21-25 Rue Etienne Marcel. (M: Etienne Marcel) 42.33.55.65. Colette-style trendy, with Miu-Miu, Prada etc.

Karine Dupont, 4 Rue Marché St-Honore (M: Tuileries) 40.27.82.82. Sassy bags, accessories, clothing. Another location in 6e.

Kazana, 9 Rue Montorgueil, (M: Etienne Marcel) 45.08.19.21. Scarves,accessories. Has several locations.

Kenzo, 3 Pl Victoires (M: Pont Neuf) 40.39.72.00. Haute couture. You will also find la Bulle Kenzo, parfums, at 1 rue Pont Neuf.

Kitchen Bazaar, 50 Rue Croix des Petits-Champs (M: Pyramides) 40.15.03.11.Hip kitchen gadgets.

Kranji, 5 Rue Turbigo (M: Etienne Marcel) 42.33.89.97. Ladies shop.

Kranji, 30 Rue Pierre Lescot (M: Les Halles) 42.36.01.49. Mens shop.

Kyo, 2 Rue de l'Echelle (M: Pyramides) 42.96.89.68. Designer timepieces and European designed watches.

L'Eclaireur, 10 Rue Hérold (M: Sentier) 40.41.09.89. Multi brand designers boutique.

La Boutique du Palais Royal, 9 Rue Beaujolais (M: Palais-Royal) 42.60.08.22. Tiny store packed with toys.

La Chaise Lounge, 30 Rue Croix des Petits Champs (M: Bourse) 42.96.32.14. Tiny store with hip home gadgets and accessories. Several locations in Paris.

La Droguerie, 9 Rue du Jour (M: Les Halles) 45.08.93.27. Colorful little shop with tons of beads, feathers, yarns, frivolous buttons.

Lavinia, 3-5 Blvd Madeleine (M: Madeleine) 42.97.20.20. Wines. See "Superlatives".

Le Prince Jardinier, 39 Rue de Valois (M: Palais-Royal) 42.60.37.13. For chic gardeners.

Les Petits, 3 Rue Montmartre (M: Etienne Marcel) 40.28.45.55. Womens wear.

Longchamp, 404 Rue St-Honore (M: Concorde) 43.16.00.16. Leather and accessories.

Loro Piana, 253 Rue St-Honore (M: Tuileries) 55.35.39.35. Fine cashmere.

Loulou de la Falaise, 21 Rue Cambon (M: Concorde) 42.60.02.66. Absolutely gorgeous, one-of-a-kind, and whimsical haute couture jewelry and accessories at couture prices. 10a-7p. Say Bonjour to Frederic and Dominique. Closed Sunday. A FAVORITE.

Louvre des Antiquaires, 2 Pl du Palais-Royal (M: Palais-Royal) 11a-7p. 250 antique dealers.

Lydia Courteille, 231 Rue St-Honore (M: Tuileries) 42.61.11.77. Antique and estate jewelry.

Madame André, 34 Rue Mont Thabor (M: Concorde) 42.96.27.24. "Pink" boutique sells Gilles Defour collection, accessories, underwear, more.

Madelios, 23 Blvd de la Madeleine (M: Madeleine) 53.45.00.00. Department store for men. Closed Sunday.

Maitre Parfumeur et Gantier, 5 Rue des Capucines (M: Opéra) 42.96.35.13. 25-year old perfume & room freshener boutique.

Mandarina Duck, 7 Blvd Madeleine (M: Tuileries) 42.86.08.00. Trendy fine leather.

Marc Jacobs, 34 Rue de Montpensier (M: Palais-Royal) 55.35.02.60. Haute couture and fine designs.

Maria Luisa, 2 Rue Cambon (M: Concorde) 47.03.96.15. Designer labels, hot swimwear.

Maria Luisa, 4 Rue Cambon (M: Concorde) 47.03.48.08. Manolo Blahnik shoes.

Maria Luisa for Men, 19 bis, Rue du Mont Thabor (M: Concorde) 42.60.89.83.

Maria Luisa for Sportswear, 38 Rue du Mont Thabor (M: Concorde) 42.96.47.81. Men and women.

Marie Stuart, 3 Galerie de Montpensier (M: Palais-Royal) 42.96.28.25. Medals and military memorabilia.

Martin Margiela, 25 bis, Rue de Montpensier (M: Palais-Royal) 40.15.07.55. Ladies boutique.

Martin Margiela, 23 Rue du Montpensier (M: Palais-Royal) 40.15.06.44. Ladies and mens wear.

Mauboussin, 20 Pl Vendôme (M: Tuileries) 44.55.10.00. Haute jewelry, prestigious designs. Another location in 8e.

1e. Louvre, Ile de Cité

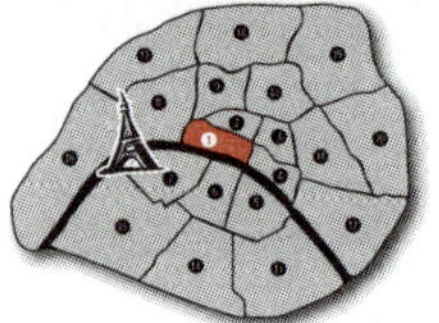

Metal Pointus, 13 Rue du Jour.(M: Les Halles) 42.33.35.38. Costume jewelry.

Minapoe, 19 Rue Duphot (M: Madeleine) 42.61.06.41. Mina D'Ornano has original and imaginative accessories.

Mora, 13 Rue Montmartre (M: Les Halles) 45.08.19.24. Baking tools.

Octopussy, 255 Rue St-Honore (M: Tuileries) 40.15.96.45. For 18 years this store has offered a good selection of moderately priced costume jewelry and accessories. Say "bonjour" to Frank Nebbot.

Papeterie Moderne, 12 Rue de la Ferronnerie (M: Châtelet) 42.36.21.72. Look through old Parisian signs for a great souvenir.

Patrice Fabre, 350 Rue St-Honore (M: Tuileries) 42.60.62.74. Unique jewelry designs. One-of-a-kind and limited series jewelry collections. Mon-Friday, 10a-7p.

Pellini, 30 Galerie Montpensier, Jardins du Palais-Royal (M: Palais-Royal) 42.96.18.68. Boutique.

Philippe Ferrandis, 346 Rue St-Honore (M: Tuileries) 42.96.36.95. Costume jewelry.

Pierre Hardy, 156 Galerie de Valois (M: Palais-Royal) 42.60.59.75. Shoes.

Pouic-Pouic, 4 Rue Herold (M: Sentier) 40.26.27.90. Collectibles such as original Barbie dolls, at good prices. 12p-7p. Closed Sunday.

Robert Capia, Galerie Vero-Dodat, (M: Louvre-Rivoli) 42.36.25.94. Specializes in antique dolls, toys, old phonographs.

Rudolpe Menudier, 14 Rue de Castiglione (M: Tuileries) 40.41.69.80 Designer shoes.

Sagil, 242 Rue de Rivoli (M: Concorde) 42.60.71.81. Parfumerie.

Saillard, 8 Rue Richelieu (M: Palais-Royal) 42.96.07.78. Find an assortment of country-inspired articles. They have been gun-makers since 1716.

Salons du Palais Royal Shiseido, 142 Galerie de Valois (M: Palais-Royal) 49.27.09.09. Fine perfumes.

Sandrine Philippe, 6 Rue Herold (M: Louvre) 40.26.21.78. Designer, elegant, glamorous clothes.

Sandro, 1 rue Juillet (M: Tuileries) 40.15.61.78. Tailored and cool.

Scooter, 10 Rue Turbigo (M: Etienne Marcel) 45.08.50.54.Great jewelry.

Shiseido, Les Salons du Palais-Royal, 142 Galerie de Valois (M: Palais-Royal) 49.27.09.09. Unusual and unique perfumes.

Stoklux, 8 Pl Vendôme (M: Opéra) 49.27.09.31. Discounts.

Surface To Air, 46 Rue d l'Arbre Sec (M: Pont Neuf) 49.27.04.54. Collections of young urban designers.

Sybele, 350 Rue St-Honore (M: Tuileries) 42.60.87.71. Funky boutique with assortment of minerals, gems, shells.

Terre et Decoration, 90 Rue St-Honore (M: Louvre Rivoli) 45.08.10.11. Home accessories, childrens, toys.

Thierry Mugler, 49 Ave Opéra (M: Opéra) 53.05.25.80. Haute Couture.

Toraya, 10 Rue St-Florentin (M: Concorde) 42.60.13.00. Japanese confectionary and tea room.

Van Cleef & Arpels, 22 Pl Vendôme (M: Opéra) 53.45.45.45. Jewelry.

Vanessa Bruno, 12 Rue de Castiglione (M: Concorde) 42.61.44.60. Designer for women. Accessories, bags. There are other locations in Paris.

Veronique Leroy, 10 Rue d'Alger (M: Tuileries) 49.26.93.59. Belgian designer with edgy styles, similar to Azzedine Alaïa.

Victoire, 4 Rue Duphot (M: Concorde) 55.35.95.01. Current designs in fashion.

W. H. Smith, 248 Rue de Rivoli (M: Concorde) 44.77.88.99. Books in English, international magazines. A FAVORITE.

Wolford, 257 Rue St-Honore (M: Tuileries) 42.97.54.56. Lots of other locations.

Yohji Yamamoto, 47 Rue Etienne Marcel (M: Etienne Marcel) 45.08.82.45. Designer of couture collections.

Zadig & Voltaire, 9 Rue du 29 Juillet (M: Tuileries) 42.92.00.80. Designer boutique, accessories, luggage, jewelry.

Zelia Boutique, 8 Rue de Richelieu (M: Palais-Royal) 40.15.00.64. Haute creation of fine robes, lingerie.

Zero One One, 2 Rue de Marengo (M: Louvre) 49.27.00.11. Modern tableware settings.

RESTAURANTS: LES PLATS DU JOUR:

Angelina, 226 Rue de Rivoli (M: Concorde) 42.60.82.00. Baroque and elegant, circa 1903. Expect long lines for fine teas, pastries, and hot chocolate.

Armand au Palais-Royal, 6 Rue Beaujolais (M: Bourse) 42.60.05.11. Romantic. Try the foie gras filled crepe. Dinner is €90 for two.

Au Pied de Cochon, 6 Rue Coquillière (M: Chatelet-Les Halles) 40.13.77.00. 24-hour brasserie that can get touristy. Dinner for two €60.

Aux Bon Crus, 7 Rue des Petits-Champs (M: Bourse) 42.60.06.45. Small wine bar with good lunches based on Lyonnais style cooking. Closed Sunday.

Barlotti, 35 Pl du Marché St-Honore (M: Concorde) 44.86.97.97. Italian. Same owners as Buddha Bar.

1e. Louvre, Ile de Cité

1

Brasserie du Louvre, Pl du Palais-Royal (M: Palais-Royal) 42.96.27.98. Open noon - midnight. $33 prix fixe menu for lunch & dinners. Old fashioned and dependable fare.

Ca d'Oro, 54 Rue de l'Arbre-Sec (M: Louvre) 40.20.97.79. Light Italian and friendly service. Open Sunday.

Café de la Comedie, 157 Rue St-Honore (M: Palais-Royal) 42.61.40.01. Great terrace for people-watching. Friendly, inexpensive and simple. A FAVORITE.

Café Marly, 93 Rue de Rivoli (in Louvre courtyard) 49.26.06.60. Less-than-dependable food and service yet it is a great courtyard terrace setting outside the Louvre. Open Sunday.

Café Ruc, 159 Rue St-Honore (M: Palais-Royal) 42.60.97.54. Owned by Costes brothers. Enjoy the scene as well as the fresh, diverse menu. Be forewarned that service can get snobby.

Chez La Vieille, 1 Rue Bailleul (M: Louvre-Rivoli) 42.60.15.78. Country French cooking with mostly Bordeaux wines. Owner Marie-José welcomes diners. Dinner is only served on Thursdays. Only five tables for lunch Mon-Wed and Thursday.

Chez Max, 47 Rue St-Honore (M: Les Halles) 45.08.80.13. Haute cuisine at low prices.

Chez Pauline, 5 Rue Villedo (M: Palais-Royal) 42.96.20.70. Authentic French in food and décor. Cozy red banquettes downstairs. Moderate prices. Popular. Closed Sun.

Cibus, 5 Rue Moliere (M: Palais-Royal) 42.61.50.19. Tiny, chic bistro for intimate Italian cuisine.

Cleret André, 11 Rue Jean Lantier (M: Châtelet) 42.33.82.68. Delicious tarts and sandwiches.

Clos Saint-Honore, 3 Rue St-Hyacinth (M: Tuileries) 40.15.09.36. Under the Tuileries, Romantic setting in cellar with attentive service and moderate prices. Classic food.

Comptoir de la Gastronomie, Epicerie Fine Restaurant, 34 Rue Montmartre (M: Etienne Marcel) 42.33.31.32. Foie gras and gourmet grocery store and restaurant. 11a - 11p.

Côstes, 239 Rue Faubourg St-Honore (M: Tuileries) 42.44.50.25. Inside the Hotel Côstes, this is the "place" to see and be seen. Eclectic menu, intimate.

Dave, 12 Rue de Richelieu (M: Palais- Royal) 42.61.49.48.Basic Chinese. Jet set love it!

Ferdi, 32 Rue Mont-Thabor (M: Concorde) 42.60.82.52. Some say the "best" cheeseburgers can be found at this tiny Spanish restaurant and only served at lunch. Mojitos, tapas, enchiladas, ravioli all delight the taste buds and served to fashionable Right Bank crowd in an inviting atmosphere. Reserve. Closed in August.

Il Cortile, 37 Rue Cambon (M: Concorde) 44.58.45.67. Good Italian. Surprisingly charming courtyard patio in Castille Sofitel Demeure Hotel.

Joe Allen, 30 Rue Pierre Lescot (M: Etienne Marcel) 42.36.70.13. Manhattan, NY in the heart of Paris.

Juvéniles, 47 Rue de Richelieu (M: Palais-Royal) 42.97.46.49. Wine bar. Cozy space, light snacks, tapas. Closed Sunday.

Kinugawa, 9 Rue du Mont-Thabor (M: Tuileries) 42.60.65.07. Expensive sushi.

L'Absinthe, 24 Pl du Marché St-Honore (M: Tuileries) 49.26.90.04. Inventive cuisine from Michel Rostang's daughter. Hit or miss. New décor. €90 dinner for two.

L'Ane et la Mule, 74 Quai des Orfèvres (M: Pont Neuf) 43.54.16.71. Cozy l'le de Cité setting. Moderate prices. Lunch, tea, dinner.

L'Ardoise, 28 Rue du Mont Thabor (M: Concorde) 42.96.28.18. Small bistro. Nouveau French. €100 for two including wine. Closed Mon/Tues.

L'Argenteuil, 9 Rue d'Argenteuil (M: Pyramides) 42.60.56.22. Small bistro. Enjoyable prix fixe menus. A FAVORITE.

L'Atelier Berger, 49 Rue Berger (M: Louvre) 40.28.00.00. Chef Jean Christiansen trained w/Rostang, presented us with a stunning tasting menu. Reserve a table upstairs. Closed Sunday.

L'Autobus Imperial, 14 Rue Mondetour (M: Etienne Marcel) 42.36.00.18. French comfort food prepared for lunch & dinner with reasonable prices. Closed Sunday.

L'Ecume Saint Honore, 6 Rue Marché St-Honore (M: Tuileries) 42.61.93.87. Fishmongers, seaside setting and bare wooden tables. Casual lunch.

L'Epi d'Or, 25 Rue Jean Jacques-Rousseau (M: Les Halles) 42.36.38.12. Traditional. Good value. Closed Sunday.

L'Escargot Montorgueil, 38 Rue Montorgueil (M: Les Halles) 42.36.83.51. 1830's Parisian decor with gold, mirrors, red banquettes. New menu with escargot sampler. Closed Sunday.

L'Estaminet Gaya, 17 Rue Duphot (M: Madeleine) 42.60.43.03. Great gem on a small, hidden street. Mosaic tile makes comfortable setting and the fresh seafood delights many. Delicious desserts. Closed Sunday.

La Cloche des Halles, 28 Rue Coquillières (M: Les Halles) 42.36.93.89. Bistro. Very popular, good food and wine. Share a table on Saturdays. Closed Sunday.

La Cordonnerie, 20 Rue St Roch (M: Pyramides) 42.60.17.42. Chef/owner Hugo Wolfer and his wife do it all at this tiny restaurant with an open kitchen and fresh menu. Moderate prices. Closed Sunday.

La Corte, 320 Rue St-Honore (M: Rue de Rivoli) 42.60.45.27. Italian.

La Fermette du Sud-Ouest, 31 Rue Coquilliere (M: Les Halles) 42.36.73.55. Southwestern classics, cozy. Low prices.

1e. Louvre, Ile de Cité

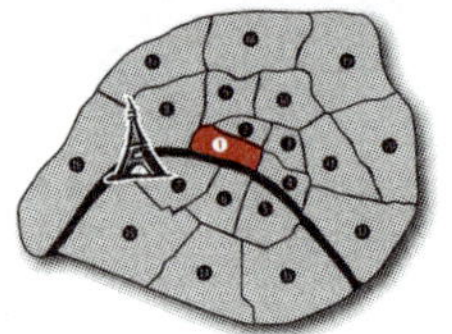

La Mousson, 9 Rue Thérèse (M: Palais-Royal) 42.60.59.46. Cambodian meals and simple décor. Good prices and good area.

La Poule au Pot, 9 Rue Vauvilliers (M: Les Halles) 42.36.32.96. Dinner for two €60. Good onion soup and crème brulee. Open til 5am.

La Robe et la Palais, 13 Rue de Lavandieres-Ste Opportune (M: Châtelet-Les-Halles) 45.08.07.41. Friendly bistro à vins serving imaginative dishes complimenting 40 wines-by-the-glass. Closed Sunday.

La Tour de Montlhéry Chez Denise, 5 Rue des Prouvaires (M: Les Halles) 42.36.21.82. Local, 33-year old bistro serving steak and classics in a lively elbow-to-elbow dining room. Open 3am. Reservations necessary.

La Tourelle, 43 Rue Croix des Petits Champs (M: Bourse) 42.61.35.41. Small bistro popular with locals for lunch of charcuterie and salads with good wine list.

Le Caveau du Palais, 19 Dauphine, facing Place Dauphine on Ile de Cité. (M: Pont Neuf) 43.26.04.28. Wonderful terrace and inside, beamed ceilings. Reliably good food and service to spend a leisurely 2-hour dinner.

Le Dauphin, 167 Rue St-Honore (M: Palais-Royal) 42.60.40.11. Charming bistro, relaxed mood and rustic Basque menu $74 for two.

Le Musset, 5 Rue de L'Echelle (M: Palais-Royal) 42.60.69.29. Cozy, classic bistro with plats du jour.

Le Pain Quotidium, 18 Pl du Marché St-Honore (M: Pyramides) 42.96.31.70. Brunch served French-style on communal tables, can be fun. Several locations in Paris.

Le Pharamond, 24 Rue de la Grande-Truanderie (M: Etienne Marcel) 40.28.45.18. Classic bistro cooking. Quaint Belle Epoque décor.

Le Poquelin, 17 Rue Molière (M: Palais-Royal) 42.96.22.19. Charming, Traditional specialties from Auvergne. Attentive service. Closed Sunday.

Le Restaurant du Palais-Royal, 110 Galerie de Valois (M: Bourse) 40.20.00.07.

Le Rubis, 10 Rue du Marché St-Honore (M: Tuileries) 42.61.03.34. Wine bar, serving lunch and charcuterie for dinner, 30 wines by the glass.

Le Soufflé, 36 Rue du Mont Thabor (M: Concorde) 42.60.27.19. Delicious souffle 3-course meal. Non-smoking room. Friendly service. Closed Sunday and August. A FAVORITE.

Les Boucholeurs, 34 Rue de Richelieu (M: Pyramides) 42.96.06.86. Mussels, fresh seafood. Intimate and nautical décor.

Lescure, 7 Rue de Mondovi (M: Concorde) 42.60.18.91. Since 1919, traditional French and very friendly atmosphere. Closed Sunday.

Maceo, 15 Rue des Petits Champs (M: Palais-Royal) 42.97.53.85. Same owners as Willi's Wine bar.

Muscade, 36 Rue Montpensier (M: Palais-Royale) 42.97.51.36. Tearoom and classic bistro fare. Salads and seafood for lunch in garden.

Pierre Au Palais Royal, 10 Rue de Richelieu (M: Palais-Royal) 42.96.09.17. M/MME Fremondiere run a cozy room with good food at reasonable prices.

Pinxo, 9 Rue d'Alger (M: Opéra) 40.20.72.03. We enjoyed our meal of small plates. This is Chef Dutournier's offshoot of gastronomique restaurant, Carre des Feuillants,

Rouge Tomate, 34 Pl du Marché St-Honore (M: Pyramides) 42.61.16.09. Fresh tomato-based menus. €15.

Saudade, 34 Rue des Bourdonnais (M: Chatelet-les-Halles) 42.36.03.65. Portugese flavors spice up classic dishes. Closed Sunday.

Scoop, 154 Rue St-Honore (M: Louvre) 42.60.31.84. 10a-7p. Upstairs/downstairs bar and crowded for lunch. Health-conscious salads, quiches, soups. Ice cream, of course.

Taverne Henry IV, 13 Pl du Pont Neuf at Rue Henri-Robert (M: Pont Neuf) on Ile de Cité. 43.54.27.90. Great pairings of wine and cheeses. Lunch and dinner. No credit cards. Closed Sunday.

Willi's Wine Bar, 13 Rue des Petits-Champs (north exit of Jardins du Palais-Royal, turn left. (M: Bourse) 42.61.05.09. Enjoy the food, wine, and conversation in this cozy wine bar. Named after Colette's first husband. Closed Sunday. A FAVORITE.

RESTAURANTS: GASTRONOMIQUE:

Carre des Feuillants, 14 Rue de Castiglione (M: Concorde/Opéra) 42.86.82.82. Elegant, Exceptional Tasting menu from Chef/Owner Alain Dutournier.

Gérard Besson, 5 Rue Coq-Héron (M: Les Halles) 42.33.14.74. Lunch menus change regularly. Well known for dinner, featuring wild game, in season. Very expensive.

Goumard, 9 Rue Duphot (M: Madeleine) 42.60.36.07. Philippe Dubois features great seafood from the House of Prunier, you'll enjoy lobster €79, John Dory €49, and the Affaire Dejeuner is a memorable meal at €60. Expensive. Open Sunday.

L'Espadon, Ritz Hôtel, 15 Pl Vendôme (M: Opéra) 43.16.30.80. Everything you'd expect from the Ritz, with violin and harp, Limoges china, and chef Michael Roth's exquisite cuisine.

Le Grand Vefour, 17 Rue de Beaujolais (M: Palais-Royal) 42.96.56.27. Now owned by Taittinger group with lively chef, Guy Martin who is getting superb reviews. Expensive. Closed Sunday.

Le Meurice, Hôtel Meurice, 228 Rue de Rivoli (M: Concorde) 44.58.10.55. Royal setting. Impeccable service. In perfect taste. Chef Yannick Alleno works wonders and has been awarded another Michelin star. Make reservations well in advance. Because there are less than 20 tables and only one sitting for lunch and one sitting for dinner. Lunch prix fixe is €69, Dinner for two at $400. A FAVORITE.

1e. Louvre, Ile de Cité

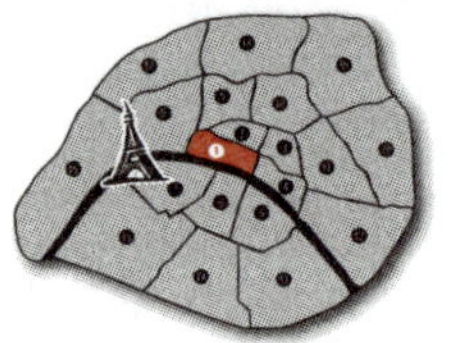

BONNE SOIREE! PARIS AT NIGHT:

Au Bec Fin, 6 Rue Thérèse (M: Pyramides) 42.96.29.35 Chansonniers.

Banana Club, 13-15 Rue de la Ferronnerie (M: Châtelet) 42.33.35.31. 90's style hot spot. Friendly.

Cabaret, 2 Pl du Palais-Royale (M: Palais-Royal) 58.62.56.25. Downstairs, trendy bars. Upstairs restaurant. Very snobby.

Café Oz, 18 Rue St. Denis (M: Châtelet) Top Ten night bars. 40.39.00.18

Café Rive Droit, 2 Rue Berger (M: Chatelet/Les Halles) 42.33.81.62. Brasserie with chanteuse or karaoke.

Côstes, 239 Rue St-Honore (M: Tuileries) 42.44.50.25. Great for before or after dinner drinks. A FAVORITE.

Châtelet-Theatre, Musical de Paris, Pl du Châtelet (M: Châtelet) 40.28.28.00. Call for concerts and schedules.

Comédie Française, 2 Rue de Richelieu (M: Palais-Royal) 44.58.15.15. 17th century théâtre presents the classics.

Hemingway Bar in Ritz Hôtel is very small and very smoky.

Kong, 1 Rue du Pont Neuf (M: Pont Neuf) 40.39.90.00. Food is an afterthought, so go for happy hour 6-8p or after 10:30 for lounge.

Duc des Lombards, 42 Rue des Lombards, 42.33.22.88, **Le Baiser Sale,** 58 Rue des Lombards, 42.33.37.71, **Sunset,** 60 Rue des Lombards, 40.26.46.60. Sunside, 40.26.21.25. Live music along Rue des Lombards is easy to find. See also, Stonewall, below.

Paris Paris, 5 Ave. de l'Opéra (M: Opéra) 42.60.64.45. Monday evenings, once a month, the fashionable store Colette hosts dance classes at 10p, followed by DJ and music until 3am. Free. Call for schedule.

Stonewall, 46 Rue des Lombards (M: Châtelet) 40.28.05.04. Dance club. Vaulted rooms.

Theatre de la Ville de Paris, 2 Pl du Châtelet (M: Châtelet) 42.74.22.77. Formerly the "Sarah Bernhardt Theatre", call Box Office to see dance, jazz, classical theatre.

Tuileries Bar, in Hotel Inter-Continental, 3 Rue de Castiglione (M: Concorde) 44.77.10.47. Piano player entertains 10p-closing Tuesdays-Saturdays.

Vendôme Bar, Ritz Hotel, is near the front entrance and has piano music for a romantic way to end the evening. Non-smoking area. A FAVORITE.

Wine & Bubbles, 3 Rue Francaise (M: Etienne Marcel) 44.76.99.84. They stock 600 bottles in the shop to take to mezzanine café til 2am.

My Special Travel Notes

1

My Special Travel Notes

2e. Bourse

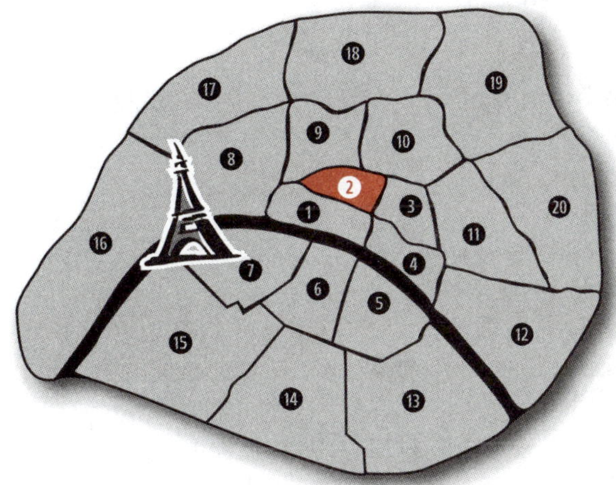

Take a stroll along **Rue Montmartre** for some eclectic fashion finds and café hop in this hip and trendy area in Paris.

Visit the boutiques in some of the oldest "passages" in Paris, **Passage du Grand Cerf** or **Passage Vivienne.**

Café Moderne is one of our favorites for lunch and is in the center of Paris' stock exchange.

Drink martinis in Paris' Best American Bar: **Harry's New York Bar.**

MAJOR METROS:

- BOURSE
- OPÉRA
- SENTIER
- RICHELIEU DROUOT
- GRANDS BOULEVARDS
- REAMUR-SEBASTOL
- ETIENNE MARCEL

2e. Bourse

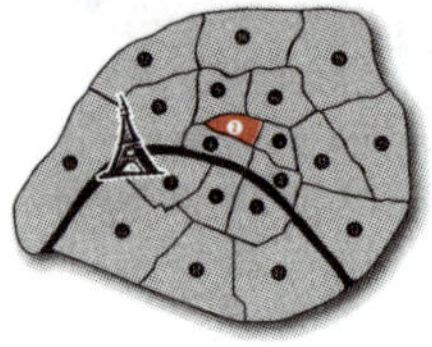

2

FAMOUS SIGHTS:

Bibliothèque Nationale, 58 Rue Richelieu (M: Bourse) 47.03.81.26. Various collections. Inside you will find the **Musée du Cabinet des Médailles,** with coins and medals, Charlemagne's chess set, and more. Call for exhibitions. Admission fee. Closed Monday.

DIVERSIONS:

Les Etoiles du Rex (at Le Grand Rex movie cinéma) 1 Blvd Poissonnière (M: Sentier) 45.08.93.40. Interactive audio tribute of movies. Open Wed-Sun 10a-7p.

Massato Salon, 5 Rue Volney (M: Opéra) 42.96.10.04. Haircut and Blow Dry $110, stylist Diego Dos Santos.

Martine Moisan gallery, 8 Galerie Vivienne (M: Palais-Royal or Bourse) north of the Palais-Royal 42.97.46.45. Martine is an art teacher who will take you and your group of 4 on a sketching tour of Paris (bring your own art supplies).

Musée du Parfum, Théâtre des Capucines, 39 Blvd des Capucines (M: Opéra) 42.60.37.14. Perfume muséum. Free, Mon-Sat.

Passage du Grand Cerf, 145 Rue St-Denis and 10 Rue Dussoubs (M: Etienne Marcel) Opens at noon and has some good boutiques such as jewelry designer

Marie-Lise Goelo jewelry, no. 10.

Passage des Princes, 3-5 Blvd des Italiens (M: Richelieu Drouot). Mostly childrens' toys and games.

Passage Sainte-Foy, (M: Strasberg St-Denis). Walk south from the Metro until you get to 236 Rue St-Denis, then cross the courtyard and climb 13 steps to 14 Sainte Foy, continuing to Rue Chemin and Rue d'Aboutier.

Passages Choiseul, 44 Rue des Petits-Champs (M: Quâtre-Septembre). Open Sat/Sun/Mon.

Passages des Panoramas, 10 Rue Saint-Marc and Blvd Montmartre (M: Bourse).Old stamps and postcards.

Walk **Rue Montorgueil** for a lively mix of fresh grocers, boutiques and cafes.

SUPERLATIVES:

Best American Bar: Harry's New York Bar, 5 Rue Daunou (M: Opéra) 42.61.71.14.

Best pastries: Stohrer, 51 Rue Montorgueil (M: Etienne Marcel) 42.33.38.20. Tarts, baba au rhum.

Best prime rib: Le Gavroche. See Restaurants.

Best sushi: Isse, 56 Rue Ste-Anne (M: 4 Septembre) 42.96.67.76. Very expensive.

Most generous champagne cocktails: Somo, 168 Rue Montmartre (M:Grands Boulevards). 40.13.08.80. Open noon-2a, Mon-Sat. Hip split-level restaurant and club.

Oldest Wine Merchants: Legrand Filles et Fils 1 Rue de la Banque (M: Bourse) 42.60.07.12. Retail wine shop and wine bar. Closed Sunday.

Traditional Bistro: Chez Georges, 1 Rue du Mail (M: Sentier) 42.60.07.11. Great reviews from friends. Authentic French, classic Paris.

Walk Rue Montorguei for a lively mix of fresh grocers, boutiques and cafes.

SHOPS :

58 M, 58 Rue Montmartre (M: Etienne Marcel) 40.26.61.01. Shoes: great brands such as Sigerson Morrison, Marc Jacobs.

A. Simon, 48-52 Rue Montmartre (M: Sentier) 42.33.71.65. Cookware, knives, etc.

Anna Moi, 65 Rue Montmartre (M: Grands Boulevards) 42.36.00.89. Ladies wear.

Anne Fontaine, 50 Rue Etienne Marcel.(M: Etienne Marcel) 40.41.08.32. Fine blouses.

Brentanos, 37 Ave l'Opéra (M: Opéra) 42.61.52.50. Book store.

Cartier, 13 Rue de la Paix (M: Opéra) 42.18.53.70. Their name says it all.

Cinna, 91 Blvd de Sébastopol (M: Reamur-Sebastopol) 40.26.99.32. Three story design studio.

Corum, 5 Rue de la Paix (M: Opéra) 44.55.07.77. Boutique for watches.

Daum, 4 Rue de la Paix (M: Opéra) 42.61.25.25. Designer glass and crystal.

Dunhill's, 15 Rue de la Paix (M: Opéra) 42.61.58.40. Exquisite antiques, one-of-a-kind cuff links, travel pepper mill, et al.

Epicare P. LeGrand, 1 Rue de la Banque (M: Bourse) 42.60.07.12. Galerie Vivienne. A must for wine lovers! 9a-7p. Closed Mon.

Jean-Paul Gaultier, 6 Rue Vivienne (M: Bourse) 42.86.05.05. Ready-to-wear. His new headquarters is in 8e.

Kiliwatch, 64 Rue Tiquetonne (M: Etienne Marcel) 42.21.17.37. Popular for hip streetwear and denim.

Kokon to Zai, 48 Rue Tiquetonne (M: Etienne Marcel) 42.36.92.41. Tiny boutique, edgy accessories by hot talents.

Kookai, 82 Rue Reamur (M: Reamur Sébastopol) 45.08.93.69. The is main store of several locations.

Lagerfeld Gallery, 12 Rue Vivienne (M: Bourse) 44.50.22.22. Boutique and photo gallery.

Le shop, 3 Rue d' Argout (M: Sentier) 40.28.95.94. One of the first concept stores. Trendy, hip accessories and clothing.

Les Néréides, 40 Rue Tiquetonne (M: Etienne Marcel) 42.33.52.00. Jewelry showroom.

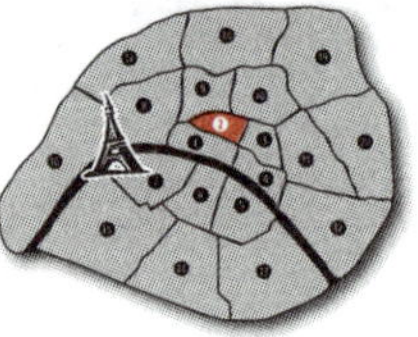

Lollipops, 60 Rue Tiquetonne (M: Etienne Marcel) 42.33.15.72. Specialize in handbags, accessories.

Massaro, 2 Rue de la Paix (M: Opéra) 42.61.00.29. Custom-made heels by appointment only.

Michel Swiss, 16 Rue de la Paix (M: Opéra) 42.61.61.11. Duty-free perfumes, cosmetics, accessories.

Morgan, 16 Rue Turbigo (M: Etienne Marcel) 44.82.02.00. Womens wear.

Nathalie Garçon, 15-17 Galerie Vivienne (M: Pyramides) 40.20.14.00. Parisien designer.

Oliviers et Co, 90 Rue Montorgueil (M: Etienne Marcel) 44.82.62.28. Olive oils.

Paul & Joe, 46 Rue Etienne Marcel (M: Etienne Marcel) 40.28.03.34.Boutique

Tartine et Chocolat, 24 Rue de la Paix (M: Opéra) 47.42.10.68. Infant and children's clothing, accessories.

Thierry Mugler, 54 Rue Etienne Marcel (M: Etiene Marcel) 42.33.06.13. Couture for men.

Urban Nature, 58 Rue d'Argout (M: Sentier) 42.21.47.47. Flowers, plants, vases.

Ventilo, 27 bis, Rue du Louvre (M: Etienne Marcel) 44.76.82.95. Women's clothing, flirty wraparound tops, layered skirts, shoes and accessories.

Ya Ya Boutique, 55 Rue Montmartre (M: Sentier) 40.39.92.89. Chic clothing boutique.

ZOR, 65 Rue Montmartre (M: Sentier) 40.41.12.70. Costume jewelry.

RESTAURANTS: LES PLATS DU JOUR:

A Priory Thé, 35-37 Galerie Vivienne (M: Bourse) Enjoy brunch or lunch in this tea room owned by an American woman.

Angl'Opera, 39 Ave Opéra (M: Palais-Royal) 42.61.86.25. Inventive cuisine by chef Gilles Choukroun. Terrace.

Aux Lyonnais, 32 Rue Saint-Marc (M: Grands Boulevards) 42.96.65.04. Perfect combination of Alain Ducasse's expertise and Christophe Saintoigne's hearty Lyonnaise meals.

Aux Trois Petits Cochons, 31 Rue Tiquetonne (M: Etienne-Marcel) 42.33.39.69. Popular.

Bistrot Vivienne, 4 Rue des Petits Champs (M: Palais-Royal) 49.27.00.50. Neighborhood favorite. Classic steak tartare, fresh salads, good soup. Hearty bistro fare. Friendly. Closed Sunday.

Café Marcel, 34 Rue Etienne Marcel (M: Etienne Marcel) 45.08.01.03. Décor is not as great as some of the other Costes restaurants.

Café Moderne, 40 Rue Notre-Dame des Victoires (M: Bourse) 53.40.84.10. We enjoy very much. €24 for 3-course lunch. Delicious eclectic menu. A FAVORITE. Say bonjour to Frederic, who now also owns Astier. Closed Sunday.

Chez Georges, 1 Rue du Mail (M: Sentier) 42.60.07.11. Paris bistro with good reports from friends.

Chez Laurent, 3 Rue St Augustin (M: Bourse) 42.97.48.09. Long bar, classy décor.

Dédé La Frite, 135 Rue Montmartre (M: Bourse) 40.41.99.90. Simple neighborhood bistrot.

Drouant, 18 Rue Gaillon (M: Opéra) 42.65.15.16. Antoine Westermann, who also owns Mon Vieil Ami, and his chef, present €70 three-course meal that comes with lots of vegetables on the side. Art déco setting. Closed Sunday

Gallopin Brasserie, 40 Rue Notre Dame-des-Victoires (M: Bourse) 42.36.45.38. Classic food and 1876 interior. Small terrace. Very typical Parisian flare and flavors.

La Fontaine Gaillon, Pl Gaillon (M: Opéra) 47.42.63.22. Gerard Depardieu's restaurant. Chef Audiot's fine cooking combined with Depardieu's insistence on freshest ingredients. Open lunch and dinner Monday-Friday. Beautiful terrace.

La Grille Montorgueil, 50 Rue Montorgueil (M: Etienne Marcel) 42.33.21.21. Classic bistro dishes, fun little terrace, friendly and popular with locals.

Le Café, 62 Rue Tiquetonne (M: Etienne Marcel) 40.39. 08.00. Fresh salads, lighter fare. Sunny terrace.

Le Celadon, in the Hotel Westminster. 15 Rue Daunou (M: Opéra) 42.61.77.42. Young chef Christophe Moisand, of the Meurice, has quickly earned a Michelin star here with his imaginative specialties. Prix-fixe lunch and dinner. Closed in August.

Le Croissant, 146 Rue Montmartre (M: Bourse) 42.33.35.04. This bar was the site of the assassination of Jean Jaurés in 1914. Closed Sat/Sun.

Le Gavroche, 19 Rue St-Marc (M: Bourse) 42.96.89.70. Traditional bistro with great prime ribs. Open til 1 am. True Parisian atmosphere. Closed Sunday.

Le Grand Colbert, 2 Rue Vivienne (M: Bourse) 42.86.87.88. Grand brasserie in Passage Vivienne. Fills with tourists since the movie "Something's Gotta Give" was filmed here.

Le Mesturet, 77 Rue de Richelieu (M: Bourse) 42.97.40.68. Owner Alain Fontaine's mix of flea market décor, new fresh menu, and inexpensive wine list is a hit. Closed Sunday.

Le Petit Vendome, 8 Rue des Capucines (M: Opéra) 42.61.05.88. Very popular at lunch with tourists and locals alike. Not inexpensive.

Le Vaudeville, 29 Rue Vivienne (M: Bourse) 40.20.04.62. Lively late-night brasserie.

2e. Bourse

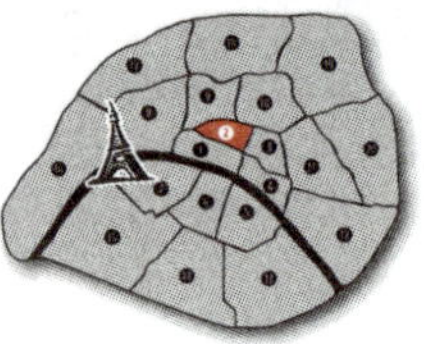

2

Legrand Filles et Fils, 1 Rue de la Banque (M: Bourse) Galerie Vivienne. 42.60.07.12. Enjoy light fare under glass roof or wine in the cozy atmosphere inside. Good wine list. Closed Sunday.

Little Italy Café, 92 Rue Montorgueil (M: Sentier) 42.36.36.25. Popular Italian on this convivial street.

Liza, 14 Rue de la Banque (M: Bourse) 55.35.00.66. Excellent Lebanese meals prepared by Chef Karim Haidar (from London restaurants) Modern décor with contemporary lighting. Try the baked lamb with five spices or the eggplant.

Mellifère, 8 Rue de Monsigny (M: Quatre Septembre) 42.61.21.71. Friendly chef/owner Alain Atibard and his wife Veronique serve good simple Basque-style food at simple prices. Friendly service. Nightly blackboard menu of food and wines. €34 3-course meal. Closed Sat. lunch/Sunday.

Mi Cayito, 10 Rue Marie Stuart (M: Etienne Marcel) 42.21.98.86. Hip Cuban.

Mori Venice Bar, 2 Rue Quatre Septembre (M: Bourse) 44.55.51.55. Designed by Philippe Starck, with Murano chandeliers. Venetian dishes of antipasti, homemade ravioli, pastas. Closed Sunday.

Somo, 168 Rue Montmartre (M: Grands Boulevards). 40.13.08.80. Open noon-2a, Mon-Sat. Hip split-level restaurant and club.

RESTAURANTS: GASTRONOMIQUE:

Isse, 56 Rue Ste-Anne (M: Quatre Septembre) 42.96.67.76. Very expensive and very fresh sushi. Some believe this is the best Japanese food in Paris.

Le Park, Hyatt Hotel, Salon Verriere, 3-5 Rue de la Paix (M: Opéra) 58.71.12.34. Chef Christophe David from Taillivent fame.

BONNE SOIREE! PARIS AT NIGHT:

Barbara Bui Café, 27 Rue Etienne Marcel (M: Etienne Marcel) 45.08.04.04. 9 pm show 3rd Thursday each month. Call.

Bar Les Chenets, in Hotel Westminster, 13 Rue de la Paix (M: Opéra) 42.61.57.46. Cozy with selection of champagne-based cocktails. Cocktail piano between 6:30p-9p. Bar open 8:30a - Midnight.

Cerise, 46 Rue de Montorgueil (M: Sentier) 46.34.57.26. Piano, Jazz.

Duke's Bar at the Hotel Westminster, 13 Rue de la Paix (M: Opéra) 42.61.57.46. Go before or after dinner, has resident pianist and jazz singer joins in on weekends.

Grand Rex Club, 5 Blvd Poissonnière (M: Sentier) 45.08.93.89. Has national acts.

Harry's New York Bar. See above "Superlatives". 5 Rue Daunou Open daily til 4 am.

La Belle Epoque, New Look, 36 Rue des Petits Champs (M: Opéra) 42.96.33.33. Cabaret.

Le Port d'Amsterdam, 20 Rue Croissant (M: Sentier) 40.39.02.63. Popular night bar.

Le Pulp, 25 Blvd Poissoniere (M: Sentier) 40.26.01.93. Hip hop/R & B/ House. Mixed crowd. Trendy.

Opéra Comique, 5 Rue Favart (M: Richelieu-Drouot) enter Pl. Boieldieu. 42.44.45.40. Call for shows and times.

Sentier des Halles, 50 Rue d'Aboukir (M: Sentier) 42.61.89.96. Call for entertainment schedule.

My Special Travel Notes

3e. Marais

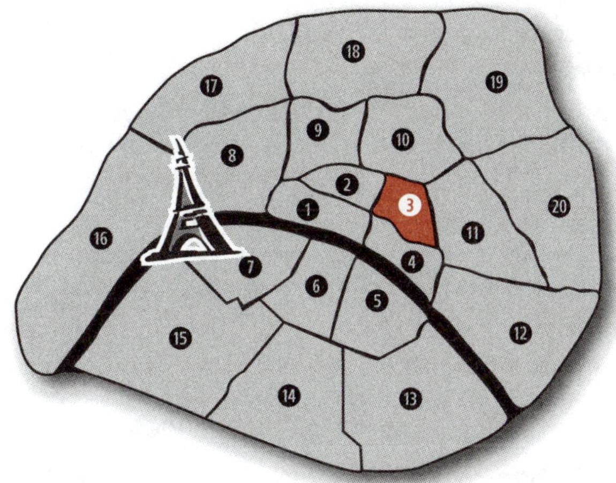

Musée Carnavelet is one of our favorites. So are **Musée Picasso** and **Musée des Arts et Métiers.**

Ennjoy shopping at **Shine** while you stroll the **haute Marais.**

We love to sip pastis at **Chez Janou,** where you can choose from over 80 selections.

You will find the **"Grand Pignon"** - a house built in 1407 by Nicolas Flamel and considered to be the oldest in Paris.

MAJOR METROS:

- RAMBUTEAU
- ARTS ET MÉTIERS
- TEMPLE
- REAMUR
- SÉBASTOPOL
- FILLES DU CALVAIRE
- CHEMIN VERT
- ST-SÉBASTIEN FROISSART

3e. Marais

3

FAMOUS SIGHTS:

Musée des Arts et Métiers, 60 Rue Réaumur (M: Arts et Métiers) 53.01.82.00. €5.50. 10a-6p. Open til 9:30p on Thurs. Closed Mondays. Founded in 1794. Housed in the abbey of Saint-Martin-Des-Champs. Bright and airy museum is devoted to scientific instruments, materials, construction, communications, energy, mechanics, and transportation. Take the No. 11 Metro line to get here so you can see this metro station which was inspired by Jules Verne's submarine, Nautilus. A FAVORITE.

Musée Carnavelet, 23 Rue de Sévigné (M: St-Paul) 44.59.58.58. Open 10a-5p. Devoted to the history of Paris. Lovely manicured garden. Hôtel le Peletier de St-Fargeau, across the courtyard, also has exhibits. A FAVORITE. Closed Monday.

Musée de la Chasse (Hunting Museum) 60 Rue des Archives (M: St-Paul) 53.01.92.40. In Hotel Guenegaud, near Carnavelet Museum. Designed by Mansart, you'll see mounted heads, a Rembrandt sketch of a lion, hunting tapestries, etc. €5.00 Closed Mon.

Musée d'Art et Histoire du Judaisme, 71 Rue du Temple (M: Hôtel de Ville) 53.01.86.60. Trace the development of Jewish culture in Paris and France as well as the best display of art from leading Jewish artists €6.00. 11a – 6p. Closed Sat.

Musée Picasso, 5 Rue de Thorigny (M: Chemin Vert) 42.71.25.21 Picasso's private collection. This is a must for art lovers. A FAVORITE. Closed Tues. €5.50.

DIVERSIONS:

Stroll the "haute Marais" bordered by Rue Vieille-du-Temple, Rue de Poitou, Rue Charlot (M: Filles du Calvaire). You will enjoy the many diverse shops and galleries in this fun and funky Bobo (bourgeois-bohemian) Marais neighborhood. Lots of shopping opportunities, fun streets, bustling activity. Many of the shops are closed on Sunday and some are closed on Monday. A FAVORITE.

Cooking classes at L'Atelier de Fred, 6 Rue des Vertus (M: Arts et Métiers) 40.29.46.04. Call in advance to reserve your place among small groups of six.

France Fiction, 6 bis Rue des Forez (M: Filles du Calvaire). Visit this gallery which has a new theme each month.

Galerie Christophe Delcourt, 125 Rue Vieille-du-Temple (M: St-Sébastien Froissart) 42.78.44.97. Furniture designer.

Galerie Thaddaeus Ropac, 7 Rue Debelleyme (M: Filles du Calvaire) 42.72.99.00. Various shows. Call for exhibitions.

Jardin St-Gilles-Grand-Veneur (M: Chemin Vert) Take the passage at 12 Rue de Villehardouin and then turn onto Rue de Hesse where you will find a 2 acre public garden amid mansions.

Musée Cognacq-Jay, Hôtel Donon, 8 Rue Elzevir (M: St-Paul) 40.27.07.21. Private mansion once owned by founders of Samaritaine. Well-displayed collection of French rococo art and also has perfume cases, snuff boxes. Closed Mondays.

3

Musée de l'Histoire de France, in **Hôtel de Soubise,** 60 Rue des Francs Bourgeois (M: Rambuteau) 40.27.60.96. Entrance €3.50. Housed in mansion built in 1705. Closed Tues.

Musée de la Poupée, French Doll muséum, Impasse Berthaud (M: Rambuteau) 42.72.73.11. Price €6. Dolls made of porcelain, fabric, etc. and displayed with accessories, furniture and old toys. Private collection, over 200 dolls, even Barbie.Closed Mon.

Passage Molière. 161 Rue St Martin (M: Rambuteau) 19th century passage with art galleries, book stores. Look for Entrée des Artists bookstore and gallery with marionettes, masks, posters and mechanical circus with lion tamer.

Passages de Poitou, Rue de Poitou (M: Filles du Calvaire) Boutiques.

Web bar, 32 Rue de Picardie (M: Filles du Calvaire) 42.72.66.55. Internet café and more. Open 11:30a - 2am.

Wine bar and board games: L'Apparemment, 18 Rue des Coutures-St-Gervais (M: St-Sébastian Froissart) 48.87.12.22.

Wine courses at Le Jardin des Vignes. 91 Rue de Turenne (M: St-Sébastien Froissart) 42.77.05.00. Evening sessions at 8-10p during the week. €85 each. No credit cards. Call Jean Radford for information.

SUPERLATIVES:

Best pain au chocolat: Au Levain du Marais, 32 Rue de Turenne (M: Chemin Vert) 42.78.07.31.

More chocolate: Joséphine Vannier, 4 Rue du Pas de la Mule (M: Chemin Vert) 44.54.03.09. Chocolate as an art form!

Oldest house in Paris: 51 Rue de Montmorency (M: Arts et Métiers) "Grand-Pignon" built in 1407 by Nicolas Flamel.

SHOPS:

AB33, 33 Rue Charlot (M: Filles du Calvaire) 42.71.02.82. Cote d'Azur fashions and boutique with stylish selections from Isabel Marant and others. Shoes, bags, too. Closed Monday.

Abou d'Abi Bazar 125, 125 Rue Vieille-du-Temple (M: Filles du Calvaire) 42.71.13.26. Multi-brand boutique, fun items. A second location is also in the Marais. Closed Sunday.

Abou D'abi Bazar, 10 Rue des Francs Bourgeois (M: Rambuteau) 42.77.96.98. Open Sunday. Many brands, reasonable prices.

Adeline André, 5 Rue Villehardouin (M: Chemin Vert) 42.77.72.56. Haute couture house.

3e. Marais

Agenda Moderne, 42 Rue Sévigne (M: St-Paul) 44.54.59.20. Stationers, fine products. I use their Agenda International.

Alain Maisonneuve, 18 Rue Charlot (M: Filles du Calvaire) 40.29.49.79. Antiques and objets d'art.

3

Altea, 41 Rue Charlot (M: Filles du Calvaire) 42.77.71.00. Teas and teapots.

Amours, Délices Orgues, 5 Rue du Perche (M: Filles du Calvaire) 44.54.98.62. Erotic items and sexy underwear.

Anne Fontaine, 12 Rue des Francs Bourgeois (M: St-Paul) 44.59.81.59.

Art 75 Galerie Yves di Maria-Paris, 58 Rue Vieille-du-Temple (M: Hôtel de Ville) 42.71.70.26. Vintage posters, photographs, art. Reasonable prices, friendly. A FAVORITE.

CSAO, 80 Rue Turenne (M: Filles du Calvaire) 44.54.55.88. A haven for West African goods, as well as a restaurant.

Calesta Kid Store, 23 Rue Debelleyme (M: Filles du Calvaire) 42.72.15.59. Trendy teen concept store. Marlene Pillici smartly included a play space and cartoons downstairs, as well as furniture and decoration items.

Camper Shoes, 9 Rue des Francs Bourgeois (M: St-Paul) 48.87.09.09. Small, but good selection.

Cecile & Jeanne, 12 Rue des Francs Bourgeois (M: St-Paul) 44.61.00.99.Jewelry. Several locations.

Celis, 72 Rue Vieille-du-Temple (M; Rambuteau) 48.87.52.73. Roxana Pecquet's handmade finger puppets make irresistible souvenirs for the child in everyone. A FAVORITE.

Clauss Didier, 26 Rue Pastourelle (M: Arts et Métiers) 42.72.00.78. Jewelry. Closed Mondays.

Comptoire de l'Image, 44 Rue du Sevigne (M: Chemin Vert) 42.72.03.92. Fashion photography bookstore.

Dominique Picquier Boutigue, 10 Rue Charlot (M: Filles du Calvaire) 42.72.23.33. Everything fabric: bags, belts, pillows, home accessories. Beautiful. Closed Monday.

Entre des Fournisseurs, 8 Rue des Francs-Bourgeois (M: St-Paul) 48.87.58.98. Tiny shop with couture selections of buttons, ribbons, to accessorize.

Et Cætera, 40 Rue de Poitou (M: Filles du Calvaire) 42.71.37.11. Antiques.

Fiesta Galerie, 43 Rue Vieille-du-Temple (M: Hôtel de Ville) 42.71.53.34. Art Deco collectibles.

Food, 58 Rue Charlot (M: Filles du Calvaire) 42.72.69.97. Gallery, bookstore, recipe books.

Galerie 213, 58 Rue Charlot (M: Filles du Calvaire) 43.22.83.23. Small, welcoming bookstore with rare titles, trendy photographers, carefully overseen by Antoine de Breaupré.

Galerie Dansk, 31 Rue Charlot (M: Filles du Calvaire) 42.71.45.95. Hip Scandinavian antiques from the mod era.

Galerie Emmanuel Perrotin, 76 Rue Turenne (M: St- Sébastian Froissart) 42.16.79.79. Art dealer.

Galerie Pierre, 22 Rue Debelleyme (M: Filles du Calvaire) 42.72.20.24. Shop & Exhibition space. Ceramics.

Galerie Yvon Lambert, 108 Rue Vieille-du-Temple (M: St-Sébastien Froissart) 42.71.09.33.

Gavilane, 8 Rue des Francs-Bourgeois (M: Rambuteau) 42.72.92.36. Jewelry and accessories. We like! They have other locations in the Marais district.

Goumanyat et son Royaune, 3 Rue Dupuis (M: Temple) 44.78.96.74. Gourmet specialty shop.

L'Artisan Fleuriste, 95 Rue Vieille-du-Temple (M: Hotel de Ville) 42.78.40.40. The bouquet is enhanced by the "bouquet."

L'Habilleur, 44 Rue de le Poitou (M: Filles du Calvaire) 48.87.77.12. Discounts on last season's couture.

Le Boudoir du Marais, 9 Rue de Perche (M: Filles du Calvaire) 42.78.26.45. A space for the body. Manicure, pedicure, "stone therapie" massages. Both sexes.

Le Boudoir et Sa Philosophie, 18 Rue Charlot (M: Filles du Calvaire) 48.04.89.79. Right out of an 18th century movie set with everything for the bedroom.

Le Palais des Thés, 64 Rue Vieille-du-Temple (M: St-Sébastien Froissart) 48.87.80.60. Rare teas.

Les Milles Feuilles, 2 Rue Rambuteau (M: Rambuteau) 42.78.32.93. Florists.

Lieu Commun, 5 Rue Filles du Calvaire (M: Filles du Calvaire) 44.54.08.30. Hip concept store: clothing, décor, CDs and seasonal collectibles. Closed Monday.

Martin Grant, 10 Rue Charlot (M: Filles du Calvaire) 42.71.39.49. Australian designer/dressmaker offers clean lines for simple tastes from third floor of apartment building with access through the courtyard.

Pierre Frey, 111 Blvd Beaumarchais (M: St-Sébastien Froissart) 48.04.30.03. Home décor accessories and furniture. Also has exhibition space.

Quidam de Revel, 24 Rue Poitou (M: Filles du Calvaire) 42.71.37.07. Tasteful vintage treasures. Closed Sun/Monday.

3e. Marais

Sans Arcidet, 117 Rue Vieille-du-Temple (M: Filles du Calvaire) 42.72.10.04. This collection of ethno-chic handmade bags, hats, accessories is created by three sisters. Closed Sun/Mon.

3

Shine, 15 Rue de Poitou (M: Filles du Calvaire) 48.05.80.10. Vinci D'Elia's magical multi-brand boutique combines rock and roll, glitz, and glamour. Clothing, bags, accessories, jewelry. One-of-a-kind styles. I always go to see the latest trends. A FAVORITE.

Tatiana Lebedev, 64 Rue Vieille-du-Temple (M: Hôtel de Ville) 42.77.80.89. New designer. Womens boutique. Great mix of fabrics. Accessories. A FAVORITE. Closed Sunday.

The White Shop, 69 Rue des Gravilliers (M: Arts et Métiers) 42.76.04.04. Each month is devoted to a new theme, i.e. everything digital, soccer-wear.

Tools Galerie, 119 Rue Vieille-du-Temple (M: St-Sébastien Froissart) 42.77.37.62. Owner Bigot showcases unique designs for the kitchen home.

Tsumori Chisato, 20 Rue Barbette (M: St-Paul) 42.78.18.88. New boutique from this designer used to collaborate w/Issey Miyake.

Villa Marais, 40 Rue des Francs Bourgeois (M: Rambuteau) 42.78.42.20. Tableware and objets d'art.

RESTAURANTS: LES PLATS DU JOUR:

404, 69 Rue des Gravilliers (M: Arts et Métiers) 42.74.57.81. Couscous and belly dancing. Trendy North African and very popular.

Al Filo Della Stagioni, 8 Rue de Beauce (M: Temple) 48.04.52.24. Savory Italian at moderate prices in comfortable décor. Closed Sunday.

Ambassade d'Auvergne, 22 Rue du Grenier St Lazare (M: Etienne Marcel) 42.72.31.22. Good value at €55 for two. Hearty, regional country-style cooking. Open Sunday.

Au Bascou, 38 Rue Reamur (M: Arts et Métiers) 42.72.69.25. Patricial Wells loved it, we have found so-so food and service for the price. Basque regional food. Closed Sunday.

Auberge Nicolas Flamel, 51 Rue de Montmorency (M: Arts et Métiers) 42.71.77.78. Some say this house, "Grand Pignon," built in 1407, is the oldest house in Paris. Rated 79 out of 100 by a French newsletter. Good wine list. Closed Sunday.

Café Baci, 36 Rue Turenne (M: Chemin Vert) 42.71.36.70. Owned by actor Jean-Pierre Bacri who serves Italian food to stylish crowd.

Cave Saint Gilles, 4 Rue St Gilles (M: Chemin Vert) 48.87.22.62. Small plates.

Chez Janou, 2 Rue Roger Verlomme (M: Chemin Vert) 42.72.28.41. Terrace. Friendly. Good Mediterranean at a reasonable price and easy pace. 80 different pastis drinks. Our favorite is Aux Epice Douces. A FAVORITE. Open Sunday.

Chez Nénesse, 17 Rue de Saintonge (M: Filles du Calvaire) 42.78.46.49. Classic bistro where the welcome is personal and the plastic coated menus aren't. Closed Sun/Monday.

Chez Omar, 47 Rue de Bretagne (M: Filles du Calvaire) 42.72.36.26. Very popular. Good Couscous. No reservations.

Innamorati, 57 Rue Charlot (M: Filles du Calvaire) 48.04.88.28. Provencal restaurant, open kitchen, friendly staff serving good food.

La Guirlande de Julie, 25 Place des Vosges (M: St-Paul) 48.87.94.07. Some say touristy, some say classic. Owned by the Terrail family of Tour d' Argent notoriety.

Le Hangar, 12 Impasse Berthaud (M: Rambuteau) 42.74.55.44. Some say imaginative, some say mediocre. Cash only. Mon-Sat.

Le Pamphlet, 38 Rue Debelleyme (M: St-Sébastien Froissart) 42.72.39.24. Good food and friendly staff. Non-smoking section. A FAVORITE. Closed Sunday.

Le Petit Marché, 9 Rue Bearn (M: Chemin Vert) 42.72.06.67. Good new neighborhood bistro. Open Sunday.

Le Réconfort, 37 Rue de Poitou (M: St-Sébastien Froissart) 49.96.09.60. Inventive Provencal cuisine in colorful Marais bistro.

Les Enfants Rouge, 9 Rue de Beuce (M: FIlles du Calvaire) 48.87.80.61. Neighborhood favorite. Menu €30.

Les Petits Marseillaise, 72 Rue Vieille-du-Temple (M: Hôtel de Ville) 42.78.91.59. Hip Marseillese menu, mixed crowd, lively provencal setting.

Orangerie Restaurant, in Hotel Beaumarchais. 5 Rue des Arquebusiers (M: St-Sébastien Froissart) 40.29.14.00. Has good prix fixe lunch.

R'Aliment, 57 Rue Charlot (M: Filles du Calvaire) 48.04.88.28. Organic meals in steel interior.Closed Sunday.

Robert et Louise, 64 Rue Vieille-du-Temple (M: Rambuteau) 42.78.55.89. Rustic communal tables. Classic food and service. No credit cards. Closed Sunday.

Si, 14 Rue Charlot (M: Arts et Metiers) 42.78.02.31. Friendly and favorably priced. Closed Sunday.

RESTAURANTS: GASTRONOMIQUE:

Chez L'Ami Louis, 32 Rue du Vertbois (M: Arts et Métiers) 48.87.77.48. You will either love it or not. Cholesterol-intense and well-known for enormous portions of foie gras and roast chicken. Expensive. A FAVORITE.Open Sunday.

3e. Marais

3

BONNE SOIREE! PARIS AT NIGHT:

Anahi, 49 Rue Volta (M: Arts et Métiers) 48.87.88.24.

Andy Wahloo, 69 Rue des Gravilliers (M: Arts et Métiers) 42.71.20.38. Fashion-forward, hip, Arabian nights club and bar. No cover.

Caveau de la République, 1 Blvd St Martin (M: République) 42.78.44.45. Chansonniers. Call ahead.

Les Bains, 7 Rue du Bourg L'Abbe (M: Etienne Marcel) 48.87.01.80. Hip nightclub with dinner served upstairs.

Tango, 11 Rue au Maire (M: Arts et Métiers) 42.72.17.78. Fun, mixed crowd. Dancing.

Web Bar, 32 Rue de Picardie (M: République) 42.72.66.55. Funky and call for concerts, poetry nights.

My Special Travel Notes

3

My Special Travel Notes

3

4e. Marais, St-Louis-En-L'Ile

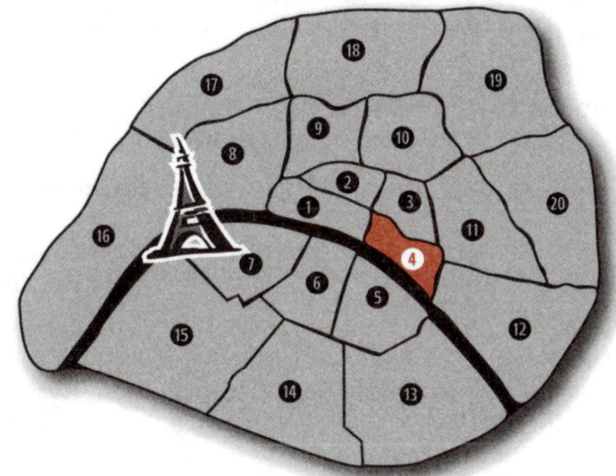

Spend time in the **Cathédrale du Notre Dame** and **Centre Pompidou.**

On Sundays, go to **Marché aux Fleurs,** a fun little flower market that has tropical birds. Follow up with ice cream at **Berthillon.**

We always enjoy our informal wine tasting and lunch at **Le Rouge Gorge,** with Francois, the owner. I show off my new jewelry that I buy at **Gian Paolo Maria** a few doors up the street.

MAJOR METROS:

- HOTEL DE VILLE
- ST-PAUL
- BASTILLE SULLY-MORLAND
- QUAI DE LE RÉPUBLIQUE

4e. Marais, St-Louis-En-L'Ile

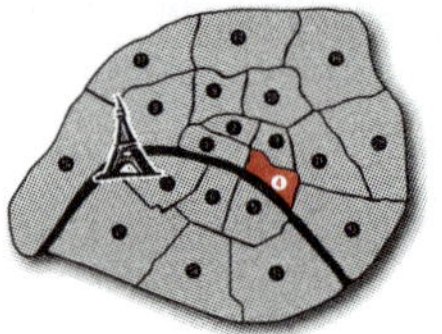

4

FAMOUS SIGHTS:

Cathédrale du Nôtre-Dame, 6 Pl du Parvis de Nôtre-Dame (M: St-Michel-Nôtre-Dame) 42.34.56.10. On Rue d'Arcole, in front of Nôtre Dame, you will notice the new space-age drinking fountain. There are only two others like it in Paris. **Tours de Nôtre-Dame,** 44.32.16.72. Climb 387 stairs to see superb view down over the steeple. The information table is on the right. If possible, enjoy mass here. A FAVORITE.

Catacombs du Parvis de Nôtre Dame, Crypte Archéologique, (M: St-Michel) 43.29.83.51. Always crowded. Open 10a-6p, Closed Mon.

Walk the square facing Nôtre Dame called **Place du Parvis-Nôtre-Dame.** In the center of Place du Parvis-Nôtre-Dame you will also find **Point Zéro** - where all distances in France are measured-from the brass compass star in the pavement in front of Nôtre Dame. You will also see **Statue de Charlemagne.**

Centre Pompidou, Pl Georges Pompidou (M: Rambuteau) 44.78.12.33. Closed Tuesdays. Open 11a-9p. Admission €5.49 gives you access to **Musée National d'Art Moderne,** the **Brancusi Studio** that has more than 140 sculptures, sketches, photos, and other exhibitions. Level 4 has Warhol. Level 5 has Matisse. The Centre also has **Flammarian Bookstore** that is A FAVORITE and **Printemps Design,** a home décor boutique. You'll get a great view while enjoying lunch at **Georges Restaurant** on the top floor

Deportation memorial, Square de L'Ile de France (M: St-Michel) is very moving. Walk down the steps to see where deportees were held and go inside to see sculptures, funeral urns and tomb. Each crystal represents one deportee. 10a – 11:30a/2p-7p. Free.

Square Jean-XXIII is at the west side of Nôtre Dame and has cherry trees, park benches, and is a good place to rest. You may be approached by gypsies; ignore them and they go away.

St-Louis-en-l'Ile lies across **Pont St-Louis.** Six blocks long, with no Metro. Lots of tourists enjoy its old-fashioned charm, distinctive art galleries and eclectic shops.

Eglise (Church) of St-Louis-en-l'Ile at 19 bis Rue St-Louis-en-l'Ile (M: Pont Marie). Inside you will find an ornate interior with white stone and gilt. Look for the 1926 plaque: "In grateful memory of St. Louis" in whose honor the city of St. Louis, Missouri USA is named. Call for church concerts 3p-7p.

DIVERSIONS:

Bains du Marais, 31 Rue des Blancs-Manteaux (M: Rambuteau) 44.61.02.02. Spa and bath. Salon opens for men and women on various days. Call ahead. Smells wonderful. Classy and peaceful.

Bibliothèque de l'Arsenal, 1 Rue Sully (M: Sully-Morland) 53.01.25.25. Library includes the prison dossier of Marquis de Sade among concentration of French literature. Open 10a-5p. Closed Sunday.

Canal Trip - Port de l'Arsenal (M: Bastille) 42.39.15.00. Begin at 9:15a/2:30p (3 hours) to La Villette by Canauxrama Boats. Please note that a lot of the canal trip is under bridges and is dark. Boats have bars, toilettes, and telephones.

Eglise Saint-Merri, 76 Rue de la Verrerie (M: Hôtel de Ville) Sat. 9p/Sunday. 4p. Free classical concerts.

Fontaine de Stravinsky on Place de Stravinsky is a wonderful place to relax and people-watch. A FAVORITE.

Haircut: Headscape, 21 Rue Vieille-du-Temple (M: Hôtel de Ville) 44.61.89.29. Phillip Starck design decor.

Hotel de Lauzun, 17 Quai d'Anjou (M: Pont Marie) 42.76.57.99. **Reserve a tour one year in advance and only on one Tuesday per month.** Visit a mansion built in 1656 and see rooms such as the "hashish room" of Baudelaire and the Chambres de parade's gaudy rooms filled with gold and gilt and velvet and nymphs.

Hôtel de Sully, 62 Rue Saint Antoine (M: St-Paul) 42.74.47.75. Call for exhibitions. Photo gallery. Garden.

Hôtel de Ville, Paris' city hall. 29 Rue de Rivoli (M: Hôtel de Ville) 42.76.51.53. Rotating exhibitions are in the salon in several small rooms. They monitor number of visitors so there may be a line. Call for exhibitions or look up in Pariscope weekly magazine. Closed Sunday.

La Balade au Cœur des Sens, 40 Rue des Blancs-Manteux (M: Rambuteau) 48.04.72.69. Making 'sense' of scents.

La Galerie d'Architecture, 11 Rue des Blancs-Manteux (M: Rambuteau) 49.96.64.00. Has café and bookshop.

Maison Européene de la Photographie, 5-7 Rue de Fourcy (M: St-Paul) 44.78.75.00. Call for exhibitions.

Mariage Frères, 30 Rue du Bourg-Tibourg (M: Hôtel de Ville) 42.72.28.11. Tea room and tea museum upstairs.

Musée de la Curiosité et Magie, 11 Rue St Paul (M: St-Paul) 42.72.13.26. Wed/Sat/Sunday. 2p-7p. €7. Magic and optical illusions.

Musée Victor Hugo, 6 Place des Vosges (M: St-Paul) 42.72.10.16. Look down over Pl. des Voges from upstairs. Free. Closed Monday.

Nomades, 37 Blvd Bourdon (M: Bastille) 44.54.07.44. Bike rentals. Call for schedule of rides.

Pavillon de L'Arsenal, 26 Blvd Morland (M: Quai de la République) Paris inside and out. Exhibitions change.

4e. Marais, St-Louis-En-L'Ile

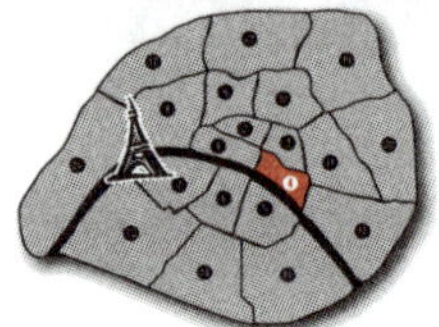

4

Place des Vosges (M: St-Paul) This used to be filled with mansions and monied extravagance fit for royalty. Now it is a lovely park with boutiques, art galleries and restaurants and may mark the end of a very nice walk meandering through the Marais.

Pilates Studio, 39 Rue du Temple (M: Hôtel de Ville) 42.72.91.74. Run by Philippe Taupiet who studied in New York under Joseph Pilates. Holds solo, duo and group classes.

Rue Rosiers is the heart of the Jewish community in Paris.

The Studio and Café la Gare, Dancing studios and little café where you can eat and watch the dancers (ballet, jazz, modern, Latin) practice. 41 Rue du Temple (M: Hôtel de Ville) 42.74.10.38. Enjoy lunch. Also has Sunday brunch.

Village St. Paul, 23-27 Rue St-Paul (M: Pont Marie) Home décor shops. Closed Tues-Wed.

SUPERLATIVES:

Best bathrooms: Café Beaubourg, 43 Rue Saint-Merri (M: Hôtel de Ville) 48.87.63.96. A great terrace faces Pompidou for great people watching. Go for atmosphere, not necessarily the food. Owned by the Côstes brothers. Open Sunday.

Best Bookstore: The Red Wheelbarrow, 22 Rue St Paul (M: St-Paul) 48.04.75.08. Say bonjour to Penelope and Abigail.

Best Boulangerie, Le Gay Choc, 45 Rue Ste. Croix de la Bretonnerie. (M: Sully-Morland) 48.87.56.88. A gay boulangerie from Richard and Dominique.

A second Le Gay is at 17 Rue des Archives. (M: Hôtel de Ville) 48.87.24.61.

Another best boulangerie: Boulangerie Martin, 40 Rue St-Louis-en-l'Ile (M: Pont Marie) 43.54.57.59. Crispy-crusted baguettes.

Best Ice Cream: Berthillon, 31 Rue St. Louis-En-l'le (M: Pont Marie) It's worth the long lines for some of the world's best ice cream. Try pistachio.

Best margaritas: La Perla Bar, 26 Rue Francois Miron (M: Hôtel de Ville) 42.77.59.40.

Best place for a picnic: Square Barye on Ile St Louis, Pont de Sully (M: Sully Morland)

Best prix fixe lunch: Le Coude Fou, 12 Rue du Bourg-Tibourg (M: St-Paul) 42.77.15.16. See Restaurants.

Best sandwiches: L'As du Fallafel, 34 Rue des Rosiers (M: St-Paul).

Best sushi: Isami, 4 Quai d' Orleans (M: Pont Marie) 40.46.06.97. Always crowded.

Best terrace view: Georges, on top of Pompidou. (M: Rambuteau) See Restaurants.

Extraordinary Spices: Izrael Epicure du Monde, 30 Rue Francois-Miron (M: St-Paul) 42.72.66.23. Tues-Sat: 9:30-1p, 7p-9p. This is where Paris chefs shop.

First "philosophy café" in Paris: Café des Phares, 7 Pl de la Bastille (M: Bastille) 42.72.04.70.

Jewish Deli: Florence Finkelsztain, 19 Rue des Rosiers (M: St-Paul) 44.61.00.20.

Largest private photography gallery: Galerie Vu, 2 Rue Jules Cousin (M: Sully-Morland) 53.01.85.81. Exhibit space located in the basement of photo agency Vu.

Most lively café: Les Philosophes, 28 Rue Vielle-du-Temple. (M: Hôtel de Ville) 48.87.49.64. Good terrace, friendly service. Great tomato tart. 2-course lunch $15.

Olive Oils: A L'Olivier, 23 Rue de Rivoli (M: Hôtel de Ville) 48.04.86.59. Founded 1860, every oil you could ever think of.

Oldest espresso machine, Brasserie de l'Ile St. Louis still has the original copper machine first used, see Restaurants.

Oldest Wine Bar: La Tartine, 24 Rue de Rivoli (M: Hôtel de Ville) 42.72.76.85. Over 60 wines. Good mix of people. Closed Tues.

Wine Bar: Bourguignon du Marais, 52 Rue François Miron (M: Pont Marie/St-Paul) 48.87.15.40. Jacques Bavard's passion for wines shows flair with food as well.

SHOPS:

2 Mille & 1 Nuits, 13 Rue des Francs Bourgeois (M: St-Paul) 48.87.07.07. Cool house-wares and décorations.

A.P.O.C. A Piece Of Cloth, 47 Rue des Francs Bourgeois (M: St-Paul) 44.54.07.05. Fun clothing line.

A L'Olivier, 23 Rue de Rivoli (M: Hôtel de Ville) 48.04.86.59. Founded 1860, huge assortment of olive oil.

Addicted, 6 Rue St Merri (M: St-Paul) 42.72.71.59. Accessories from hip, young designers.

Agathe Gaillard, 3 Rue du Pont Louis-Philippe (M: Pont Marie) 42.77.38.24. Photo gallery, over 30 years old.

Alain Carion, 92 Rue St-Louis-en-l'Ile (M: Pont Marie) 43.26.01.16. Between Rues Le Regrattier and Jean-du-Bellay. Rock collector and jeweler.

Allicante, 26 Blvd Beaumarchais (M: Bastille) 43.55.13.02. Over 150 cooking oils, with tasting table. Owner Colette Boudarel keeps inventory interesting and knows her oils. 10a-7:30p. Closed Sundays.

Antik Batik, 18 Rue Turenne (M: St-Paul) 44.78.02.00. Trendy shop. Fun bags & accessories.

Aska, 2 Rue du Pas-de-la-Mule (M: Chemin Vert) 40.27.00.67.

4e. Marais, St-Louis-En-L'Ile

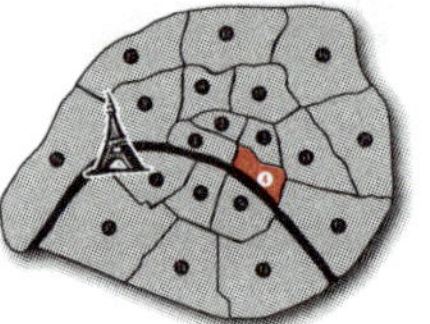

Au Petit Bonheur La Chance, 13 Rue St Paul (M: St-Paul) 42.74.36.38. Serendipity, surprises, and reasonably priced antiques. Friendly Maria Pia Varnier welcomes you in French or English.

Autour d' Elles, 20 Rue des Tournelles (M: Bastille) 42.72.90.35. Vintage designers and Dior shoes.

4

Azzadine Alaia, 7 Rue de Moussy. (M: Hôtel de Ville) 42.72.19.19. Only boutique in the world. Ask about **The Salon,** 18 de la Verrerie, for discounts.

BGN, 21 Rue des Francs Bourgeois (M: Chemin Vert) 42.72.22.73. Hip, trendy fashions. Another location in 6e.

BHV, 52-56 Rue de Rivoli (M: Hôtel de Ville) Old department store, similar to Sears. Basement café Bricolo holds do-it-yourself demonstrations.

Berthillon, 31 Rue St-Louis-En-l'le (M: Pont Marie). It's worth the long lines for some of the world's best ice cream. Try pistachio. A FAVORITE.

Bijoux (Monic) 5 Rue des Francs Bourgeois (M: Rambuteau) 42.72.39.15. Inexpensive jewelry.

Bo, 8 Rue St Merri (M: Hôtel de Ville) 42.72.84.64. Objets d'art in table settings.

Brontibay Boutique, 6 Rue Sevignes (M: St-Paul) 42.76.90.80. Fancy travel totes and handbags.

Buzz, 8 Rue du Trésor (M: Hôtel de Ville) 44.54.80.26. Home design boutique arranged by rooms in a small house. Original objets du jour, made-to-order curtains, furniture. Say bonjour to Martine and Natalie, the owners. 11a-7:30p.

Calligrane, 4,6 bis, Rue du Pont Louis-Philippe (M: Pont Marie) 48.04.31.89. Stationery shop w/limited luxury editions. A FAVORITE.

Comptoir des Cotonniers, 33 Rue des Francs Bourgeois (M: Hôtel de Ville) 42.76.95.33. Riviera chic and cool cotton. Several locations.

Cosy Cocoon, 13 Rue du Blancs Monteaux (M: Rambuteau) 42.71.21.71. Art deco tableware and gifts. Noon – 8p. Closed Monday.

D'un Marais l'Autre, 51 Rue des Francs Bourgeois (M: Rambuteau) 42.78.11.33. Art, posters, books, publishers.

Decalage, 33 Rue des Francs Bourgeois (M: Rambuteau) 42.77.55.72. Jewelry.

Délice Planète, 15 Rue du Bourg-Tibourg (M: Hôtel de Ville) 48.04.75.07. Fun boutique.

France Ma Douce, 27 Rue du Bourg-Tibourg (M: Hôtel de Ville) 44.59.38.08. Shoes, soaps, linens – from all regions of France. Good for gifts and souvenirs.

Galerie Agathe Gaillard, 3 Pont Louis Philippe (M: Pont Marie) 42.77.38.24. Art and photographs. Good selection.

Galerie d'Art, 32 Rue St-Louis-en-Ile. (M: Pont Marie) 43.25.73.35. Posters. A FAVORITE.

Galerie Vu, 2 Rue Jules Cousin (M: Sully-Morland) 53.01.85.81. Exhibit space located in the basement of photo agency Vu.

Gavilane, 14 Rue Malher (M: St-Paul) 48.87.73.13. Jewelry designs.

Gian Paolo Maria, 12 Rue St Paul (M: St-Paul) 40.27.00.12. Jewelry designers. Haute couture costume jewelry. We splurged because we couldn't resist! A FAVORITE.

Issey Miyake, 3 Pl du Voges (M: Chemin Vert) 47.87.01.86.

Izrael Epicure du Monde, 30 Rue Francois-Miron (M: St-Paul) 42.72.66.23. Tues-Sat: 9:30-1p, 7p-9p. This is where Paris chefs shop. It's a worth a visit. A FAVORITE.

K. Jacques, 16 Rue Pave (M: St-Paul) 40.27.03.57. St-Tropez-wear.

Kazana, 15 Rue Vieille-du-Temple (M: St-Paul) 42.78.20.38. Scarves & accessories. Several locations.

Kookai, 70 Rue Saint-Antoine (M: Bastille) 40.29.91.63. Cool stuff.

L'Art & Action, 19 Rue de Turenne (M: St-Paul) 42.71.45.46. Fun and funky stuff.

L'Art du Bureau, 47 Rue des Francs Bourgeois. (M: Rambuteau) 48.87.57.97.

L'Ecritoire, 61 Rue St Martin (M: Hôtel de Ville) 42.78.01.18. Sophie Bastide stocks fountain pens, colored inks, and creative handmade cards.

L'Image du Grenier sur L'Eau, 45 Rue des Francs Bourgeois.(M: Rambuteau) 42.71.02.31. Art/Posters. Run by Yves & Sylvain Di Maria. Pricey by comparison.

La Belle Hortense, 31 Rue Vieille-du-Temple (M: Hôtel de Ville) 49.04.71.60. Book Store/literary bar.

La Chaise Lounge, 20 Rue des Francs Bourgeois (M: Rambuteau) 48.04.36.37. Funky home décor. Several Locations.

La Licorne, 26 Rue des Jardins Saint-Paul (M: St-Paul) 42.72.46.02. Antiques.

Les Mots á la Buche, 6 Rue Ste Croix la Bretonnaire (M: Hôtel de Ville) 42.78.88.30. Gay bookstore.

Les Touristes, 17 Rue Blancs Manteaux (M: Rambuteau) 42.72.10.84. Fun gifts, tableware, décor.

Lobato, 6 Rue Malher (M: St-Paul) 48.87.68.14. Shoes, bags, and other designer pieces.

Lora Lune, 22 Rue du Bourg Tibourg (M: Hôtel de Ville) 48.04.00.30. Body lotions.

Lulu Castagnette, 61 Rue de Rennes (M: Reamur-Sebastopol) 45.08.53.30. Nouveau designer where you will find chic designs and glamorous denim.

4e. Marais, St-Louis-En-L'Ile

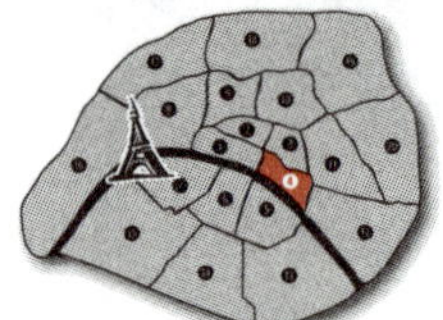

4

Max Spira, 21 Pl des Vosges (M: Chemin Vert).42.77.15.78. Antiques and art deco items.

Métropolies, 5 bis, Rue Saint-Paul. (M: Pont Marie) 42.77.58.71. Mme. Hardy is the proprietor. We like this art deco objets and antique store.

Mona Lisa, 9 Rue St. Martin (M: Châtelet) 42.74.03.02. Trendy shop.

Mouton a Cinq pattes, 15 Rue Vieille-du-Temple (M: Hôtel de Ville) 42.71.86.30. Cash & Carry.

Nina Jacobs, 23 Rue des Francs Bourgeois (M: Chemin Vert) 42.77.41.20. Women's fashions.

PWS (Price Without Surprise) 13 Rue Sevigne (M: St-Paul) 44.54.09.09. Mens/womens discounts.

Papier Plus, 9 Rue du Pont Louis-Philippe (M: Pont Marie).42.77.70.49. Custom designed notebooks and albums.

Paris-Musées Boutique. Hotel d'Albert, 29 bis, Rue des Francs Bourgeois (M: Rambuteau) 42.74.13.02.

Photofactory, 21 Rue du Renard (M: Hôtel de Ville) 40.29.05.90. Gilles Dubourg's showroom includes provocative black & white photos.

Pleats Please, 3 bis, Rue des Rosiers (M: St-Paul). 40.29.99.66. Womens fashions.

Pretty Perle, 23 Rue du Renard (M: Hôtel de Ville) 42.77.47.88. Tiny shop with diverse selection of beads, pearls, gems to make your own jewelry. Design a necklace for yourself or a friend's souvenir. €4.

Pylônes, 57 Rue St-Louis-en-l'Ile (M: Pont Marie) 46.34.05.02. Novelties. Items change depending on what's new and trendy. Teens.

Satellite, 23 Rue des Francs Bourgeois. (M: St-Paul) 40.29.45.77. Costume jewelry designs. A FAVORITE.

Sentou Galerie, 24 Rue du Pont Louis-Philippe (M: Hôtel de Ville) 42.71.00.01. Trendy home décor.

Stella Cadente, 4 Quai Celestins (M: Sully-Morland) 44.78.05.95. Ladies wear designer.

Stock Griffes, 17 Rue Vieille-du-Temple (M: Hôtel de Ville) 48.04.82.34. Bargains.

The Red Wheelbarrow, 22 Rue St Paul (M: St-Paul) 48.04.75.08. Wonderful bookstore. Say bonjour to Penelope and Abigail. A FAVORITE.

TRA Galerie, 16 Rue Turenne (M: Chemin Vert) 42.71.81.15. Eclectic gallery.

Tumbleweed, 19 Rue de Turenne (M: St-Paul) 42.78.06.10. Handcrafted toys. Mon-Sat. 11a-7p.

Vert d'Absinthe, 11 Rue d'Ormesson (M: St-Paul) 42.71.69.73. Absinthe and accoutrements.

Why, 12 Rue des Lombards (M: Châtelet). Gadgets and knick-knacks.

RESTAURANTS: LES PLATS DU JOUR:

Amici Mei, 53 Blvd Beaumarchais (M: Chemin Vert) 42.71.82.62. Pizza.

Au Petit Fer á Cheval, 30 Rue Vielle-du-Temple (M: Hôtel de Ville) 42.72.47.47. Dependable food and friendly. Good wine list from smaller vineyards. Horseshoe-shaped bar and Metro bench add to its charm.

B4. 6-8 Square Sainte Croix de la Bretonnerie (M: Hôtel de Ville) 42.72.16.19. Glass walls, Fusion cooking. Upscale, gay crowd. Sunday brunch.

Baracane, 38 Rue des Tournelle (M: Pont Marie) 42.71.43.33. Terrific cassoulet. Good wine list. Small, so reserve ahead. Closed Sat. lunch / Sunday.

Bel Canto, 72 Quai de l'Hôtel de Ville (M: Hôtel de Ville) 42.78.30.18. Italian, where waiters sing opera. Food gets less-than-rave reviews.

Benoît, 20 Rue St-Martin. (M: Châtelet) 42.72.25.76. Some call this the "most traditional" in all of Paris. Ducasse offers €38 3-course lunch. Dinners at €100. We think over-priced. Open Sunday.

Bistrot du Dôme, 2 Rue de la Bastille (M: Bastille) 48.04.88.44. Fresh fish, bistro style. Good wine list.

Bofinger, 5-7 Rue de la Bastille (M: Bastille) 42.72.87.82. Open daily. Historic old spectacular brasserie. Tiered shellfish platters. A Parisian classic. Open til 1am. Reserve. Open Sunday.

Bourguignon du Marais, 52 Rue François Miron (M: Pont Marie/St-Paul) 48.87.15.40. Jacques Bavard's passion for wines shows flair with food as well.

Brasserie de L'Ile de St Louis, 55 Quai Bourbon (M: Pont Neuf) 43.54.02.59. Simple. Choucroute plates, onion tarts. Terrace.

Cacao et Chocolat, 36 Rue Vieille-du-Temple (M: Hôtel de Ville) 42.71.50.06. Hot chocolat, pastries, ganache.

Café Beaubourg, 43 Rue Saint-Merri (M: Hôtel de Ville) 48.87.63.96. A great terrace faces Pompidou for great people-watching. May get pretentious, depending on maitré d. Owned by the Côstes brothers. Open Sunday. A FAVORITE.

Café Trésor, 5-7 Rue du Trésor (M: St-Paul) 42.71.35.17. Hip and casual café. Terrace. Friendly.

Chez Marianne, 2 Rue des Hospitalieres St Gervais (M: St-Paul) 42.72.18.86. Very popular. Tunisian food, fallafel, grilled eggplant. Sawdust floor, terrace.

Coconnas, 2 bis Pl des Vosges (M: St-Paul) 42.78.58.16. Another Terrail-family (they own Tour L'Argent) restaurant. Casual restaurant with terrace. Open Sunday.

Epices et Delices Restaurants, 53 Rue Vielle-du-Temple (M: Hôtel de Ville) 42.71.14.14. Traditional Bistro.

4e. Marais, St-Louis-En-L'Ile

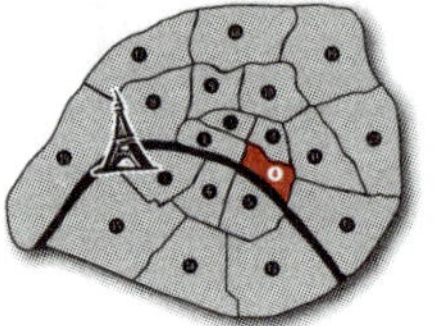

4

Georges, Top floor of Pompidou. (M: Rambuteau) 44.78.47.99. Owned by Costes brothers. Good view of Paris from outside terrace. Open Sunday. Direct access from plaza by elevator til 9p. Escalator from Rue Rambuteau.

Goldenberg Delicatessen, 7 Rue du Rosiers (M: St-Paul) 48.87.20.16. Since 1920. Kosher delicatessen.

Isami, 4 Quai d' Orleans (M: Pont Marie) 40.46.06.97. Always crowded. Exceptional sushi and sashimi.

L'Alivi, 27 Rue du Roi de Sicile (M: St-Paul) 47.87.90.20 Good Corsican meals €30 on the terrace.

L'As du Fallafel, 34 Rue des Rosiers (M: St-Paul) for a great lunch.

L'Enoteca, 25 Rue Charles (M: St-Paul) 42.78.91.44. Italian food. Over 400 Italian wines. Lunch, dinner. Cozy décor and friendly Italian servers. Fresh pasta. A few tables upstairs. A FAVORITE. Open Sunday.

L'Excuse, 14 Rue Charles V. (M: St-Paul) 42.77.98.97. Intimate, romantic. Delicious New French cuisine and good service. Wine from the Rhone Valley. Upstairs is non-smoking. Closed Sunday.

L'Impasse, 4 Impasse Guémenée (M: Bastille) 42.72.08.45. Wood-beamed dining room and Francoise Mainguy welcomes you. Everything is homemade. Make reservations.

L'Orangerie, 28 Rue St-Louis-en-L'Ile (M: Pont Marie) 46.33.93.98. Romantic. New chef presents a fresh menu. Reserve ahead. A FAVORITE.

L'Osteria, 10 Rue de Sévigné (M: St-Paul) 42.71.37.08. Great Italian and "local secret" so call ahead. Good risotto. Closed Sunday.

La Castafiore, in Hotel Chenizot, 51 Rue St-Louis-en-l'Ile. (M: Pont Marie) 43.54.78.62. Italian. Reservations recommended.

La Rose de France, 24 Pl Dauphine (M: Pont Neuf) 43.54.10.12. Stephane Dupuis uses fresh ingredients. Good €18 entrees. Tiny terrace. Lunch and dinner, non-stop.

La Tête Ailleurs, 20 Rue Beautreillis (M: St-Paul) 42.72.47.80. The glass rooftop adds to the arty décor and good Mediterranean dishes.

Le Caveau-de-L'Ile, 36 Rue St-Louis-en-L'Ile (M: Pont Marie) 43.25.10.26. Tiny, gracious, good and inexpensive.

Le Colimacon, 44 Rue Vielle-du-Temple (M: Hôtel de Ville) 48.87.12.01. Dinner-only in two-story house, circa 1732. Good wine list. Reservations needed.

Le Coude Fou, 12 Rue du Bourg-Tibourg (M: St-Paul) 42.77.15.16. Cozy neighborhood bistro serves good food. Friendly service. Mixed crowd.

Le Coupe Gorge, 2 Rue de la Coutellerie (M: Hôtel de Ville) 48.04.79.24. Choose your wine from the well-stocked cellar and then sit back and enjoy bistrot-style food at reasonable prices. Open Sunday.

Le Dôme du Marais, 53 bis Rue des Francs Bourgeois. (M: St-Paul) 42.74.54.17. Chef Pierre Le Coutre serves solid French with Asian accents, but slim wine list. Reservations needed. Closed Sunday.

Le Grizzli, 7 Rue St Martin (M: Hôtel de Ville) 48.87.77.56. Moderate prices, good food. Upstairs is quieter. Open Sunday, friendly. A FAVORITE.

Le Murano, 13 Blvd du Temple (M: Hôtel de Ville) 42.71.20.00. In the Murano Urban Resort hotel. Modern, edgy décor with talented team of young chefs who present delicious meals. Fame produces somewhat snotty service.

Le Rouge Gorge, 8 Rue St Paul (M: Pont Marie) 48.04.75.89.Say bonjour to François who knows his wine. Wine bar and very small dining room for lunch and dinner. Closed Sunday. A FAVORITE.

Le Sergent Recruteur, 41 Rue St-Louis-En-L'Ile (M: Pont Marie) 43.54.75.42. Classic meals in Louis 14th décor. €38 for 4 course prix fixe.

Le Trumilou, 84 Quai de l'Hôtel de Ville. (M: Hôtel de Ville) 42.77.63.98. Very popular. Casual, €18 3- course lunch. Open Sunday.

Le Vieux Bistro, 14 Rue du Cloître Nôtre-Dame (M: Cité) 43.54.18.95. Good frogs legs, escargots, hangar steak, profiteroles. Lyonnaise-style meals. Fills with tourists.

Les Bourgeoises, 12 Rue des Francs-Bourgeois (M: St-Paul) 42.72.48.30. Make reservations for good food. Try the lamb stew.

Les Philosophes, 28 Rue Vielle-du-Temple. (M: Hôtel de Ville) 48.87.49.64. Great terrace and tarte tatin. A FAVORITE.

Ma Bourgogne, 19 Pl des Vosges, (M: St-Paul) 42.78.44.64. Classic French bistro. Steak tartare. This is where the locals go for Sunday breakfast. No credit cards. Open Sunday.

Ma Salle à Manger, 26 Pl Dauphine (M: Pont Neuf) 43.29.52.34. Try the crème brulee.

Mon Vieil Ami, 69 Rue St-Louis-en-l'Ile. (M: Pont Marie) 40.46.01.35. Fresh seafood, traditional meals, with especially creative vegetables. €39 3-course dinner. Tight seating. Open Saturdays and Sundays. Closed Monday. A FAVORITE.

Nos Ancestres Les Gaulons, 39 Rue St-Louis-en-Ile (M: Pont Marie) 46.33.66.07. All you can eat/drink.

Oz0, 37 Rue Quincampoix (M: Mademoiselle) 42.77.10.03. The mix and match menu appeals to young adults and is also ideal for families.

Piétons, 8 Rue Lombards (M: Châtelet) 48.87.82.87. Tapas bar.

Pitchi Poi, 7 Rue Caron (M: St-Paul) 42.77.46.15. Jewish all-you-can-eat Sunday Brunch. Blinis and vodka. Closed Sat.

4e. Marais, St-Louis-En-L'Ile

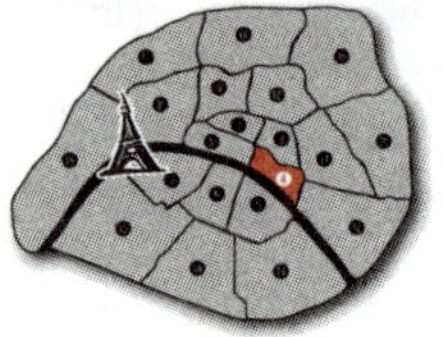

RESTAURANTS: GASTRONOMIQUE:

Aboard the Don Juan II, Dinner cruise with 5-course gourmet meal presented by Chef Jean Pierre Vigato. 2 hours, $300 pp, excluding wines. Port Henri IV in front of 10 bis Quai Henri IV (M: Quai de la Rapée) 44.54.14.70. A FAVORITE. **Yachts de Paris** offers other Seine dinner cruises at other price ranges.

L'Ambroisie, 9 Pl des Vosges (M: St-Paul) 42.78.51.45. One of Paris' best. Reserve well ahead. Closed Sunday.

4

BONNE SOIREE! PARIS AT NIGHT:

7 Lézards, 10 Rue de Rosiers (M: St-Paul) 48.87.08.97. Street level bar with tapas and improv theatre or music downstairs. Sunday night jam sessions. Call ahead for music and covers.

Café du Trésor, 5-7 Rue du Trésor (M: St-Paul) 44.78.06.60. Wed-Sunday. Dancing to DJ's, along with lounge and terrace.

La Chaise au Plafond, 10 Rue du Trésor (M: St-Paul) 42.76.03.22. Night bar. After dinner wine.

Franc Pinot, 1 Quai de Bourbon (M: Pont Marie) 46.33.69.64. Live music, jazz concerts at 9p downstairs. Free on Tuesdays. They also serve prix fixe dinner €35-55. A FAVORITE. Closed Sun/Monday.

Le Bistro Latin, 20 Rue Vieille-du-Temple (M: Hôtel de Ville) 42.77.21.11. Latin menu and tango dancing Thu-Sat. International crowd.

The Lizard Lounge, 18 Rue Bourg-Tibourg (M: Hôtel de Ville) 42.72.81.34. Popular favorite of American expats. Three floors of fun, food, music. Saturday and Sunday American brunch.

My Special Travel Notes

4

My Special Travel Notes

4

5e. Panthéon, Latin Quarter

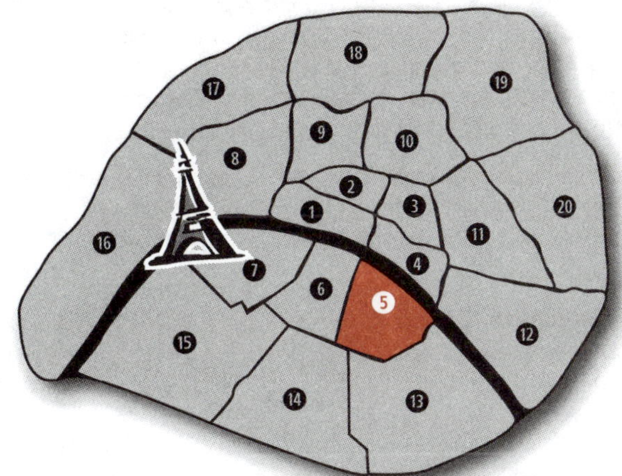

You will find the **Oldest Street,** the **Oldest Church** and the **Oldest Tree** in this quarter.

Walk Rue Mouffetard or Rue des Ecoles, past the **Sorbonne,** or visit **Musée du Moyen-Age.**

My first stop in Paris is always **Diptyque** to stock up on their perfect candles.

MAJOR METROS:

- ST-MICHEL
- MAUBERT-MUTUALITE
- CLUNY LA SORBONNE
- CARDINAL LEMOINÉ
- JUSSIEU
- MONGE

5e. Panthéon, Latin Quarter

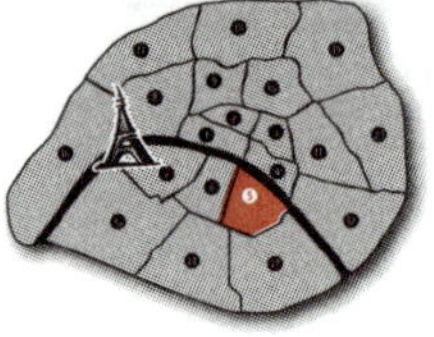

FAMOUS SIGHTS:

Musée Nationale d'Histoire Naturelle, Jardin des Plantes, 57 Rue Cuvier (M: Jussieu) 40.79.30.00. You may visit several pavilions within the Jardin des Plantes: the history of evolution at **La Grande Galerie de l'Evolution,** "cristaux géants"-boulder-sized crystals in the **Galerie de Minéralogie,** and fossils, insects, and skeletons in the **Galerie de Paléontologic.** There is also a tropical greenhouse, Alpine Garden, Botanical Garden, rose garden with more than 300 varieties and Le Ménagerie is France's oldest public zoo. Limited English. €5-7 individual galleries. 10-6p/10p on Thursdays.Closed Tuesday. Very kid-friendly.

5

Panthéon, Pl du Panthéon (M: Cardinal-Lemoine) 44.32.18.00. Open daily 10a-5:15p. €7. Dedicated as a "temple of reason" and crypt houses Voltaire, Rousseau, Victor Hugo, along with Pierre and Marie Curie. Go up the steps for wonderful view of the city.

Eglise Val-de-Grace, 1 Pl Alphonse-Laveran (M: Port Royal) 40.51.51.92. Church commissioned by Louis XIII in 1619, with dome by Le Duc, Mansart the main architect, Mignard did the frescoes. €5, 5p is last entrance.

DIVERSIONS:

Bibliothèque Ste-Genevieve, 10 Pl du Panthéon (M: Cardinal Lemoine) 44.41.97.97. You will find a rare book and manuscript division in this librairy with over one million books.

Grains Nobles Wine Courses and Soirées, 5 Rue Laplace (M: Cardinal Lemoine) 43.54.93.54. Soirées €65, single class €85, courses from €250. Since 1991, André Bessou opens vintage bottles during his regional surprise wine selections followed by a meal. In French. No credit cards.

Gym at Club Quartier Latin, 19 Rue Pontoise (M: Maubert Mutualité) 55.42.77.88. €15 Day pass. 55.42.77.88.

Gym: Club Jean de Beauvais, 5 Rue Jean de Beauvais (M: Maubert Mutualité) 46.33.16.80. Daily/weekly passes. Aerobics, yoga, equipment. Clean and friendly.

Institut du Monde Arab, 1 Rue des Fosses-St-Bernard (M: Cardinal Lemoine) 40.51.38.38. Restaurant and salon de tea are among the most beautiful rooms in Paris. Stunning view from the beautiful terrace on 9th floor. Open till about 10 pm. Closed Monday.

La Maison des Trois Thés, 33 Rue Gracieuse (M: Monge) 43.36.93.84. Tea room with hundreds of varieties.

Manufacture des Gobelins (Gobelins Tapestry Factory) 42 Ave des Gobelins (M: Les Gobelins) 44.08.52.00. Take a tour of weavers using ancient techniques on century-old looms. Tues-Thurs. €8. Guided tours only at 2 and 2:45 pm. Call ahead to see when tours are in English.

Musée du Moyen Age/Hotel de Cluny, 6 Pl Paul-Painleve (M: Cluny La Sorbonne) 53.73.78.00. Médiéval Paris: Gallo-Roman baths. Visit Gallery 13 to see the tapestry of "The Lady and The Unicorn" and stained glass windows. 9:30a – 5:45p. Closed Tuesday. Jardin de Cluny is free. Entrance is on Blvd St. Michel or Rue de Cluny.

Picnic in Arènes de Lutèce, Rues Monge and Navarre (M: Jussieu).

Rent Bikes at Paris Vélo, 2 Rue du Fer a Moulin (M: Censier Dauberton) 43.37.59.22.

Some nice strolls: Frederic Sauton, Pl Maubert, Ste Geneviève, Rue Blainville, Rue Descartes, Rue Mouffetard (M: Maubert Mutualité) Begin at **Marché Maubert's** open-air market Tues/Thurs/Sat. 8a-noon. We enjoy its sights and smells. From M: St-Michel, walk **Rue de la Huchette,** literary landmark from "The Last Time I Saw Paris".

Spend Sunday mornings at "Marché Mouffetard" on Rue Mouffetard (M: Monge) in the square in front of St-Medard church. Musicians gather here to play accordions, dance and sing. Song sheets are distributed and everyone joins in the fun! 11a-1p.

SUPERLATIVES:

Best Baguette: Ste. Boulangerie Kayser, 8 Rue Monge (M: Maubert Mutualité) 44.07.01.42.

Another Best Baguette: Boulangerie Beauvallet Julien, 6 Rue de Poissy (M: Maubert-Mutualité) 43.26.94.24. Freshly baked out of the oven 7am, 11am, 1pm. Closed Wed.

Best bookstore: Shakespeare & Co., 37 Rue de la Bucherie (M: St-Michel) 43.25.40.93. Sylvia runs this friendly book store, loaded with character and characters. Say Bonjour to Jenna and John.

Best éclairs: Sadaharu Aoki, 56 Blvd Port Royal (M: Port Royal) 45.35.36.80. Pastry chef from Crillon Hotel.

Best greasy-spoon diner: Breakfast in America, 17 Rue des Ecoles (M: Maubert Mutualité) 43.54.50.28.

Favorite pétanque/boules field: Arènes de Lutèce, 49 Rue Monge (M: Monge).

Good wine bar: Café de la Nouvelle Marie, 19 Rue des Fosses Saint Jacques (M: Luxembourg) 44.07.04.41. Open til midnight. Closed Sat/Sun. No credit cards.

Lunch deal: Le Buisson Ardent, 25 Rue Jussieu. (M: Jussieu) 43.54.93.02. Good traditional food in 1920's setting. Closed Sunday.

Most fun on a Sunday: join in at Marché Mouffetard (see "diversions") from 11am - 1pm. Year 'round, except rain.

Oldest church: Eglise St. Julien le Pauvre, 1 Rue St Julien le Pauvre. (M: St-Michel) 42.50.96.18. Call for schedule of candlelight concerts.

5e. Panthéon, Latin Quarter

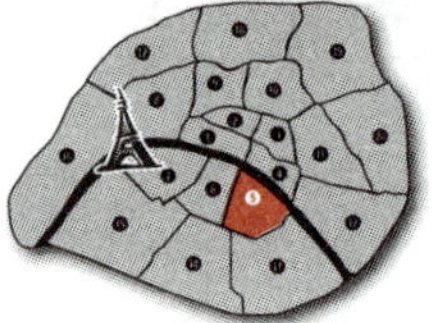

5

Oldest street: Rue Mouffetard (M: Monge) and Rue St-Jacques (M: Maubert Mutualité).

Oldest Tree in Paris: the "Robinier" in front of Eglise St Julien le Pauvre. 400 years old. Only Gallo-roman remains to be seen in Paris, at 47 Rue Monge (M: Cardinal Lemoine).

Perfect candles: Diptyque, 34 Blvd Saint Germain. (M: Maubert Mutualité) 43.26.45.27. A FAVORITE.

Shortest Street: Rue Chat-qui-Pêche (M: St-Michel) 6 feet long.

Best souvenirs: La Tuile à Loup, 35 Rue Dauberton (M: Censier Dauberton) 47.07.28.90. Good selection of French crafts and hand-made gifts.

Teas, over 1,000 varieties at Maison des Trois Thés. 1 Rue St-Medard (M: Monge) 43.46.93.84.

Largest vintage print and poster shop: L'Imagerie. 9 Rue Dante (M: Maubert Mutualité) See Shops.

Best Wine Bar: Café de la Nouvelle Marie, 19 Rue des Fosses Saint-Jacques (M: Luxembourg) 44.07.04.41. Open til Midnight, Closed Sat/Sunday. No credit cards.

Wine market: Le Cuvier (La Halle aux Vins) 47 Blvd St Germain (M: Maubert Mutualité) 43.54.57.96. Closed Sunday. Family owns château in Fronsac and stocks smaller producers of wines as well as the big names.

SHOPS:

Album, 6,7 Rue Dante (M: Monge) 43.54.67.09. Old comic books.

Aoki Sadaharu, 56 Blvd Port Royal (M: Port Royal) 45.35.36.80. Delicious pastries.

Boulanger de Monge, 123 Rue Monge (M: Censier Daubenton) 43.37.54.20. Dominique Saibron bakes tasty baguettes and is so popular there are two other locations in the neighborhood.

Claude Nature, 32 Blvd Saint Germain (M: Maubert Mutualité) 44.07.30.79. Taxidermists. Glass cabinets hold pink flamingos, heads of deer, exotic butterflies, insects.

Danielle Bouyer, 9 Rue Blainville (M: Monge) 43.25.04.24.Small boutique. Closed Sunday.

Ding Dong Bazaar, 24 Rue Mouffetard (M: Monge) 43.37.58.68. 18th century vintage collectibles.

Diptyque, 34 Blvd Saint Germain (M: Maubert Mutualité) 43.26.45.27. Perfect candles and aromatic scents for the home and body. A FAVORITE.

Embellie, 11 bis Rue Vauquelin (M: Censier Daubenton) 43.31.43.51. Young & funky vintage brands.

FNAC-Micro, 71 Blvd Saint Germain (M: Cluny) 44.41.31.50. Computer supplies.

L'Imagerie, 9 Rue Dante (M: Maubert Mutualité) 43.25.18.66. Original Art Deco, Art Nouveau posters and prints. Stamps. Closed Sunday.

La Quincaillerie, 3 & 4 Blvd St Germain (M: Cardinal Lemoine) 46.33.67.71. Hardware store.

La Tuile à Loup, 35 Rue Dauberton (M: Censier Dauberton) 47.07.28.90. French crafts and hand-made gifts.

Le Cuvier (La Halle aux Vins) 47 ter Blvd St Germain (M: Maubert Mutualité) 43.54.57.96. Family owns château in Fronsac and carries smaller producers of wines as well as the big names.

Le Rouvray, 1 Rue Bûcherie (M: Maubert Mutualité) 43.25.00.45. Quilt shop with thousands of bolts of fabrics. Owner is from Michigan, USA. Quaint.

Les Deux Tisserino, 3 Rue des Bernardins (M: Maubert Mutualité) 46.33.88.68. Marie-Claude Leblois owns this unusual toy shop and famous line of children's clothing.

Librairie Gourmands, 4 Rue Dante (M: Maubert Mutualité) 43.54.37.27. Gourmet cook books, new and old titles.

Maison des Trois Thés, 1 Rue St-Medard (M: Monge) 43.46.93.84.

Shakespeare & Co., 37 Rue de la Bucherie (M: St-Michel) 43.25.40.93. Bookstore. Expats meet here. Seems to be open at all hours.

RESTAURANTS: LES PLATS DU JOUR:

Anahuacalli, 30 Rue des Bernardins (M: Maubert Mutualité) 43.26.10.10. Good for margaritas and Mexican food.

Asia-Tée, 47 Rue de la Mont Ste-Genevieve (M: Cardinal Lemoine) 43.26.39.90. Chef/owner Renji serves original "sakana" tasting dishes fusing Japanese and French tastes.

Atelier Maître Albert, 1 Rue Maître Albert (M: St-Michel). 56.81.30.01. Overseen by Guy Savoy. Modern décor, huge fireplace, and communal bar in back room. Adequate wine list. Closed Sunday.

Bar à Huîtres, 33 Rue Saint-Jacques (M: Maubert Mutualité) 44.07.27.37. Shellfish. There are two other locations in 3e. and 11e.

Brasserie Balzar, 49 rue des Ecoles (M: Cluny) 43.54.13.67. Classic, old Parisian bistro. We like it for lunch.

Café de la Nouvelle Marie, 19 Rue des Fosses Saint-Jacques (M: Luxembourg) 44.07.04.41. Wine and food pairings. See Best Wine Bar, above. Open til Midnight, Closed Sat/Sunday. No credit cards.

5e. Panthéon, Latin Quarter

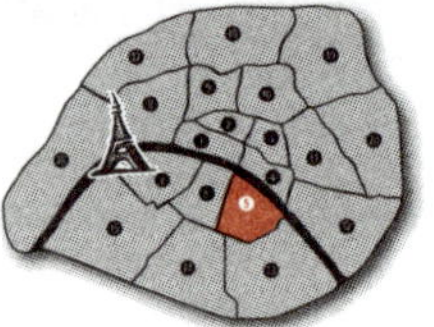

5

Chez René, 14 Blvd Saint Germain, (M: Maubert Mutualité) 43.54.30.23. The best boeuf bourguignon and good crème caramel.

Chieng-Mai, 12 Rue Frederic-Sauton (M Maubert Mutualité) 43.25.45.45. Reservations a must for good Thai food. Service can be iffy.

L'AOC, 14 Rue des Fosses St-Bernard (M: Cardinal Lemoine) 43.54.22.52. Pleasant service and memorable dining. Non-smoking section. Moderate prices. Closed Sunday.

L'Equitable, 3 Rue Fosses Saint-Marcel (M: St Marcel) 43.31.69.20. Voted best start-up by one newsletter.

La Brouette, 41 Rue Descartes (M: Cardinal Lemoine) 43.25.41.10. Fondue.

La Marée Verte, 9 Rue de Pontoise (M: Maubert Mutualité) 43.25.89.41. Recommended for meat and seafood. $40. Closed Sunday.

La Methode, 2 Rue Descartes (M: Maubert Mutualité) 43.54.22.43. Traditional cuisine, plat du jour and wine. Terrace. Music on Friday nights.

La Rôtisserie du Beaujolais, 19 Quai de La Tournelle (M: Jussieu) 43.54.17.47. Rotisserie overlooks the room and the owner's cat is not far away.
Good coq au vin.

La Table de Fabrice, 13 Quai Tournelle (M: Maubert Mutualité) 44.07.17.57. Recommended by our good friend in Paris, Flavien. Fabrice and his wife, Brigitte, offer a warm welcome and delicious meals. He used to work at L'Arpege and Laserre. 3-course dinner, including 1998 Margaux for €122. A FAVORITE. Closed Sunday.

La Truffière, 4 Rue Blainville (M: Monge) 46.33.29.82. Pl de la Contrescope. Good value, delicious food, pleasant service. Downstairs is very romantic. Memorable. A FAVORITE.

Le Buisson Ardent, 25 Rue Jussieu (M: Jussieu) 43.54.93.02. Popular newer bistro with the right combination of good food, friendly service and pretty décor. Closed Sunday.

Le Cosi, 9 Rue Cujas (M: Luxembourg) 43.29.20.20. Good Corsican meals. Closed Sunday.

Le Coupe-Chou, 3 Impasse Chartiere (M: Maubert Mutualité) 46.33.68.69. Fresh homemade foie gras, roasted rack of lamb and 3-tier chocolate cake for €100 for two. Closed Sunday.

Le Jardin d'Ivy, 75 Rue Mouffetard (M: Monge) 47.07.19.29. Locals like it. Enjoy the garden.

Le Mauzac, 7 Rue de l'Abbe de l'Epee (M: Luxembourg) 46.33.75.22. Wine bar and bistro. Closed Sat/Sunday.

Le Moulin á Vent (Chez Henri) 20 Rue des Fosses Saint-Bernard (M: Cardinal Lemoine) 43.54.99.37. Traditional French. Very popular. Closed Sunday.

Le Petit Pontoise, 9 Rue de Pontoise (M: Maubert Mutualité) 43.29.25.20. Small bistro. Blackboard menu. A FAVORITE.

Le Petit Prince de Paris, 12 Rue de Lanneau (M: Maubert Mutualité) 43.54.77.26. Classic French food in quite a gay atmosphere! Entertaining waiters, a bit campy.

Le Pré Verre, 8 Rue Thenard (M: Maubert Mutualité) 43.54.59.47. Chef Philippe Delacourcelle serves imaginative meals in a jazzy setting, upstairs and downstairs. Closed Sunday.

Le Reminet, 3 Rue des Grands-Degres (M: Maubert Mutualité) 44.07.04.24. Tiny, cute contemporary bistro. Call ahead. Open Sunday.

Le Ziryab, 1 Rue des Fosses Saint-Bernard (M: Cardinal Lemoine) 53.10.10.16. French Moroccan cuisine w/orchestra nightly. Terrace with good river view.

Les Bouchons de Fr. Clerc, 12 Rue de l'Hôtel Colbert (M: Maubert Mutualité) 43.54.15.34. Highly recommended and usually crowded. Wines sold at "cost" Mon-Sat. Reserve well in advance.

Les Fontaines, 9 Rue Soufflot (M: Luxembourg) 43.26.42.80. Classic French bistro. Local clientele.

Les Papilles, 30 Rue Gay-Lussac (M: Luxembourg) 43.25.20.79. Grocery store, wine store and bistro that serves good Southwestern fare that recently won a food award. Buy a bottle of wine and pay a small corkage fee or select from wines by the glass. 4 course €39. A FAVORITE. Closed Sunday.

Les Pipos, 2 Rue de l'Ecole Polytechnique (M: Maubert Mutualité) 43.54.11.40. The façade is a registered monument and the owner Christophe's charming presence adds to your welcome. Simple meals, good wines.

Louis Vins, 9 Rue Montagne Ste Genevieve (M: Maubert Mutualité) 43.29.12.12. Good meals under €30. Nice neighborhood location.

Maresco, 5 Rue Pontoise (M: Maubert Mutualité) 43.25.56.81. Provencal cooking. Live jazz on Thurs. and Friday nights. Closed Sunday.

Moissonnier, 28 Rue des Fossés-St-Bernard (M: Jussieu) 43.29.87.65. Simple country French with generous portions. May get smoky.

Perraudin, 157 Rue St Jacques (M: Cluny) 46.33.15.75. Homey, simply good French cooking at moderate prices. Quaint Latin Quarter décor. Reserve. Closed Sunday.

RESTAURANTS: GASTRONOMIQUE:

La Tour d'Argent, 15-17 Quai de la Tournelle (M: Cardinal Lemoine) 43.54.23.31. Gastronomique French. Open Sunday.

5e. Panthéon, Latin Quarter

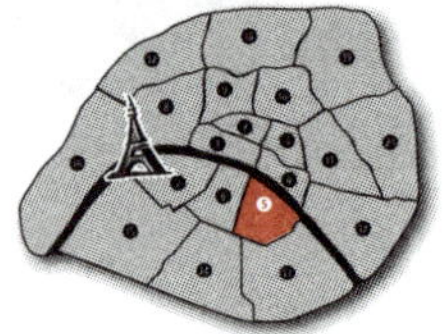

BONNE SOIREE! PARIS AT NIGHT:

Café Universel, 267 Rue St Jacques (M: Luxembourg) 43.25.74.20. Live jazz. No cover. Call for concerts.

Caveau de la Huchette, 5 Rue de la Huchette (M: St-Michel) 43.26.65.05. Call for Listings.

Caveau des Oubliettes, 52 Rue Galande (M: St-Michel). 46.34.23.09. Live improv sessions Monday nights.

5

Le Café Maure de la Mosque, 39 Rue Geoffroy St-Hilaire (M: St Marcel) 43.31.18.14. Peaceful, alcohol-free.

Le Paradis Latin, 28 Rue Cardinal-Lemoine (M: Jussieu) 43.25.28.28. Cabaret show. Nudity. French and English speaking.

Les Trois Maillets, 56 Rue Galande (M: St-Michel) 43.54.00.79. Live music. Cover. Call for headliners and times. 43.54.42.94.

Petit Journal Saint Michel, 71 Blvd St Michel (M: Luxembourg) 43.26.28.59. Live music starts at 10p.

The Hideout, 11 Rue du Pot de Fer (M: Monge) 45.35.13.17. Top Ten night bars. Tango dancing til dawn, quai Saint Bernard (M: Gare d'Austerlitz) is east of Notre Dame near Jardin des Plantes.

My Special Travel Notes

5

My Special Travel Notes

5

6e. Luxembourg, St-Germain-des-Prés

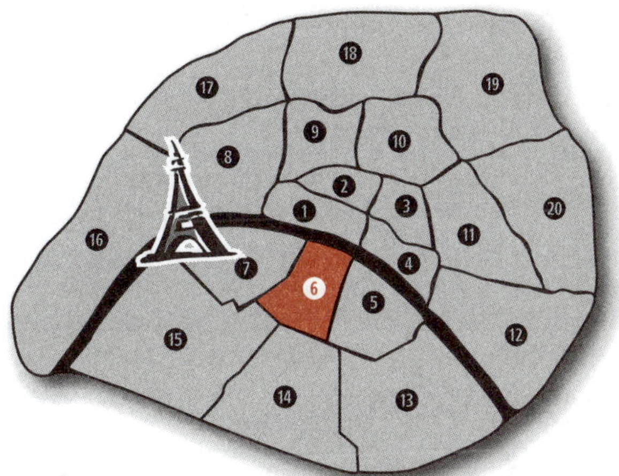

Welcome to **St. Germain des Prés,** probably the most famous district on the Left Bank. Walk hand-in-hand along **Boulevard Saint Germain** and people watch at **Café Flore.**

I get my hair cut at **Institute Marianne Gray**.

Pack a picnic lunch with items from our **Superlatives Listings** (macaroons from **Pierre Hermè** come to mind) and head to **Luxembourg Gardens.**

You'll enjoy the best prixe fix dinner in Paris at **Le Comptoir** and then go to **Café Laurent** for live music and champagne cocktails.

MAJOR METROS:
- ST-GERMAIN-DES-PRÉS
- ODEON
- MABILLON
- ST. SULPICE
- SEVRES-BABYLONE
- VAVIN

6e. Luxembourg, St-Germain-des-Prés

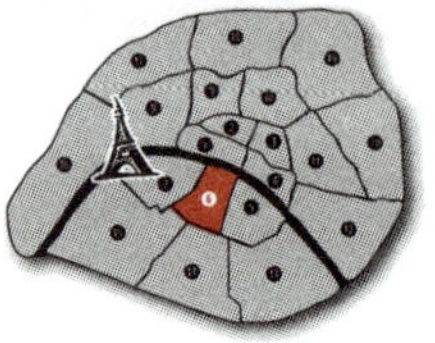

FAMOUS SIGHTS:

Jardin du Luxembourg, (M: Luxembourg) 44.61.21.66. A must! Enjoy the gardens, water basin, puppet shows, watch boules. Enter via Rue Odeon to see the beautiful **Fountain de Medicis**. A FAVORITE.

Palais du Luxembourg tours are available on the first Sunday of each month at 10:30 a.m. Call in advance for reservation.

Musée de Jardin du Luxembourg, 19 Rue de Vaugirard (M: Luxembourg) 42.22.16.20. Free. Open daily.

Orangerie du Sénat et Jardin du Luxembourg, 19 Rue de Vaugirard. (M: Luxembourg) 42.34.33.99. Free.

6

St-Sulpice Church, Rue St-Sulpice (M: St-Sulpice) Free admission. See the fountain of Visconti outside, and inside you will find the Chapelle de la Madonna. The Delacroix frescoes are in the Chapelle des Anges on your right as you enter. This is the only church in Paris where holy water may be taken home.

DIVERSIONS:

Antique and Arts district: Rue Jacob, Rue de Cherche-Midi, Rue Dragon, Rue du Saints Peres (M: St-Germain-des-Prés). A FAVORITE.

Centré de Dégustation Jacques Vivet Wine Courses, 48 Rue de Vaugirard (M: St-Sulpice) 43.25.96.30. Jacques Vivet has operated this tasting centre for more than 20 years. Mon/Tues/Thu evenings. €185 for four introductory courses/€200-300 four advanced classes. No credit cards. Call in advance.

Compagnie Bleue. 100 Rue de Cherche-Midi (M: Vaneau) 45.44.47.48. Gym + weight rooms, relaxation areas, group sessions.

Couvert des Cordeliers, Université de Paris, 15 Rue de l'Ecole de Medecine (M: Cluny Sorbonne) 42.34.68.68. Call for exhibitions. €5. We enjoyed a stunning display of 75 photographers' portraits of Isabelle Huppert, for example.

Ecole Nationale Supérieure des Beaux-Arts Galerie, 13 Quai Malaquais (M: St-Germain-des-Prés) 46.03.50.00. Call for rotating exhibitions from top students as well as from the school's extensive collections.

Eglise Saint-Germain-des-Prés, 3 Pl St-Germain-des-Prés (M: St-Germain-des-Prés) 43.25.41.71. Built in AD 990. Check on concert listings.

Galerie 54, 54 Rue Mazarine (M: Odeon) 43.26.89.96. Sculpture garden.

Galerie Art of This Century, 22 Rue Mazarine (M: Odeon) 43.25.81.65. Call for exhibitions.

Galerie Breheret, 9 Quai Malaquais (M: St-Germain-des-Prés) 42.60.74.74. Art selection displayed in 17th century townhouse. Closed Sun/Mon.

Galerie Claude-Bernard, 7-9 Rue des Beaux-Arts (M: St-Germain-des-Prés) 43.26.97.07. Call for exhibits.

Haircut at Institut Marianne Gray, 52 Rue St André des Arts (M: St-Michel) 43.26.58.21. See if Sandra or Nicola are there. €70 Haircut/Blowdry/Tip.

Musée Delacroix, 6 Pl de Fürstenberg (M: St-Germain-des-Prés) 44.41.86.50. Admission. Former home of Eugene Delacroix displaying his works and memorabilia. Closed Tues.

Musée des Lettres et Manuscrits, 8 Rue de Nesle (M: St-Michel) 43.25.25.41. Three levels of preserved, private letters and manuscripts. Thematic by floors: basement holds European monarchs, the Holocaust, Napoleon. The mezzanine houses the temporary exhibitions. The upper floor is devoted to the arts where you will find music scores by Mozart, letters from Matisse, manuscripts from Colette, Descartes. 1p-9p Wed/10a-6p Thur-Sunday. Closed Mon/Tues.

Musée Zadkine, 100 bis, Rue d'Assas (M: Vavin) 45.44.47.48. Sculpture gardens, Closed Mon. 11a-5:00p.

Postal Muséum, 34 Blvd Vaugirard (M: Montparnasse or Pasteur) 42.79.24.24. Personalized French stamps @ $9.00/sheet of 10.

Rue Vavin is a wonderful street at south exit of Luxembourg Gardens. Walk south to get to Le Select on **Blvd Montparnasse** to sit and enjoy pastis and people watching.

St-Germain-des-Prés is one of the most famous streets in Paris.

SUPERLATIVES:

Best Baguette: Eric Kayser Artisan Boulangerie, 10 Rue de l'Ancienne (M: Odeon) 43.25.71.60. Enjoy lunch at his new sandwich bar, Cuisine du Bar. Closed Sun.

Best confectionery: Les Bonbons, 6 Rue Brea (M: Vavin) 43.26.21.15. Candies from all regions of France.

Best cosmetics: Amin Kader Pharmacy, 2 Rue Guisarde (M: Mabillon) 43.25.86.88. This is the only place to find perfumes and beauty products by Santa Maria Novella.

Best cassoulet: La Table d'Aude, 8 Rue Vaugirard. See Restaurants, below.

Best crepes: Creperie des Arts, 27 Rue St Andre des Arts. (M: St-Michel) 43.26.15.68. Delicious combinations in a warm, surprising, and funky setting. Truly only in Paris!

Best croissants: Bread and Roses, 62 Rue Madame (M: Rennes) 42.22.06.06. Bakery, confectionery, a few tables. Delicious.

Best Made-to-order panini sandwiches at Cosi, 54 Rue de Seine (M: Odeon) 46.33.35.36. Opéra music + lots of students.

6e. Luxembourg, St-Germain-des-Prés

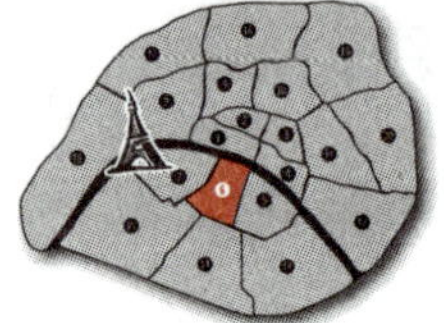

6

Best Pastis stop/Bar a vins: La Dernière Goutte, 6 Rue de Bourbon-La-Château (M: St-Germain-des-Prés) 43.29.11.62.

Best Pâtisserie, Croissants/Pastries: Gérard Mulot, 76 Rue de Seine (M: Odeon) 43.26.85.77.Closed Wed.

Best Pharmacy: Pharmacie Fouhety, 26 Rue du Four (M: St-Sulpice) 46.33.20.81. Markdowns + best selection. Two floors. Crowded. Closed Sunday.

Best Place to Kiss: Place du Fürstenberg, off Rue Jacob (M: St-Germain-des-Prés) (notwithstanding Sacre Coeur, Pont Neuf, the Eiffel Tower, Tuileries Gardens and everywhere in Paris)!

Best Prix Fixe Lunch: Café Aux Délices. See Restaurants. Sample the shrimp.

Best Prix Fixe Dinner: Le Comptoir. See Restaurants. 43.29.12.05.

Best Selection of Oils: L'Huilerie Artisanal J. Leblanc et Fils, 6 Rue Jacob. (M: St-Germain-des-Prés) 46.34.61.55. Great! Try pistachio oil. A FAVORITE. Closed Sundays.

Best pizza: Le Golfe de Naples, 5 Rue de Clement (M: Mabillon) 43.26.98.11. Over 17 varieties of pizza. Sidewalk terrace.

Best soup bar: What'Soup, 18 Rue du Dragon (M: St-Germain-des-Prés) 42.22.06.06. Two floors. All soups made daily.

Best Left Bank Terrace: Les Deux Magots, 6 Pl St-Germain-des-Prés (M: St-Germain-des-Prés) 45.48.55.25. Lots of history. Even more tourists.

Best Selection of Wines: La Maison des Millesimes, 137 Blvd St-Germain (M: St-Germain-des-Prés) 40.46.80.01. This tiny store stocks over 1,500 bottles of vintage Bordeaux wines in every price range. The only place you will find a bottle of 1928 Chateau Lafite Rothschild. Will is friendly and very knowledgeable. A FAVORITE. Closed Sundays.

Landmark Parisien Bistro: La Palette, 43 Rue de Seine (M: Odeon) 43.26.69.15. Lively atmosphere, focus on drinks and conversation. Great terrace on corner for people-watching and enjoying evening aperitifs.

More liquor, with over 130 flavors: La Rhumerie, 166 Blvd St-Germain-des-Prés (M: Mabillon) 43.54.28.94. Snacks, too. Til 2am.

More photography: La Chambre Claire, 14 Rue St Sulpice. Two levels of 10,000+ works. See Shopping, below.

Most Famous Café: Café Flore, 172 Blvd St-Germain (M: St-Germain-des-Prés) 45.48.55.26. Great location for people-watching and can be expensive, but worth it, at least once! Upstairs is where the locals, movie stars and politicians sit. A FAVORITE.

Most famous Flower Shop: Christian Tortu, 6 Carrefour de l'Odeon (M: Odeon) 43.26.02.56. Call ahead to take a floral arrangement class for one hour. Make sure you reconfirm day before.

Most Famous bridge in Paris: Pont Neuf, simply stroll up Rue Dauphine (M: Odeon) and you'll find it! A FAVORITE.

Most offbeat bookstore: Un Regard Moderne. See Shops, below.

Oldest church in Paris: Eglise Saint-Germain-des-Prés, 3 Pl St-Germain-des-Prés (M: St-Germain-des-Prés) 43.25.41.71. Built in AD 990.

Second Oldest street in Paris: Rue Serpente, existing from pre-war Paris. (M: St-Michel).

World-renowned pâtisserie & pastries: Pierre Hermè, 72 Rue Bonaparte (M: St-Sulpice) 43.54.47.77. Absolutely everything is scrumptious! Well worth the possible wait, if there is a line. A FAVORITE.

SHOPS:

Accessoire, 6 Rue Cherche Midi (M: Sèvres-Babylone) 45.48.36.08. Leather, shoes, accessories.

Adelline, 54 Rue Jacob (M: St-Germain-des-Prés) 47.03.07.18. Adeline Roussal presents gold and semiprecious stones.

Agatha Ruiz de la Prada, 9 Rue Guénégaud (M: Odeon) 43.25.86.88. Stylish women's wear.

Allison, 3 Rue de Buci (M: Odeon) 43.26.88.82. Boutique with trendy multi-brands. Several locations.

Amin Kader Pharmacy, 2 Rue Guisarde (M: Mabillon) 43.25.86.88. This is the only place to find perfumes and beauty products by Santa Maria Novella.

Anne Fontaine, 64-66 Rue des Saint-Peres (M: Sèvres-Babylone) 45.48.89.10. Great blouses.

Annick Goutal, 12 Pl St Sulpice (M: St-Sulpice). 46.33.03.15. Beautiful fragrances.

Au Gré du Vent, 10 Rue des Quatre Vents (M: Odeon) 44.07.28.73. Vintage collection as well as jewelry.

Aux Armes de Furstenberg, 1 Rue Furstenberg (M: St-Germain-des-Prés) 43.29.79.51. Antique shops with maritime objects and collectibles, model boats, maps, globes, telescopes.

Avant-Scène, 4 Pl de l'Odeon (M: Odeon) 46.33.12.40. Fun furniture designs and objets d'art featuring designer Hubert Le Gall. Imaginative pieces will make you smile.

BGN, 59 ter, Rue Bonaparte (M: St-Sulpice) 40.46.89.77. Trendy, modern fashions. Also in 4e.

Burberry, 55 Rue de Rennes (M: Rennes) 45.48.52.71.

Cacharel, 64 Rue Bonaparte, (M: St-Germain-des-Prés) 40.46.00.45. Designs at affordable prices.

6e. Luxembourg, St-Germain-des-Prés

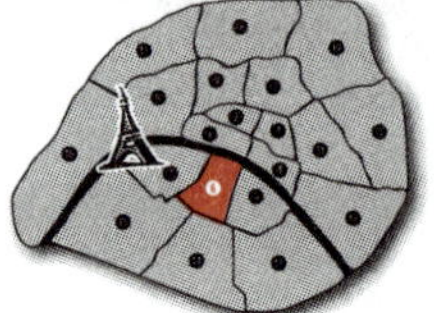

Carine Gilson, 6 Rue Bonaparte (M: St-Sulpice) 43.26.46.71. Subtle and sexy lingerie designer. A FAVORITE.

Castelbajac Concept Store, 26 Rue Madame (M: St-Sulpice) 45.48.40.55. Funky, young line of accessories and housewares.

Catherine B, 3 Rue Guisarde (M: Mabillon) 43.25.64.92. Vintage Hermès.

Cécile + Jeanne, 4 Rue de Sèvres (M: Sèvres-Babylone) 42.22.82.82. Jewelry. One of several locations.

Céline, 58 Rue de Rennes (M: St-Germain-des-Prés) 45.48.58.55.

Cesaree, 11 Rue du Dragon (M: St-Germain-des-Prés) 45.48.86.86. Jewelry.

6

Christian Dior, 16 Rue de l'Abbaye (M: St-Germain-des-Prés) 56.24.90.53. Ready-to-wear collections.

Christian Tortu, 6 Carrefour de l'Odeon (M: Odeon) 43.26.02.56. Beautiful floral designs. Call ahead to take a floral arrangement class for one hour. Make sure you reconfirm the day before.

Coiff'Inst, 44 Rue du Four (M: St-Germain-des-Prés) 45.44.84.39. Three stories of hair styling in a country house setting. Relaxing baths and exclusive VIP floor.

Comoglio, 22 Rue Jacob (M: St-Germain-des-Prés) 43.54.65.86. 18th and 19th century antiques. Two floors, including a selection of Comoglio fabrics.

Cop Copine, 3 Rue Montfaucon (M: Odeon) 42.34.70.26. Stylish fashions not available in U.S. A FAVORITE.

Da Rosa, 62 Rue de Seine (M: Odeon) 40.51.00.09. Wonderful store with whole rooms devoted to olive oils, charcuterie and spices. Eat in or Takeout. A FAVORITE.

David Hicks France, 12 Rue de Tournon (M: Odeon) 55.42.82.82. Design shop.

Dépôt-Vente du Buci-Bourbon, 6 Rue de Bourbon-le-Chateau (M: Mabillon) 46.34.45.05. Good vintage design collection. 11a-8p.

Emilia Cosi, 20 Rue St Sulpice (M: St-Sulpice) 43.54.78.66. Boudoir boutique with pink walls and a feather chandelier. Finest lingerie.

Emporio Armani, 149 Blvd St Germain (M: St-Germain-des-Prés) 53.63.33.50. Visit the Ofr Bookshop upstairs, beside the Café.

Eres, 4 bis, Rue du Cherche Midi (M: Sèvres-Babylone) 45.44.95.54. Bathing suits. Several locations.

Fabrice, 33 Rue Bonaparte (M: St-Germain-des-Prés) 43.26.57.95. Jewelry.

Feel Good, 9 Rue Cherche Midi (M: Sèvres-Babylone) 45.44.88.66. Flirty, well-made dresses/bodysuits.

Flamant, 8 Rue de l'Abbaye (M: St-Germain-des-Prés) 56.81.12.40. Home décor emporium.

FNAC, 136 Rue de Rennes (M: St-Placide) 49.54.30.00. Well known for selection of French books, CDs, music tickets, etc.

Galerie Claude Bernard, 7-9 Rue des Beaux-Arts (M: St-Germain-des-Prés) 43.26.97.07. Important gallery of photography and contemporary art. Works by Robert Doisneau, Martine Franck, Cartier-Bresson and other artists.

Galerie De Conti, 1 Quai de Conti (M: Pont Neuf) 43.25.81.33. Elegant gallery with originals by Chagall, Picasso, and limited-edition Bronzes. By appointment at 06.85.02.24.92. Closed Sun/Monday.

Galerie Doria, 1 Rue des Beaux-Arts (M: St-Germain-des-Prés) 43.25.43.25. Furniture and decorative arts from the 1920's. Call for exhibitions. Closed Sun/Monday.

Galerie Helena Poree, 1 Rue de l'Odeon (M: Odeon) 43.54.17.00. Jewelry. Closed Sun/Mon.

Galerie Larock-Granoff, 13 Quai de Conti (M: Pont Neuf) 43.54.41.92. Modern art.

Galerie Vallois, 41 Rue de Seine (M: Mabillon) 43.29.50.84. Art Deco treasures.

Galerie Yves Gastou, 12 Rue Bonaparte (M: St-Germain-des-Prés) 53.73.00.10.

Galeries Documents, 53 Rue de Seine (M: Odeon) 43.54.50.68. Vintage advertising posters and art. Fair prices and friendly. A FAVORITE.

Garderobe, 18 Rue St Sulpice (M: St-Sulpice) 56.24.22.99. Nothing but womens pants - all made in France.

Gien, 13 Rue Jacob (M: St-Germain-des-Prés) 46.33.46.72. Boutiqe sells the "Jolie Paris" faïence plates, tableware. €44 set of 4 canape plates.

Hervé Chapelier, 1 bis Rue du Vieux-Colombier (M: St-Sulpice) 44.07.06.50. Brightly colored nylon bags, all sizes, trendy.

Honoré, 38 Rue Madame (M: St-Sulpice) 45.48.96.86. Hand-knit sweaters and home-made tees. Trendy, like Agnes B. stores.

Isa Parvex, 15 Rue du Dragon (M: St-Germain-des-Prés) 45.44.88.00. Jewelry.

Jnf, Flammarian Publishers, 17-19 Rue Visconti (M: Odeon) 44.41.19.60. Rare and unique French publications and art books. A FAVORITE.

Judith Lacroix, 61 Rue Bonaparte (M: St-Germain-des-Prés) 43.26.02.58. Another boutique location for offbeat collections of irresistible children's clothes.

Kamel Mennour, 60 Rue Mazarine (M: Odeon) 56.24.03.63. Photo gallery with eclectic showings.

Karine Dupont, 16 Rue du Cherchè Midi (M: St-Sulpice) 42.84.06.30. Sassy fashions, bags, accessories. A FAVORITE.Another boutique is in 1e.

Kenzo, 60 Rue Rennes (M: St-Germain-des-Prés) 45.44.27.88. Designer boutique.

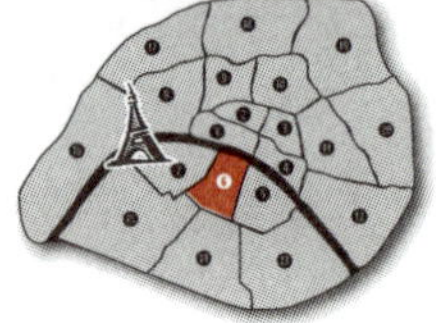

Kim and Garo, 7 Rue des Quatre Vents (M: Odeon) 40.46.89.29. Marrakesh designer Ludovic Petit's sleek creations.

Kristina Popovitch, 59 bis, Rue Bonaparte (M: St-Germain-des-Prés) 53.10.88.38. Designer boutique.

L'Angelot, 28 Rue Bonaparte (M: St-Germain- des-Prés) 56.24.21.22. Infants and children clothing.

L'Huilerie Artisanal J. Leblanc et Fils, 6 Rue Jacob. (M: St-Germain-des-Prés) 46.34.61.55. Great! This tiny shop has so many flavored oils. Try the pistachio oil. A FAVORITE.

6

La Chambre Claire, 14 Rue St Sulpice (M: Odeon) 46.34.04.31. Two levels of 10,000+ photographic works of art. Numbered and signed Helmut Newton's.

La Crémerie Caves Miard, 9 Rue des Quatre Vents (M: Odeon) 43.54.99.30. Wine store and small wine bar. Good selection of Rhones and wines from smaller producers. Serves simple, fresh lunch, too.

La Cornue, 18 Rue Mabillon (M: Mabillon) 46.33.83.15. Famous makers of beautiful and expensive ovens, this small store sells kitchen accessories and offers cooking lessons in French on Thursdays.

La Dernière Goûte, WINES, 6 Rue de Bourbon le Château (M: St-Germain-des-Prés) 43.29.11.62. Good selection. Saturday wine tastings.

La Maison des Millesimes, WINES, 137 Blvd St-Germain (M: St-Germain-des-Prés) 40.46.80.01. This tiny store stocks over 1,500 bottles of vintage Bordeaux wines in every price range. The only place you will find a bottle of 1928 Chateau Lafite Rothschild. Will is friendly and very knowledgeable. A FAVORITE. Closed Sundays.

Lagerfeld Gallery, 40 Rue de Seine (M: Odeon) 55.42.75.51. High fashion.

Lancel, 43 Rue de Rennes (M: St-Germain-des-Prés) 42.22.94.73. Leather handbags.

Le Monde en Marche, 34 Rue Dauphine (M: Odeon) 43.29.09.49. Toy store.

Les Néréides, 23 Rue du Four (M: St-Sulpice) 43.26.33.55. Jewelry designs.

Les Bonbons, 6 Rue Brea (M: Vavin) 43.26.21.15. Candies from all regions of France.

Leroux, 32 Rue Jacob (M: St-Germain-des-Prés) 55.42.00.39. Design boutique.

Librairie du Moniteur, 7 Pl de l'Odeon (M: Odeon) 44.41.15.75. The bookstore for architects and urban designers.

Lionel Poilane, 8 Rue du Cherche Midi (M: Sèvres-Babylone) 45.48.45.69. Bread.

Louise Della, 55 Rue des Saints-Peres (M: St-Germain-des-Prés) 42.84.30.08. Fashion designer Blandine Della Torre presents colorful Bohemian-chic styles.

Maison de Famille, 29 Rue St Sulpice (M: St-Sulpice) 40.46.97.47. 3 floors of various household items, and a bridal registry.

Mandarina Duck, 51 Rue Bonaparte (M: St-Germain-des-Prés) 43.26.68.38. Fine leather.

Marie-Helene de Taillac, MHT, 8 Rue de Tournon (M: Odeon) 44.27.07.07. Jewelry. Precious stones, crystals. Mobiles. Expensive.

Marie Mercie, 23 Rue St Sulpice (M: St-Sulpice) 43.26.45.83. Hats, accessories.

Marie Papier, 26 Rue Vavin (M: Vavin) 43.26.46.44. Hand-made stationery, gift papers, albums. A FAVORITE.

Maud Frizon, 83 Rue des Sts Peres (M: Sèvres-Babylone) 42.22.06.93. Haute couture footwear.

Métal Pointus, 13 Rue du Cherchè Midi (M: Sèvres-Babylone) 45.44.96.99. Costume jewelry.

Mis En Demeure, 27 Rue du Cherchè Midi, (M: Sèvres-Babylone) 45.48.83.79. Home décor boutique. Good selections.

Mona, 17 Rue Bonaparte (M: St-Germain-des-Prés) 44.07.07.27 Shoes.

Monoprix, 50 Rue de Rennes (M: St-Germain-des-Prés) 45.48.18.08. Don't let appearances fool you, you can get some stylish steals in this department store. Look for M Café (has takeout food). A FAVORITE. Several locations in Paris.

Muji, 27 Rue St Sulpice (M: St-Sulpice) 46.34.01.10. New concept store. Men, office, gifts.

Odorantes Paris, 9 Rue Madame (M: St-Sulpice) 42.84.03.00. Florists Sammartino and Hervé design mysterious, dark floral creations. Their arrangements are popular with movie and fashion crowd.

Olivier Pitou, 23 Rue des Saints-Pères (M: Sèvres-Babylone) 49.27.97.49. Outstanding florist, beautiful ceramic vases.

Oliviers & Co., 28 Rue de Buci (M: Odeon) 44.07.15.43. Many types olive oil.

Onward, 147 Blvd St Germain (M: Odeon) 55.42.77.55. Boutique with cool fashion designs, accessories+basement with makeup, etc.

Oona L'Ourse, 72 Rue Madame (M: St-Sulpice) 42.84.11.94. Children's clothing.

Parallèle, 9 Rue de Sèvres (M: Sèvres-Babylone) 45.44.31.92. Chic, understated shoes.

Patrick Roger, 108 Blvd St Germain (M: Odeon) 43.29.38.42. Modernist chocolatier. Chocolate sculptures in window.

Peggy Huyn Kinh, 11 Rue Coëtlogon (M: St-Sulpice) 42.84.83.83. Bags and jewelry.

Pharmacie Fouhety, 26 Rue du Four (M: St-Sulpice) 46.33.20.81. French beauty

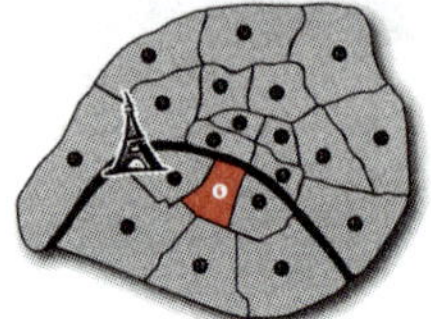

crèmes, etc. Markdowns + best selection. Two floors. Crowded. Closed Sunday.

Pierre Hermè, 72 Rue Bonaparte (M: St-Sulpice) 43.54.47.77. Absolutely everything is scrumptious! Well worth the possible wait, if there is a line. A FAVORITE.

Pierre Marcolini, 89 Rue de Seine (M: Mabillon) 44.07.39.07. World renowned chocolatier. 60 varieties.

Quartz Diffusion, 12 Rue des Quatre Vents (M: Odeon) 43.54.03.00. Glass designers.

Sabbia Rosa, 73 Rue des Saint-Peres (M: St-Germain-des-Prés) 45.48.88.37. Finest lingerie.

Séverine Perraudin, 5 Pl St Sulpice (M: Odeon) 43.54.67.33. Haute creations. Closed Sunday.

Shu Uemera, 176 Blvd St Germain (M: St-Germain-des-Prés) 45.48.02.55. Cosmetics and perfumes.

Sonia Rykiel, 175 Blvd St Germain (M: St-Germain-des-Prés) 49.54.60.60. Women. Rykiel Body & Soul is a new line of sportswear. Upstairs, you will find her erotic collection.

Stephane Kelian, 25 Rue du Four (M: St-Sulpice) 40.46.08.06. Shoes.

Un Regard Moderne, 10 Rue Git Le Coeur (M: St-Michel) 43.29.13.93. Off beat and very tiny book store that has old editions of American underground, rock, erotic books.

Ustencia, 95 Rue de Seine (M: Odeon) 56.24.20.20. Funky home accessories.

Vallois Sculptures, 35 Rue de Seine (M: Mabillon) 43.25.17.34. Art dealer in 20th century sculpture. Closed Sun/Monday.

Vanessa Bruno, 25 Rue St Sulpice (M: St-Sulpice) 43.54.41.04. Womens' wear designer. Also handbags & accessories.

Village Voice, 6 Rue Princesse (M: Mabillon) 46.33.36.47. Odile Helliers is convivial owner of this English-speaking book store.

Vogica, 91 Blvd Raspail (M: Sèvres-Babylone) 44.39.38.70. Kitchen and bath design with funky accessories on sale in boutique in front. We always find unusual décor items to buy. A FAVORITE.

Y's Yohji Yamamoto, 69 Rue des Sts Peres (M: St-Germain-des-Prés) 45.48.22.56. High end Japanese designer.

Yesterday Never Dies, 53 Rue du Four (M: St-Sulpice) 45.49.14.80. Vintage hippy-chic. Pretty Box accessories.

Zadig & Voltaire, 1 Rue du Vieux Colombier (M: St-Sulpice). 43.29.18.29. Ladies.

RESTAURANTS: LES PLATS DU JOUR:

Alcazar, 62 Rue Mazarine (M: Odeon) 53.10.19.99. Owned by Conran. Reserve table in corner for less noise. Hip bar, **Mezzanine,** is upstairs with live music. Jazz brunch on Sundays.

André Allard, 41 Rue St Andre des Arts. (M: St-Michel) 43.26.48.23. Good food, country style servings and seatings. Good wine list. A FAVORITE. Closed Sunday.

Au Bon St-Pourcain, 10 bis. Rue Servandoni (M: St-Sulpice) 43.54.93.63. Owner Francois serves wonderful cassoulet. Only 26 seats.

Au Gourmand, 22 Rue de Vaugirard (M: Odeon) 43.26.26.45. New owners in this good location. Closed Sunday.

Aux Charpentiers, 10 Rue Mabillon (M: Mabillon) 43.26.30.05. 130 years old, traditional bistro food. Open Sunday.

Aux Saveurs de Claude, 12 Rue Stanislas (M: Vavin) 45.44.41.74. Chef Lamain used to work with Guy Savoy and now runs his own restaurant with art deco and open kitchen. Fair prices for good meals and fresh vegetables. Closed Sunday.

Azabu, 3 Rue André Mazet (M: Odeon) 46.33.72.05. Teppanyaki restaurant to find some of the best Japanese meals. Check out the bathrooms while you wait.

Barroco, 23 Rue Mazarine (M: Odeon) 43.26.40.24. Latin and Spanish food and drinks.

Bistrot d'Alex, 2 Rue Clément (M: Mabillon) 43.25.77.66. Good, unpretentious, Lyonnais/Provençal meals. When busy, service sometimes gets testy.

Brasserie Lipp, 151 Blvd St Germain (M: St-Germain-des-Prés) 45.48.53.91. Classic and average. Go for onion soup and atmosphere à la Hemingway. Don't go upstairs.

Bread and Roses, 62 Rue Madame (M: Rennes) 42.22.06.06. Bakery, confectionery, a few tables. Delicious.

Café de la Mairie, 8 Pl St Sulpice (M: St-Sulpice) 43.26.67.82. Large terrace with view of church. Snacks.

Café Délices, (used to be Le Chat Gripp), 87 Rue d'Assas (M: Port Royal) 43.54.70.00. Food and service vary. Closed Sun.

Chez Fernand, 9 Rue Christine (M: Odeon) 43.25.18.55. We had wonderful truffle noir ravioli and delicious lamb. Moderate wine list. Small front room for non-smokers and larger main room for diners who smoke. Red/white checkered tablecloths. Friendly. They operate other "Fernand" restaurants in 6e. Open Sunday.

Chez (Jean-Claude) Gramond, 5 Rue de Fleurus (M: Rennes) 42.22.28.89. Brasserie food. House specialty is roasted squab.

xembourg, St-Germain-des-Prés

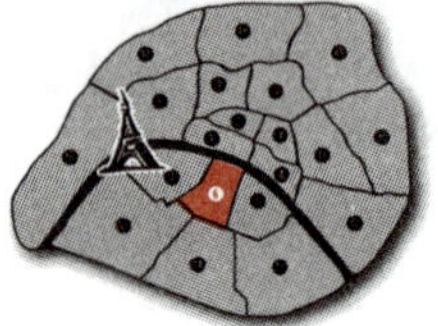

re Paul, 12 Rue Monsieur le Prince (M: Odeon) 43.54.74.59. Good bistro dly service. Downstairs is preferable. Open Sunday.

cel, 7 Rue Stanislas (M: Notre Dame des Champs) 45.48.29.94. Classic Lyonnais cooking. Cozy. Closed Sunday.

des Arts, 56 Rue St Andre des Arts. (M: St-Michel) 46.33.92.00 Friendly and ancake and creperie house. No set hours.

a Boissonnerie, 69 Rue de Seine (M: Odeon) 43.54.34.69. Wine bar and informal ood restaurant with terrace. Open Sunday.

gon Saint-Julien, 45 Quai des Grands-Augustin (M: St-Michel) 43.54.31.33. hef/owner Herraiz offers tasty Spanish tapas and meals in a modern décor. Open the private drawer and you will find your flatware. Popular.

Fromagerie 31, 64 Rue de Seine (M: Mabillon) 43.26.50.31. Cute cheese bar and shop with wine. A FAVORITE.

Gattopardo Café, 29 Rue Dauphine (M: Odeon) 46.33.75.92. Pizza, pasta, and tiramisu to-die-for. Affordable and friendly. Closed Sunday.

Il Viccolo, 34 Rue Mazarine (M: Odeon) 43.25.01.11. Great Italian. Enclosed sidewalk café.

Joséphine (aka Chez Dumonet) 117 Rue du Cherche Midi (M: Duroc) 45.48.52.40. WE LOVE IT HERE! Since 1898, one of the oldest in Paris. A real Paris bistro, wonderful meals. A FAVORITE. Closed Sunday.

L'Epi Dupin, 11 Rue Dupin (M: Sèvres-Babylone) 42.22.64.56. Must reserve because this is always on the top-ten list. WE LIKE the food a lot. A FAVORITE. Closed Sunday.

L'Espadon bleu, 25 Rue des Grands Augustin (M: St-Michel) 46.33.00.85. Jacques Cagna, seafood. Simple preparations. Closed Sunday.

L'O à la Bouche, 157 Blvd du Montparnasse. (M: Edgar Quinet) 43.26.26.53. Chef studied with Guy Savoy, mixed reviews. Terrace dining. Closed Sun-Mon.

La Bastide Odeon, 7 Rue Corneille (M: Odeon) 43.26.03.65. Provençal food. Closed Sunday.

La Brasserie Italiana, 81 Rue de Seine. (M: Odeon) 43.25.00.28. Late night dining.

La Closerie de Lilas, 171 Blvd Montparnasse (M: Vavin) 40.51.34.50. Famous old bistro. Reliable good food. Open Sunday.

La Creperie Saint Germain, 33 Rue St Andre des Arts (M: St-Michel) 43.54.24.41. Inviting blue tiled front. Delicious combinations in a warm, surprising, and funky setting. Only in Paris!.

La Ferrandaise, 8 Rue Vaugirard (M: Cluny-La Sorbonne) 43.26.36.36. Small, friendly, under €35.

La Main de la Paté, 35 Rue Dauphine (M: Odeon) 46.33.58.97. Fresh pizzas, pastas served with a smile. Very affordable, €19.50. Open 7/7. A FAVORITE.

La Maison de la Chine, 76 Rue Bonaparte (M: St-Sulpice) 40.51.95.00. Japanese.

La Maison du Jardin, 27 Rue de Vaugirard (M: Rennes) 45.48.22.31. A FAVORITE. Prix fixe is a good value. New French. A jewel of a restaurant.

La Marlotte, 55 Rue du Cherche-Midi (M: Sèvres-Babylone) 45.48.86.79. Good value, traditional food. Try the lamb.

La Maxence, 9 bis, Blvd Montparnasse (M: Edgar Quinet) 45.67.24.28. Chef David van Laer, $124 for 2. Good lamb. Closed Sunday.

La Méditerranée, 2 Pl. de l'Odeon (M: Odeon) 43.26.02.03. Bistro food. locals like it.

La Palette, 43 Rue de Seine (M: Odeon) 43.26.69.15. Lively atmosphere, focus on drinks and conversation. Great terrace on corner for people-watching and enjoying evening aperitifs. Lunch menu only, noon til 3p, modest prices. Closed Sunday.

La Petite Cour, 8 Rue Mabillon (M: Mabillon) 43.26.52.26. We LIKE it. Small, private terrace + garden. Good food, €40 3-course meal.

La Rhumerie, 166 Blvd St Germain (M: Mabillon) 43.54.28.94. Good simple café for drinks and snacks.

La Rotisserie d'en Face, 2 Rue Christine (M: St Michel) 43.26.40.98. Jacques Cagna. We have been disappointed. Seafood specialties, like bouillabaisse.

La Table d'Aude, 8 Rue Vaugirard (M: Odeon) 43.26.36.36. Chef/owner Bernard Patou and his wife serve delicious cassoulet. Their secret is grilling the meats separately to reduce fat. Closed all day Sun/dinner Monday.

Le Bélier in L'Hôtel, 13 Rue des Beaux Arts (M: St- Germain-des-Prés) 44.41.99.01. Tightly seated dinners. New French. Closed Sunday.

Le Bistro d'Henri, 16 Rue Princesse (M: Mabillon) 46.33.51.12. Simple French. Wine list reasonably priced.

Le Christine Restaurant, 1 Rue Christine (M: St-Michel) 40.51.71.64. In Dauphine Passage, recommended for lunch. Prix fixe is good value. Closed Sunday.

Le Comptoir, 9 Carrefour de l'Odeon (M: Odeon) 44.27.07.97. Hotel Relais Saint-Germain for reservations. Yves and Claudine Camdeborde offer fresh, creative, and delicious prix fixe dinners for €40. Our meal was perfect in every way. Must reserve dinner months in advance. No reservations taken for lunch. A FAVORITE.

Le Dedicace Café, 7 Rue St-Benoit (M: St-Germain-des-Prés) 42.61.12.70. Modern bistro specials. Open Sunday.

Le Golfe de Naples, 5 Rue de Clement (M: Mabillon) 43.26.98.11 Over 17 varieties of pizza. Sidewalk Terrace. See Superlatives

6e. Luxembourg, St-Germain-des-Prés

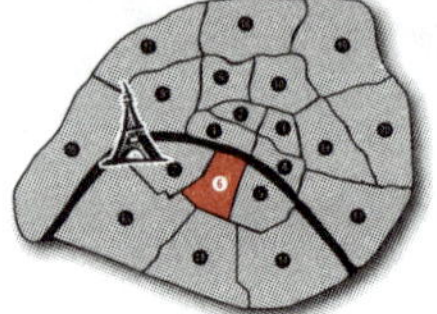

Le Parc aux Cerfs, 50 Rue Vavin (M: Vavin) 43.54.87.83. Art gallery atmosphere. Well-prepared Lyonnaise. Little patio in back.

Le Petit Saint-Benoît, 4 Rue St-Benoît (M: St-Germain-des-Prés) Good simple food. Outdoor dining.

Le Petit Zinc, 11 Rue St-Benoît (M: St-Germain-des-Prés) 42.86.61.00. Vintage 1930's setting. Outdoor dining. Now a franchise. Noon-2am.

Le Procope, 13 Rue de l'Ancienne Comedie (M: Odeon) 40.47.79.00. Circa 1689 with gold, gilt, and lavish banquettes and silver trays heaped high with fresh seafood. Open Sunday.

Le Pub Saint Germain, 17 Rue Ancienne Comédie (M: Odeon) 56.81.13.13. Sportsbar and sporty food. Upstairs is non-smoking. Open 24/7 non-stop.

Le Timbre, 3 Rue Ste-Beauve (M: Vavin) 45.49.10.40. Chef Christopher Wright from London pairs good wine with new menu. Closed Sunday.

Les Bookinistes, 53 Quai des Grands Augustins. (M: Odeon) 43.25.45.94. Trendy bistro. Has vegetarian menu. Closed Sunday.

Les Caves Miard, 9 Rue des Quatre-Vents (M: Odeon) 43.54.99.30. New owner and still popular, serving light Italian and good French wine list. Closed Sunday/Monday.

Les Deux Magots, 6 Pl St-Germain-des-Prés (M: St-Germain-des-Prés) 45.48.55.25. Lots of history and even more tourists. Great terrace. FYI, if someone sketches you while you sit, you do not have to purchase the picture unless you really like it or enjoyed the artist.

Les Editeurs, 4 Carrefour de l'Odeon (M: Odeon) 43.26.67.76. Sit at sidewalk table and enjoy snacks. Meals only at dinner.

Peres et Filles, 81 Rue de Seine (M: Mabillon) 43.25.00.28. Friendly service, classic food. Same owners as Bistrot Vivienne.

Polidor, 41 Rue Monsieur le Prince (M: Odeon) 43.26.95.34. Very old. We like it, Communal tables, basic fare.

Positano, 15 Rue Canettes (M: St-Germain-des-Prés) 43.26.01.62. Pizza, pasta, Italian. Great for when you need a break from the French foie gras and fromage.

Relais de l'Entrecote Saint-Germain, 20 bis, Rue St Benoit (M: St-Germain-des-Prés) 45.49.16.00. Friendly, dependable menu.

Roger la Grenouille, 26-28 Rue des Grands Augustins (M: St-Michel) 56.24.24.34. Frogs legs and traditional French food. Friendly service. Closed Sunday.

Sensing, 19 Rue de Bréa (M: Vavin) 43.27.08.80. Guy Martin, ex-Le Grand Vefour, opens with Chef Remi to present fresh tasting combinations.

Vagenende, 142 Blvd St Germain (M: St-Germain-des-Prés) 43.26.68.18. Belle Epoque brasserie. A FAVORITE. Open Sunday.

Visconti, 25 Rue Mazarine (M: Odeon) 44.07.38.98. Roberto offers good Italian, moderately priced in cozy setting. Open 7/7.

Wadja, 10 Rue de la Grande Chaumière (M: Vavin) 46.33.02.02. Good, inexpensive food, diner-like setting. We LIKE. Closed Sunday.

Yakijapo Mitsuko, 8 Rue du Sabot (M: St-Sulpice) 44.22.17.74. Sushi.

Ze Kitchen Galerie, 4 Rue des Grand Augustin (M: St-Michel) 44.32.00.32. Chef William Ledeuil of Bookinistes. Reliably good meals. Closed Sunday.

RESTAURANTS: GASTRONOMIQUE:

Jacques Cagna, 14 Rue des Grands Augustins (M: Odeon) 43.26.49.39. Gastronomique. Recent reports from friends very mixed about food, but all say service slow and lacking. Closed Sunday.

Laperouse, 51 Quai des Grands Augustin (M: St-Michel) 43.26.68.04. Romantic & classic. Reserve a table in one of the boudoir-dining rooms. Received 90 out of 100 rating by French newsletter. Upstairs café is less-costly. A FAVORITE. Closed Sunday.

Hélène Darroze, 4 Rue d'Assas (M: Rennes) 42.22.00.11. Gastronomique upstairs/Tapas downstairs. We enjoyed everything here. She just received another Michelin star. A FAVORITE. Closed Sunday.

Le Paris, Hotel Lutetia, 23 Rue de Sèvres (M: Sèvres-Babylone) 49.54.46.90. Haute cuisine with Sonia Rykiol décor. Solid, classic meals Closed Sunday

Relais Louis XIII, 8 Rue des Grands-Augustins (M: Odeon) 43.26.75.96. Intimate ambiance and classic meals prepared by ex-Tour d'Argent chef Manuel Martinez. Tasting menu and good wine list complete this fine dining experience. Closed Sun/Mon.

BONNE SOIREE! PARIS AT NIGHT:

Au Caveau de la Bolée, 25 Rue de l'Hirondelle (M: St-Michel) 43.54.62.20. Cabaret and Dinner.

Balle Au bond, 3 Quai Malaquais (M: Pont Neuf or St-Germain-des-Prés) 40.51.87.06. Music sets vary, call first.

Bar Lutèce, 45 Blvd Raspail (M: Sèvres-Babylone) 49.54.46.46. Piano bar with live jazz in Hôtel Lutetia.

Bilboquet, 13 Rue St-Benoit (M: St-Germain-des-Prés) 45.48.81.84. Open since 1947. Jazz music. Can get smoky downstairs. A FAVORITE. Instead of cover, you are charged mightily for your first drink. Dinner is also served.

6e. Luxembourg, St-Germain-des-Prés

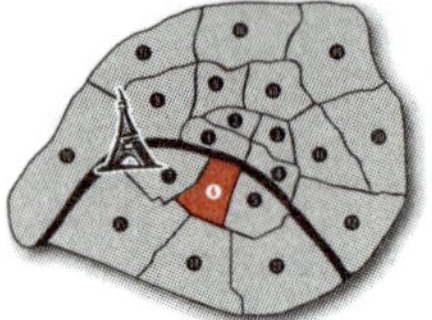

Birdland, 20 Rue Princesse (M: Mabillon) 43.26.97.59. Jazz bar. Mon-Sat 7p-dawn. Sundays noon-dawn.

Café Laurent, 33 Rue Dauphine, inside the Hotel D'Aubusson (M: Odeon) 43.29.43.43. Flavien manages a lively bar and good jazz. Ask for one of his champagne cocktails. A FAVORITE.

Castel's, 15 Rue Princesse (M: Mabillon) 43.26.90.22. Private club. Disco downstairs and bistro is on ground level.

Cavern, 21 Rue Dauphine (M: St-Michel) 43.54.53.82. Concerts at 9:30p. Call ahead to check schedule.

Le Bar, 27 Rue de Condé (M: Odeon) 43.29.06.61. Cozy room, ambiance.

Le Bar 10 (Dix), 10 Rue de l'Odeon (M: Odeon) 43.26.66.83. 5p-2a, except Sun, 12:30 am. Inside this "dive" bar, with hippy French and expats, you will find a jukebox with an even hipper selection.

Le Bob Cool, 15 Rue des Grands Augustins (M: Odeon) 46.33.33.77. Le Bob has cool cocktails, a cool oak bar, cool board games, cool music and a cool clientele. Not-so-cool is how smoky it gets. 5p-2a.

Le Caveau de la Bolée, 25 Rue de L'Hirondelle (M: St-Michel) Live music, chansons.

Mezzanine, 2nd floor of Alcazar, 62 Rue Mazarine (M: Mabillon) 53.10.19.99.

New Riverside, 7 Rue Grégoire (M: Odeon) 43.54.46.33. Cellar club. 1970's style music.

My Special Travel Notes

6

My Special Travel Notes

6

7e. Invalides, Tour d'Eiffel

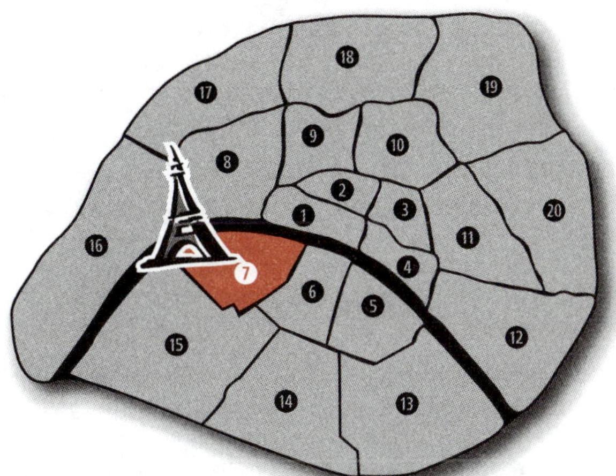

You shouldn't miss the **Eiffel Tower, Rodin Museum** and the **Musée d'Orsay.**

Visit **Loulou de la Falaise's** boutique of original jewelry and accessories.

Chefs **Christian Constant** and **Schmidt** prepare savory meals and Catherine Constant graciously greets you at **Le Violon D'Ingrés**.

MAJOR METROS:
- RUE DU BAC
- ASSEMBLÉE NATIONALE
- INVALIDES
- LA TOUR-MAUBOURG
- VARENNE
- ECOLE MILITAIRE
- SOLFERINO
- SEVRÉS-BABYLONE

7e. Invalides, Tour d'Eiffel

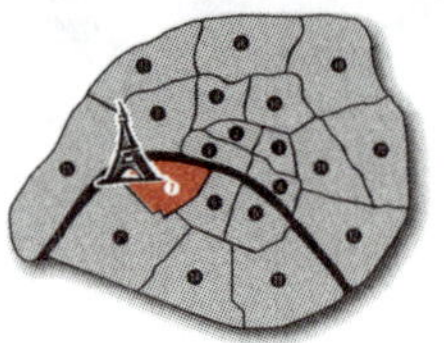

FAMOUS SIGHTS:

Hôtel des Invalides, Pl des Invalides, 129 Rue de Grenelle (M: Invalides) 44.42.38.77/ 44.42.37.72 Open daily 10a-5p. €6. Impressive masterpiece of French architecture circa 1670. Includes **Musée de L'Armée,** the world's greatest military museum, with suits of armor, Napoleon's bedroom, and his "flag of farewell." Through the west wing is the **Musée des Plans-Reliefs** which shows French towns and monuments down to scale. Across the Cour d'Honneur is the **Eglise du Dôme,** the second-tallest monument in Paris, where you will see **Napoleon's Tomb.** A FAVORITE. Open daily. $7 adults/$5.50 youth. 10a-6p.

Musée d'Orsay, 1 Rue de la Légion d'Honneur (M: Solferino) 40.49.48.14. 10a-6p. Call for special exhibitions. 19th century art, sculptures and huge Impressionists collection. A FAVORITE. €7.50. Open 10a-6p and until 9:30p on Thursdays. On the terrace is **Cafe des Hauteurs** for simple snacks with good view. Enjoy an elegant lunch or tea at the **Musée d'Orsay Restaurant,** 45.49.47.03. on the middle floor. Closed Monday.

7

Musée du Quai Branly, 37 Quai Branly (M: Pl de Alma) 56.61.70.00. Exterior features a "living wall" and inside you will find primitive art and artifacts from Africa, Asia and the Americas. Three mezzanine floors offer rotating exhibitions. Jacques Chirac is responsible for moving these works from the Louvre. Two restaurants: a casual garden café at ground level and Les Ombres rooftop which requires reservation for lunch and dinner, call 47.71.69.73. Museum is closed Monday.

Musée Rodin, 77 Rue de Varenne (M: Varenne) 44.18.61.10. A FAVORITE. Open Tues-Sunday. Famous sculptures and lovely gardens. Admission fee.

Tour d'Eiffel, Parc du Champs de Mars (M: Bir Hakeim) 44.11.23.23. Open 9:30a-11p. Admission depends on which of three levels you choose. Mail your friends souvenir postcards from a post office atop the tower. Don't forget the carrousel! Lights twinkle at night for ten minutes on-the-hour.

It's fun to have a picnic in **Jardin du Champ-de-Mars.** (M: Bir Hakeim). Look for the **Wall of Peace** in front of the Eiffel Tower.

DIVERSIONS:

American Church, 65 Quai d'Orsay. (M: Solferino) 40.62.05.00. Interdenominational church serving the English-speaking community in Paris. Free classical concerts on Sunday evenings.

Antique and Arts district: Rue de l'Universite, Rue de Beaune, Rue de Verneuil, Rue du Bac, Rue de Lille (M: Rue du Bac).

Le Bon Marché Department Store, 24 Rue de Sèvres (M: Sèvres-Babylone) 44.39.80.00. Good collections from designers PLUS, Epicerie de Paris is within Bon Marché and has its own entrance from the street, at 38 Rue de Sèvres. It is a deluxe food market that quite a few believe is better than Fauchon, with lower prices.

Bateaux Parisiens, Tour d'Eiffel (M: Trocadéro) 44.11.33.55. River cruises along the Seine. A FAVORITE. Reserve in advance.

Bateaux Vedettes, Port de Suffren (M: Bir Hakeim) 47.05.71.29. River cruises on Seine. Reservations required, open seating.

Boffi Cuisines, 234 Blvd St Germain (M: Solferino) 42.84.11.02. Culinary design studio.

Deyrolle, 46 Rue du Bac (M: Rue du Bac) 42.22.30.07. Open since 1880, famous taxidermist - go upstairs and see stuffed animals.

Four Seasons Fountain, circa 1739. 57-59 Rue de Grenelle (M: Rue du Bac)

Galerie Maeght, 42 Rue du Bac (M: Rue du Bac) 45.48.45.15. Prestigious contemporary art gallery. Open Tues-Sat.

Galerie Martine Gossieux, 56 Rue de l'Université (M: Solferino) 45.44.48.55. Drawings by French illustrator Jean-Jacques Sempé. Open Tues-Sat.

Jardin de Babylone, (M: Sèvres-Babylone) West of Metro and Bon Marché department store.

La Chapelle Miraculeuse, Hotel de Chatillon, 140 Rue du Bac (M: Sèvres-Babylone) Virgin Mary appeared here in 1760.

La Clo, Les Vins du Terroir Wine Classes, 34 Ave Duquesne (M: St Francois-Xavier) 40.61.91.87. Alexandre Gerbe's wine shop runs evening classes once a month, usually 8:30p-10p. €65 per class, includes tasting 7 wines. Maximum 12 people. Call in advance.

Market: Rue Cler, between Ave de la Motte-Picquet and Rue de Grenelle (M: Ecole Militaire) Tues-Sat. mornings on cobblestone street. Best on Saturdays.

Musée Maillol, Fondation Dina-Vierny, 61 Rue de Grenelle (M: Rue du Bac) 42.22.59.58. Sculptures, paintings, tapestry with works by Matisse, Kadinsky. Open Wed-Mon 11a-6p. Admission fee. Call for exhibitions.

Palais Bourbon/Assemblée Nationale, 33 Quai d'Orsay (M: Assemblée Nationale) 40.63.64.08. Free admission. Hours vary. Government building. Tight security check. Celebrate 14th Juillet, Fetes Nationales aka Bastille Day, here.

Picnic on the lawn on **Esplanade des Invalides** (M: Invalides).

Pont Alexandre III, (M: Invalides) Belle-Epoque, lamp-lined bridge that many say epitomizes Paris. Sunset makes a good backdrop for romance.

Sewers of Paris (Les Egouts) think of Les Miserables and go underground with tours beginning at Pont de l'Alma (M: Alma-Marceau) and wait in line. Tour consists of film, museum, trip through maze which can be stinky. €4.

Sennelier, 3 Quai Voltaire (M: Rue du Bac) 42.60.72.15. Three stories of artists' supplies.

7e. Invalides, Tour d'Eiffel

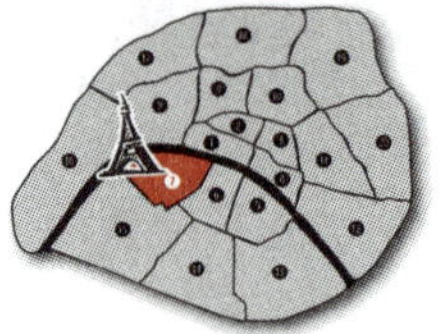

Serge Gainsbourg's home at #5 bis Rue de Verneuil (M: Rue du Bac) Might become new museum very soon. A favorite Parisian cult-singer.

Square Récamier, 6 Rue Récamier (M: Sèvres-Babylone) Pretty public square with Espace Electra, an art space, one of the most interesting places for art in Paris.

SUPERLATIVES:

All roses: Au Nom de la Rose, 4 6 Rue du Bac (M: Rue du Bac) 40.56.05.15.

Best Bread: Poujauran, 20 Rue Jean Nicot (M: La Tour-Maubourg)43.17.35.20.

Best Cheese: Fromagerie Quatrehomme, 62 Rue de Sèvres (M: Sèvres-Babylone) 47.34.33.45. Try the house goat cheese.

Best chocolate dessert: la delice mousse at Le Télégraphe. See Restaurants.

7

Best ham and popular grocer: Bellota-Bellota, 18 Rue Jean Nicot (M: La Tour-Maubourg) 53.59.96.96. Has a few stools. Good for picnic supplies before heading to the Eiffel Tower on a sunny day.

Best Meal in a 2 acre garden: Restaurant of the Maison de l'Amerique Latine, 217 Blvd St Germain (M: Rue du Bac) 49.54.75.10. Inside this hotel is a beautiful and quiet garden setting to enjoy lunch or dinner.

Best Pain au Chocolate: Jean Millet, 103 Rue St Dominique (M: Ecole Militaire) 45.51.49.80. You can also have an espresso and St-Marc pastry, sandwiches, salads at one of the tables.

Best rooftop dining: Les Ombres, 37 Quai Branly, rooftop of Musée du Quai Branly. 47.53.68.00. See Restaurants below.

Best seafood soup: L'Affriole's mussel soup. See Restaurants.

Best Wine Bar: Sancerre, 22 Ave Rapp (M: Alma-Marceau) 45.51.75.91. Closed Sat. lunch and Sunday.

Cheese Market: Saxe Breteuil Market (behind Eiffel Tower) Place de Breteuil (M: Sevres-LeCourbe) Thu-Sat. 9a-1p. Great selection of cheeses.

Finest Cheese Shop: Barthélemy, 51 Rue Grenelle (M: Sèvres-Babylone) 42.22.82.24. Closed Sun-Mon.A FAVORITE. They do not speak much English.

Famous Cheese Shop: Marie-Anne Cantin, 12 Rue du Champ de Mars. (M: Ecole Militaire) 45.50.43.94. Open 9a-1p 4p-7p. Closed Sun-Mon. Ask for époisses de Bourgogne.

Finest Foie Gras: Ambassade du Sud Ouest, 108 Rue St Dominique (M: Ecole Militaire) 45.55.59.59. See Restaurants.

Great souvenirs: Fragonard, 196 Blvd St Germain (M: Rue du Bac) 42.84.12.12. Silk, cotton, organdy drawstring embroidered bags for $6-$36.

Society Hangout: Restaurant le Voltaire, 27 Quai Voltaire (M: Rue du Bac) 42.61.17.49.

Superb Bakery/Cannelonis: Jean-Luc Poujauran Boulangerie, 20 Rue Jean Nicot (M: La Tour-Maubourg) 43.17.35.20.

Unusual and modern view of Eiffel Tower, from Rue de Monttessuy RER Pont de l'Alma or in the reflection on the wall of Musée du Qaui Branly.

SHOPS:

Anne Fontaine, 68 Rue Sts Peres (M: Rue du Bac) 45.48.89.10. Classy blouses. Several locations.

Aryllis, 141 Rue St Dominique (M: Ecole Militaire) 47.05.86.26. Master florist.

Au Liégeur, 17 Ave de la Motte-Picquet (M: Ecole Militaire) 47.05.53.10. Everything about cork, corkscrews. Take a look at the bouchon universal, a cork designed to fit any sized bottle.

Barthélémy, 51 Rue Grenelle (M: Sevrés-Babylone) 42.22.82.24. Our favorite when shopping for cheese. They do not speak much English.

Bellota-Bellota, 18 Rue Jean Nicot (M: La Tour-Maubourg) 53.59.96.96. Food store and tasting bar serving Spanish hams, cheeses. Good for picnic supplies before heading to the Eiffel Tower on a sunny day. Closed Sunday.

Bonpoint, 42 Rue de l'Université (M: Solferino) 40.20.10.55. Childrens' clothes. Expensive.

Boulangerie Poujauran, 20 Rue Jean Nicot (M: La Tour-Maubourg) 43.17.35.20. Patisserie. Delicious pastries and treats. Closed Sun/Monday.

Bruno Frisoni, 34 Rue de Grenelle (M: Rue du Bac) 42.84.12.30. Shoe designer.

Chahan Minassian, 12 Rue de Beaune (M: Rue du Bac) 42.96.88.88. Opulent new interior designer.

Colors do Brasil, 4 Rue Perronet (M: St-Germain-des-Prés) 45.44.20.80. Bikinis, tunics, beach and club wear.

Conran, 117 Rue du Bac (M: Rue du Bac) 42.84.10.01. Eclectic décor and gifts. closed Sunday. There is another location in 9e.

Debauve & Gallais, 30 Rue des St Pères (M: St-Germain-des-Prés) 45.48.54.57. Fine chocolates.

Décembre En Mars toy shop, 65 Ave de La Bourdonnais (M: Ecole Militaire) 45.51.15.45. Stuffed animals, dolls, wooden trains, French hand puppets and unique variety to bring out the child in all of us. Closed Sun-Mon and August.

Deyrolle, 46 Rue du Bac (M: Rue du Bac) 42.22.30.07. Open since 1880, famous taxidermist - go upstairs and see stuffed animals. A FAVORITE.

7e. Invalides, Tour d'Eiffel

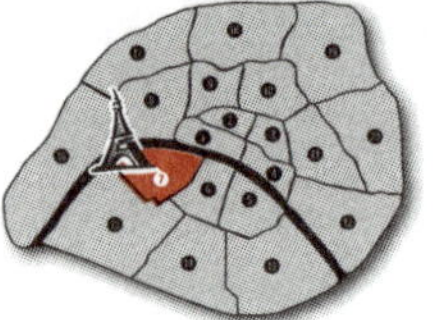

Éclair de Lune, 30 Rue de Grenelle (M: Rue du Bac) 45.49.27.61. Fun and eclectic boutique. A FAVORITE.

Editions de Frederic Malle, 37 Rue de Grenelle (M: Rue du Bac) 42.22.77.22. Famous for perfume "misting" chambers.

Fragonard, 196 Blvd St Germain (M: Rue du Bac) 42.84.12.12. Silk, cotton, organdy drawstring embroidered bags for $6-$36 make great souvenirs.

Galerie Altero, 21 Quai Voltaire (M: St-Germain-des-Prés) 42.61.19.90. Third generation antique shop. Trés chic and trés expensive.

Galerie J. Kugel, 25 Quai Anatole-France (M: Musée d'Orsay) 42.60.86.23. Exclusive antique dealer. Huge space. Priceless.

Galerie Maeght, 42 Rue du Bac (M: Rue du Bac) 45.48.45.15. Prestigious contemporary art gallery. Open Tues-Sat.

Galerie Martine Gossieux, 56 Rue de l'Université (M: Solferino) 45.44.48.55. Drawings by French illustrator Jean-Jacques Sempé and other collections. Open Tues-Sat.

Galerie Robert Four, 8 Rue des Saints-Pères (M: St-Germain-des-Prés) 40.20.44.96. Rugs and tapestries, including designs by Klee, as well as d'Aubusson tapestries. Closed Sun/Mon.

Gosselin, 258 Blvd St Germain (M: Solferino) 45.51.53.11. Famous baker and confectioner. Delicious assortments.

Iris France, 28 Rue de Grenelle (M: Sèvres-Babylone) 42.22.89.81. Cool mix of designer shoes.

Iunx, 48-50 Rue de l'Universite (M: Rue du Bac) 45.44.05.14. New line of scents from Olivia Giacobetta of Shiseido. Modern and minimalist.

Karry 'O, 62 Rue des Saints Peres (M: St-Sulpice) 45.48.94.67. Karine Berredi designs original costume jewelry and hand-selects vintage pieces.

Kenzo, 16 Blvd Raspail (M: Rue du Bac) 42.22.09.38. Ladies' designer clothing.

L'Artisan Parfumeur, 24 Blvd Raspail (M: Rue du Bac) 42.22.23.32. Fine perfumes.

La Boîte à Musique, 96 Rue du Bac (M: Rue du Bac) 42.22.01.31. Antique music boxes.

Le Bon Marché, 24 Rue de Sèvres (M: Sèvres-Babylone) 44.39.80.00. Department store that has good selection of designers. A FAVORITE. Enjoy the epicurean food hall that has a separate entrance from the department store. The Délicabar has interesting snacks and wonderful pastries.

Le Cabinet de Curiosité, 23 Rue de Beaune (M: Rue du Bac) 42.61.09.57. Collector-owner Claudine Guerin. The name of the shop says it best.

Le Cabinet de Porcelaine, 37 Rue de Verneuil (M: Rue du Bac) 42.60.25.40. Tiny shop with porcelain figures and chandeliers. Closed Sun/Monday.

Le Pain de Marie, 85 Rue St Dominique (M: Ecole Militaire) 45.51.88.77. Hervé Guillot prepares the finest pastries. Closed Sunday.

Le Rideau de Paris, 32 Rue du Bac (M: Rue du Bac) 42.61.18.56. Florence Maeght offers exclusive Provençal embroidered linens.

Librairie 7L, 7 Rue Lille (M: Solferino) 42.92.03.58. Bookstore where Karl Lagerfeld shops. Rare and hard-to-find titles.

Les Prairies de Paris, 6 Rue de Pre Aux Clercs (M: Rue du Bac) 40.20.44.12. Romantic indie label with lots of florals and peasant frocks.

Librairie de Lattre, 56 Rue de l'Université (M: Rue du Bac) 45.44.75.30. Extraordinary collection of posters in a tiny space. We have made several purchases. Dominique, her sister Marie Anne, and Gabriel offer fair prices and are very nice. Open 10:30a-6p. A FAVORITE. Closed Sunday and summer holiday.

Loulou de La Falaise, 7 Rue de Bourgogne (M: Varenne) 45.51.42.22. Haute creator of beautiful, whimsical jewelry designs, accessories and clothing. Priceless. You always get compliments when wearing Loulou's pieces. A FAVORITE.

Lucien Pellat-Finet, 1 Rue Montalembert (M: Rue du Bac) 42.22.22.77. Very fine, expensive cashmere.

Madeleine Gely, 218 Blvd Saint Germain (M: Rue du Bac) 42.22.63.35. Umbrellas of all sorts, since 1834.

Maitre Parfumeur et Gantier, 84 bis Rue de Grenelle (M: Rue du Bac) 45.55.61.57. Jean-Francois Laporte's perfumes.

Marianne Robic, 39 Rue Babylone (M: Sérves-Babylone) 53.63.14.00. Beautiful floral designs.

Marie-Anne Cantin, 12 Rue du Champ de Mars (M: Ecole Militaire) 45.50.43.94. Open 9a-1p 4p-7p. The cheese to ask for is Epoisses de Bourgogne. Closed Sun/Mon.

Marie-Pierre Boitard, 9-11 Pl du Palais Bourbon (M: Assemblée Nationale) 47.05.13.30. Gifts such as crystal glasses with floral design motifs for $400, hand-painted tableware and silver objects from $32.

Martine Sitbon, 13 Rue de Grenelle (M: Rue du Bac) 44.39.84.44. Ladies' fashions.

Maud Perl, 39 Rue de Grenelle (M: Rue du Bac) 45.44.26.27. Chic fashion.

Maxalto, 43 Rue du Bac (M: Rue du Bac) 45.44.00.99. Top quality Italian furniture,tableware, etc.

Michel Chaudun, 149 Rue de l'Universite (M: La Tour-Maubourg) 47.53.74.40. Chocolate confections of all sizes, shapes, tastes. Closed Mon/Sunday and in August.

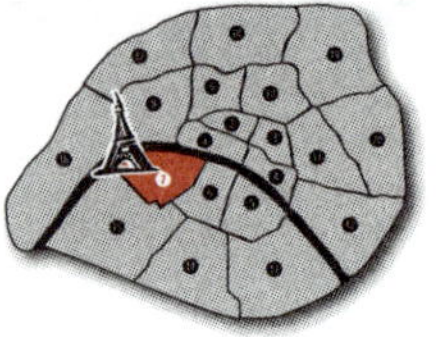

Miu Miu, 16 Rue de Grenelle (M: St-Sulpice) 53.63.20.30. Boutique for men and women, shoes and handbags.

Moss, 60 Rue des Saints Peres (M: St-Sulpice) 42.22.01.43. Fun shoes and accessories in tiny shop.

Moulie, 8 Pl du Palais-Bourbon (M: Assemblée Nationale) 45.51.78.43. Lovely flowers.

Muriel Grateau Boutique, 37 Rue Beaune (M: Solferino) 40.20.42.82. Tableware.

Ombeline, 17 Rue de Bourgogne (M: Assemblée Nationale) 47.05.56.78. Maud deMarco aka Maud Frizon (famous for shoes).

Paul & Joe, 62 Rue des Sts Peres (M: St-Sulpice) 42.22.47.01. Ladies clothing.

7

Paul Smith, 22-24 Blvd Raspail (M: Rue du Bac) 42.84.15.30. British designer for men and women.

Petrossian, 18 Blvd De La Tour-Maubourg (M: La Tour-Maubourg) 44.11.32.22. Since the 1920's, famous for caviar, smoked salmon, foie gras, truffles. Shop has a few tables. Silver caviar bowls and crystal vodka glasses.

Pharmacie Rapp, 23 Ave Rapp at Rue Edmond-Valentin at RER Pont de l'Lama. 47.05.41.25. Corner pharmacy since 1899, complete with blue glass pharmacie jars and medicinal plants.

Puyricard, 27 Ave Rapp at RER: Pont de l'Alma. 47.05.59.47. Chocolates from Aix-en-Provence, marzipan, apricot truffles and more irresistible confections. Closed Sunday.

Ryst Duperon, 79 Rue du Bac (M: Rue du Bac) 45.48.80.93. Mon-Sat. Nathalie was a huge help and very nice. Founded 1905. Grand wines of Bordeaux and fine armagnac collection. Take home an Eiffel Tower filled with wine.

Saxe Breteuil Market (behind Eiffel Tower) Pl de Breteuil (M: Sèvres-LeCourbe) Thu-Sat. 9-1p. Great selection of cheeses.

Sennelier, 3 Quai Voltaire (M: Rue du Bac) 42.60.72.15. Three stories of artists' supplies.

Siècle, 24 Rue du Bac (M: Rue du Bac) 47.03.48.03. Chic, two-story boutique specializing in ultra-stylish gifts in every price range. Each gift is packaged in one of their amethyst and emerald colored padded silk boxes. A FAVORITE.

Stephane Kelian, 13 bis, Rue de Grenelle (M: Rue du Bac) 42.22.93.03. Shoes/accessories by designer who used to work with Gaultier. A FAVORITE.

Sylvain Levy-Alban, 14 Rue de Beaune (M: Assemblée Nationale) 42.61.25.42. High-end antique dealer.

Thomas Boog, 52 Rue de Bourgogne (M: Varenne) 43.17.30.03. Exclusive decorators.

RESTAURANTS: LES PLATS DU JOUR:

7 eme. Sud, 159 Rue Grenelle (M: La Tour-Maubourg) 44.18.30.30. Small. Good reviews. Wine cellar.

Aïda, 1 Rue Pierre Leroux (M: Duroc) 43.06.14.18. Tasty Japanese at high end of the price spectrum, €72.

Altitude 95, Tour Eiffel, Champ-de-Mars (M: Bir Hakeim) 45.55.20.04. First level. Panoramic view and classic meals. Reserve a window table 15 days in advance. Fills with tourists.

Ambassade du Sud-Ouest, 46 Ave de la Bourdonnais (M: Ecole Militaire) 45.55.59.59. Foie gras and Southwestern French. Get paté to go, too. Closed Sunday.

Au Bon Accueil, 14 Rue de Monttessey (M: Alma-Marceau) 47.05.46.11. "Find of the Year" because of its fresh, creative menu. Closed Sunday.

Au Sauvignon, 80 Rue des Saints-Peres (M: Sèvres-Babylone) 45.48.49.02. We love to enjoy lunch and sip wines while people watching, although it can get smoky. Closed Sunday.

Auguste, 54 Rue Bourgogne (M: Varenne) 45.51.61.09. Recommended by Parisian chef. Chef Orieux prepares gastronomique meals at moderately high prices. Modern décor. Closed Sunday.

Aux Fins Gourmets, 213 Blvd St Germain, (M: Rue du Bac) 42.22.06.57. Hearty Southwestern dishes. Classic bistro. Musty and smoky inside.

Café Constant, 139 Rue St Dominique (M: Ecole Militaire) 47.53.73.34. Christian Constant's down to earth wonderful bistro near his gastronomique Le Violon d'Ingres. Closed Sunday. A FAVORITE.

Café des Lettres, 53 Rue de Verneuil (M: Solferino) 42.22.52.17. Nice courtyard location for Scandinavian simple meals.

Café Max, 7, Ave de la Motte-Picquet (M: Ecole Militaire/La Tour-Maubourg) 47.05.57.66. Chef Max Gerchambeau serves typical Parisian fare in funky flea market setting and décor. Great cassoulet. Closed Sunday.

Caffé Toscano, 34 Rue des Saints-Peres (M: St-Germain-des-Pres) 42.84.28.95. Simple Tuscan. Open Sunday.

Chez Germaine, 30 Rue Pierre Leroux (M: Duroc/Vaneau) 42.73.28.34. Good food+ real value so gets crowded by 9p. Has non-smoking. Warning: old style wc/restroom.

Chez les Anges, 54 Blvd la Tour-Maubourg (M: La Tour-Maubourg) 47.05.89.86. Jacques Lacipiere, from Au Bon Accueil fame, serves good meals for €50. Closed Sat. lunch/Sunday.

Cinq Mars, 51 Rue Verneuil (M: Solferino) 45.44.69.13. Good local reviews. €35. Closed Sunday.

7e. Invalides, Tour d'Eiffel

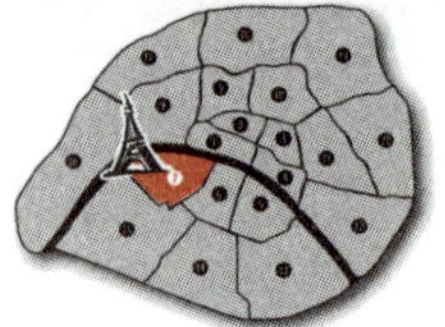

7

Cook Book, 9 Rue Surcouf (M: Invalides) 45.51.92.82. Steaks and meat from around the world complimented by a global wine list. Closed Sunday.

D'Chez Eux, 2 Ave de Lowendal (M: Ecole Militaire) 47.05.52.55. The bistro every one looks for in Paris. Highly recommended by chefs in US. Closed Sunday.

Fables of Fontaine, 131 Rue St Dominique (M: Ecole Militairs) 44.18.37.55. Another by Christian Constant and his lovely wife. €40 à la carte. Closed Sun.

Gaya Pierre Gagnaire, aka **Gaya Rive Gauche,** 44 Rue du Bac (M: Rue du Bac) 45.44.73.73. Fresh fish, imaginative preparation, simple presentations all score a hit. Closed Sun/Monday.

L'Affriole, 17 Rue Malar (M: Invalides) 44.18.31.33. Good food in cozy atmosphere. Protégé of Jacques Cagna. Modern bistro cooking. Good value.

L'Ami Jean, 27 Rue Malar (M: La Tour-Maubourg) 47.05.86.89. Classic and cozy with traditional Basque menu. Awarded 2003 Le Fooding prize. Under €100 for two. Reservations needed.

L'Auvergne Gourmande, 127 Rue St Dominique (M: Ecole Militaire) 47.05.60.79. €45 for two, at communal tables. No credit cards.

L'Esplanade, 52 Rue Fabert (M: Invalides) 47.05.38.80. We enjoy. This entry from the Côstes brothers has a dependable menu and service varies. Open Sunday.

L'Oeillade, 10 Rue de St Simon (M: Rue du Bac) 42.22.01.60. Good value/pleasant. Skate, stuffed tomatoes. Closed Sunday.

La Cigale Recamier, 4 Rue Recamier (M: Sèvres-Babylone) 45.48.86.58. Recently renovated. Souffles are house specialty. Closed Sunday.

La Cuisine, 14 Blvd de La Tour-Maubourg (M: La Tour-Maubourg) 44.18.36.32. Classy and classic meals with good service at moderate prices. Open 7/7.

La Ferme Saint-Simon, 6 Rue de St Simon (M: Rue du Bac) 45.48.35.74. Classic French. Three dining rooms. Closed Sunday.

La Fontaine de Mars, 129 Rue St Dominique (M: Ecole Militaire) 47.05.46.44. Classic French bistro with good sole. Terrace. Reasonable prices. Try the delicious frozen pear cognac after dinner.

La Poule Au Pot, 121 Rue de l'Universite (M: La Tour-Maubourg) 47.05.16.36. Late night chicken stew and wee hours of the morning for breakfast. Closed Sunday.

Le 20 de Bellechasse, 20 Rue de Bellechasse (M: Solferino) 47.05.11.11. Good bistro. Moderate prices for generous meals and good service. Closed Sunday.

Le Bamboche, 15 Rue de Babylone (M: Sèvres-Babylone) 45.49.14.40. Tiny space, not-so-tiny prices for "new" French cuisine.

Le Bistrot de Breteuil, 3 Pl de Breteuil (M: Duroc) 45.67.07.27. Good food/reasonably priced. Terrace.

Le Bistrot de Paris, 33 Rue de Lille (M: Rue de Bac) 42.61.16.83. Eric Corailler serves $35 prix fixef dinner. Open Sunday.

Le Clos des Gourmets, 16 Ave Rapp (M: Ecole Militaire) 45.51.75.61. Chef trained with Guy Savoy. Tables very close. Closed Sunday.

Le Club de la Maison Polytechniciens, 12 Rue de Poitiers (M: Solferino) 49.54.74.54. Enjoy dinner prepared by Sebastien Sevilla in this private country-style house built in 1840. Romantic. €80.

Le Maupertu, 94 Blvd de la Tour Maubourg (M: Ecole Militaire) 45.51.37.96. Terra-cotta marble décor and finely prepared French specialties make this delightful at affordable prices. Excellent wine list. Romantic glass roof. Reserve. Closed Sunday.

Le Petit Niçois, 10 Rue Amelie (M: La Tour-Maubourg) 45.51.83.65. Neighborhood seafood restaurant with bouillabaisse and paella. Corsican-style. Lunch and dinner.

Le Petit Troquet, 28 Rue de L'Exposition (M: Ecole Militaire) 47.05.80.39. Good food. Only 8 tables. A FAVORITE.

Le Perron, 6 Rue Perronet (M: St-Germain-des-Pres) 45.44.71.51. Good Italian at more than moderate prices. Less crowded at night Closed Sunday.

Le Quai, Quai Anatole France, Port de Solferino (M: Solferino) 44.18.04.39. Enjoy lunch on this houseboat on the Seine.

Le Rouge Vif, 48 Rue de Verneuil (M: Rue du Bac) 42.86.81.87. Southwestern fare at reasonable prices. Highly recommended. Closed Sat/Sunday.

Le Télégraphe, 41 Rue de Lille (M: Rue du Bac) 42.92.03.04. Has garden for lunch dining, weather permitting.

Le Voltaire, 27 Quai Voltaire (M: Rue du Bac) 42.61.17.49. Very French, very good. €150 for two. Closed Sunday.

Les Deux Abeilles, 189 Rue de l'Université (M: Pont d l'Alma) 45.55.64.04. Light lunch and tea. Closed Sunday.

Les Olivades, 41 Ave de Ségur (M: Ségur) 47.83.70.09. Chef Bruno Deligne and his wife, Chantal, offer good meals and friendly service. Closed Sunday.

Les Ombres,37 Quai Branley, rooftop of Musée du Quai Branly (M: Alma Marceau) 47.53.68.00. Infinity edge pool surrounds terrace and modern décor inside. €35 lunch/€75 dinner. The chef trained with Joel Robuchon.

Les Ormes, 22 Rue Surcouf (M: La Tour-Maubourg) 45.51.46.93. Chef Molé earned 1 Michelin star for his consistent preparations of good food. Traditional menu, 4 course at €44. A FAVORITE. Closed Saturday lunch and all day Sunday.

Maison de l'Amerique Latine, 217 Blvd St-Germain (M: Rue du Bac) 49.54.75.00. Enjoy lunch or dinner in the beautiful and quiet garden of this hotel.

7e. Invalides, Tour d'Eiffel

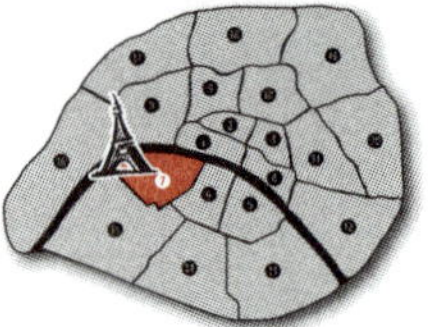

Nabuchodonosor, 6 Ave Bosquet (M: Ecole Militaire) 45.56.97.26. New bistro, good reports.

Pasco, 74 Blvd la Tour-Maubourg (M: La Tour-Maubourg) 44.18.33.26. Mediterranean flavors. Affordable prix fixe menus at €25.

Tan Dinh, 60 Rue de Verneuil (M: Rue du Bac) 45.44.04.84. Vietnamese, good wine cellar. No credit cards. Closed Sunday.

Tante Marguerite, 5 Rue de Bourgogne (M: Assemblée Nationale) 45.51.79.42. Owned by the late renowned Bernard Loiseau it is one of the more peaceful "Aunts." Closed Sat-Sunday.

Taverna de Gli Amici, 16 Rue du Bac (M: Rue du Bac) 42.60.37.74. Big antipasto and cheese platters. Good selection of Italian wines. Closed Sunday.

Thiou, 49 Quai d'Orsay (M: Invalides) 40.62.96.50. Thai cuisine, with original touches. Upscale prices. The most popular of the "Thiou chain." Reserve. Closed Sunday.

Thoumieux, 79 Rue St Dominique (M: Ecole Militaire) 47.05.49.75. Classic, traditional. Mirrored walls. Open Sundays.

Veramente, 2 Rue Sedillot (M: Alma-Marceau). 45.51.95.82. Art deco, Classic French, small.

Vin sur Vin, 20 Rue de Monttessuy (M: Alma-Marceau) 47.05.14.20. Tiny and noted for wine list. Innovative menu with interesting prices: €18 appetizers, €34 dinner, €16 deserts. Closed Sunday.

RESTAURANTS: GASTRONOMIQUE:

Jules Verne, Tour Eiffel, 2nd level (M: Bir-Hakeim) 45.55.61.44. Magic panorama of Paris with less-than-magical food and out-of-the-world prices. Open Sunday.

L'Arpége, 84 Rue Varenne (M: Varenne) 45.51.47.33. Alain Passard presents a very expensive €340 pp. tasting menu that is mostly vegetarian. Expensive wine list. Closed Sat/Sunday.

L'Atelier de Joel Robuchon, Pont Royal Hotel, 5 Rue Montalembert, (M: Rue du Bac) 42.22.56.56. Worthwhile indulgence for small plates.

Le Chamarre, 13 Blvd de la Tour-Maubourg (M: La Tour-Maubourg) 47.05.50.18. €150 for two. Chef Jerome Baudereau presents nouvelle French, with good reviews. French Mauritian in both preparation and decor.Closed Sunday.

Le Divellec, 107 Rue de l'Université (M: Invalides) 45.51.91.96. Mecca for seafood and foie gras that melts in your mouth, Decor needs updating. Closed Sunday.

Le Violon D'Ingres, 135 Rue St Dominique (M: Ecole Militaire) 45.55.15.05 A FAVORITE. Chef/Owner Christian Constant and Chef Schmidt serve delicious and delightful meals. Superb dining experience. Closed Sunday/Monday.

Le 144 Petrossian, 18 Blvd de la Tour-Maubourg (M: La Tour-Maubourg) 44.11.32.32. New chef Rougun Dia adds a spicey flare to delicious meals. Of course, as the name implies, you can still get their famous caviar. Closed Sunday.

BONNE SOIREE! PARIS AT NIGHT:

Don Camillo, 10 Rue des Sts-Peres (M: Sèvres-Babylone) 42.60.82.84. Comedy and music and dinner. Cabaret. Call. Can be slightly risqué.

Club des Poètes, 30 Rue de Bourgogne (M: Varennes) 47.05.06.03. Poetry readings and shows at 10p by actors, singers, artists, every night except Sunday. Traditional food, €20 dinner.

My Special Travel Notes

7

8e. Elysée, Champs Elysées

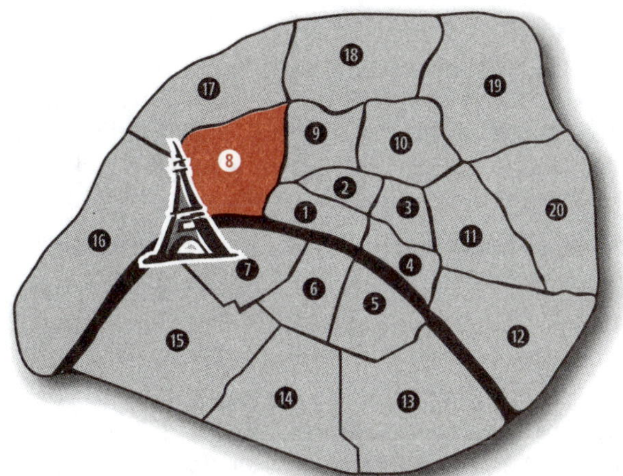

Welcome to **Champs Elysées,** probably the most famous Avenue on the right Bank.

Visit one of our favorite museums: **Musée Jacquemart-André.**

Treat yourself to an **Hermès** scarf and then celebrate with vodka and caviar at **Caviar Kaspa.**

Say "Bon soir" to Elizabeth Epié at **Citrus Etoile** and feast on sumptious meals prepared by Giles Epié, the chef/owner and her husband.

MAJOR METROS:
- CONCORDE
- CHAMPS-ELYSÉES
- FRANKLIN-D-ROOSEVELT
- GEORGE V
- ALMA-MARCEAU
- CHARLES-DE-GAULLE-ETOILE
- MADELEINE
- GARE ST-LAZARE

8e. Elysée, Champs Elysées

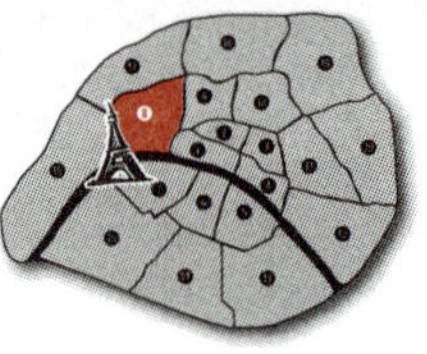

FAMOUS SIGHTS:

American Embassy: 2 Ave Gabriel (M: Concorde) 43.12.22.22.

Arc de Triomphe, Pl Charles de Gaulle (M: Charles-de-Gaulle-Etoile) 55.37.73.77. Climb the 284 stairs or take the elevator (daylight hours only) for the view of the twelve grand boulevards of Paris. €7. Open 10a-11p.

Galeries Nationales du Grand Palais, 3 Ave Général Eisenhower (M: Champs-Elysées-Clemenceau) 44.13.17.30. You can't miss this ornate Belle Epoque building which was constructed for the 1900 World's Fair. Stunning interior of iron and glass. Adjoining galleries hold exhibitions, call. €11.10 before 1pm/€10 after 1p. Closed Tuesday.

Musée Cernuschi, 7 Ave Velasquez (M: Monceau) 53.96.21.50. Extensive collection of Chinese and Japanese art.

8

Musée Jacquemart-André, 158 Blvd Haussmann (M: Miromesnil) 45.62.11.59. 10a-6p. Mansion/residence features an exquisite art collection. The audio tour is very fun. A FAVORITE.

Musée Nissim de Camondo, 63 Rue de Monceau (M: Monceau) 53.89.06.40. 18th century three-story mansion owned by Camondo family. You will enjoy one of the greatest collections of late 18th century French decorative arts and furnishings, room-by-room. A FAVORITE. Closed Mon/Tuesday.

Palais de L'Elysée, 55 Rue du Faubourg St-Honore 9 (M: Miromesnil) Official residence of the French President.

Petit Palais, 1 Ave Winston Churchill (M: Champs-Elysées-Clemenceau) 42.65.12.73. The Palais itself is a fine example of the architectural eclecticism in the 1900's. Art Nouveau objects, sculptures, religious paintings. Louis XV and Louis XVI collections, Renaissance art, all surround a lovely garden and café. Closed Mon.

Place de la Concorde (M: Concorde) is the largest square in Paris. See the Egyptian Obelisk of Luxor, 3,300 years old and weighing 220 tons.

DIVERSIONS:

American Cathedral of the Holy Trinity, 23 Ave George V (M: George V) 53.23.84.00. Free admission. Fine example of Gothic Revival architecture. Choral concerts, lectures, art shows.

Anne Semonin Spa, 108 Rue du Faubourg St-Honore (M: St-Philippe-du-Roule) 42.66.24.22. Custom beauty treatments and "Jet Lag Special". $75 will get you a manicure with Bastien, a favorite among movie stars, if he's still here!

Antiques along Rue du Faubourg St-Honore: Arianne Dandois, Didier Aaron Galerie, and Perrin Antiquaires to name some of the best in Paris.

Artcurial, 7 rond-pt Champs Elysées (M: Franklin D Roosevelt) 42.99.16.16. Contemporary art, prints, sculpture, jewelry.

Atelier Renault, 53 Ave des Champs Elysées. (M: Franklin D Roosevelt) 49.53.70.00. Fashion gallery. Enjoy lunch/wine on the top floors – lots of windows. Funky and fun.

Atelier des Chefs, 10 Rue de Penthiève (M: Miromesnil) 53.30.05.82. Foodies partake in quick lunchtime cooking classes taught by rotation of Parisian chefs. In French, $35.

Bateaux-Mouches, Pont de l'Alma (M: Alma-Marceau) 40.76.99.99. Seine River cruises. Call for day/evening schedule.

Chamber music: Salle Gaveau, 45 Rue la Boétie (M: Miromesnil) 49.53.05.07. Intimate and beautiful hall also used for meetings. Call Box Office for concerts. Closed in August.

Centre National de la Photographie, 11 Rue Berryer. (M: George V) 53.76.12.32. Closed Tues. Call for exhibitions, €4.60.

Drouot Richelieu, 2nd location of famous auction house. 15 Ave Montaigne (M: Alma-Marceau) 48.00.20.85.

Ecole de Cuisine Alain Ducasse, 55 Blvd Malesherbes (M: St-Augustin) 40.90.90.00. Classes at this prestigious cooking school are presented by themes. In French, translators can be arranged. Maximum 8 students. €125-290.

Eglise de la Madeleine, church at Place de la Madeleine (M: Madeleine) 47.42.13.09. Classical concerts.

Galerie Makassar-France, 19 Ave Matignon (M: Franklin D Roosevelt) 53.96.95.85. Art Deco objets d'art. Mon-Sat.

Gymnase Club, 26 Rue de Berri (M: George V) 43.59.04.58. Largest gym in Paris with five floors of aerobics studios, equipment, saunas solarium.

Hair salon: Alexandre de Paris, 3 Ave Matignon (M: Franklin D Roosevelt) 42.25.57.90.

Haircut - Camille Albane, 86 Rue de Miromesnil (M: Miromesnil) 45.63.32.50. She is very well known.

Hair salon - Carita Paris, 11 Rue du Faubourg St-Honore (M: Concorde) 44.94.11.11.

Haircut -unique dry cut at Claude Maxime, 27 Ave George V (M: George V) 53.23.03.03. Another location at 122 Rue du Faubourg St-Honore 45.62.75.06.

Institut Lancôme, 29 Rue du Faubourg St-Honore (M: Madeleine) 42.65.30.74. Face and body.

Joya, 7 Rue de la Renaissance (M: Alma-Marceau) 40.70.16.49. Spa aromatherapy massages. Their special body oils are sold at Collette.

Le Drugstore Publicis, 133 Ave des Champs Elysées (M: George V) 47.20.78.00. This complex seems like an airport and has boutiques and cinema. Open Sunday.

8e. Elysée, Champs Elysées

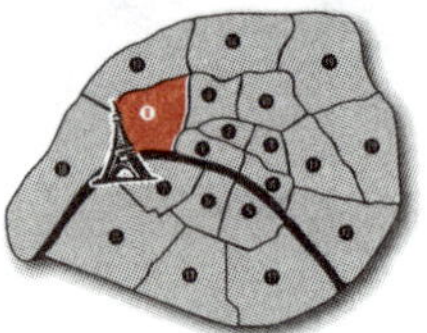

Parc du Monceau, (M: Monceau) Lovely park located in the northwest section of this arrondissment. A FAVORITE.

Pavillon Elysées, 10 Ave des Champs Elysées (M: Champs-Elysées-Clemenceau) 42.65.85.10. Kitchen Boutique and a restaurant called Café Lenôtre, plus, a cooking school, where you can attend 3-4 hour classes, 8 students. €105 adults/€38 children.

Place de Madeleine (M: Madeleine) Fun shops. Flower Market.

Salon de Thé Bernardaud, Galerie Royale, 11 Rue Royale (M: Concorde) 42.66.22.55. Exceptional tea room.

Shiseido's cosmetic lounge, 3-5 Blvd Malesherbes (M: Madeleine) 53.05.97.81. Book a private 80 minute treatment in La Cabine.

Spa - Carita, 11 Rue du Faubourg St-Honore (M: Madeleine) 44.94.11.11. Everything from haircut to lunch in this three-level salon with patio and fountain.

Spa-facials at Institut de Beauté Auriège, 36 Rue de l'Arcade (M: Madeleine) 27.28.00. €45-56 Facials 55.27.28.00.

8

Spa - Daniel Jourane Espace Mer, 91 Ave des Champs Elysées (M: Franklin D Roosevelt) 47.23.48.00.

Spa-massage at Espace France-Asie, 11 Rue du Chevalier de St-George (M: Madeleine) 49.26.08.88. Thai massage. Extraordinary. €65 one hour. 10:30a-8p. Closed Sunday.

Spa - Hotel du Plaza Athénée, 25 Ave Montaigne (M: Franklin D Roosevelt) 53.67.75.00.

Sothy's Institut Spa, 128 Rue du Faubourg St-Honore (M: St-Philippe du Roule) 53.93.91.53. €56-€80 for facial. Book ahead.

Spa - Yves Rocher, 102 Ave des Champs Elysées (M: George V) 53.53.94.93.

Spa - Les Thermes du Royal Monceau. Hotel Monceau, 35 Ave Hoche (M: Charles-Du-Gaulle-Etoile) 42.99.85. 86. Massages, treatments, sauna, steam, gym & pool.

Spa Mosaic, Hilton Arc de Triomphe, 51 Rue de Courcelles (M: Courcelles) 58.36.68.09. Signature treatment is Sensation Mosaic- a 2-hour facial, massage, stone treatment.

Venus et Mars Spa, 26 Ave Marceau (M: Alma-Marceau) 56.89.10.01. Unisex salon and spa with library bar, tea room, hair stylists, facials, massages.

SUPERLATIVES:

All truffles - all the time: Terres de Truffes. A FAVORITE. See Restaurants.

Antique Dealer: Jean-Marie Rossi at Aveline, 94 Rue du Faubourg St-Honore (M: St-Philippe-du-Roule) 42.66.60.29. World-renowned.

Best foie gras: Laurent. See Restaurants.

Best hamburgers: De Vèz. Christian Valette imports all his beef from his ranch in the Aubrac region of France. See Restaurants.

Best silversmith: Puiforcat, 2 Ave Matignon (M: Champs-Elysées-Clemenceau) 45.63.10.10. Baby spoons, vases, accessories.

Best Sommelier is at **Alain Ducasse Plaza Athénée.** See Restaurants.

Best Wine List: Le Bistrot du Sommelier, 97 Blvd Haussmann. (M: Havre-Caumartin) 42.65.24.85. See Restaurants.

Biggest takout: Be, 73 Blvd de Courcelles (M: Courcelles) 46.22.20.20. Alain Ducasse and Eric Kayser (master baker) team up to offer a wide variety of take-away items and freshly baked delicacies.

Chocolate: La Maison du Chocolate, 56 Rue Pierre Charron (M: Franklin D Roosevelt) 47.23.38.25. Mon-Sat. 10a-7:30p.

Classic Dinner: Bath's. 40.70.01.09. See Restaurants.

Classic Dinner: Stella Maris, 4 Rue Arsene-Houssaye (M: Charles-de-Gaulle-Etoile) 42.89.16.22. Chef/owner Yoshino trained with Joel Robuchon.

Finest delicacies: Epicerie Granterroirs, 30 Rue de Miromesnil (M: Miromesnil) 47.42.18.18. Gourmet food store that serves fresh light lunches. Jean Francois Ginenez is very friendly. A FAVORITE.

Gourmet Food shop: Dalloyau, 99-101 Rue du Faubourg St-Honore (M: St-Philippe-du-Roule) 42.99.90.00. Since 1802 it has been serving quality foods, similar to Fauchon. Also voted Best Macaroons. Open Sunday.

Grand Prix de la Baguette 2006: Jeanne-Pierre Cohier, 270 Rue de Faubourg St-Honore. There may be a line, be patient.

Rare Wines & Spirits: Au Verger de la Madeleine, 4 Blvd Malesherbes (M:Madeleine) 42.65.51.99. Since 1937, family-owned épicerie sells rare wines. You will find old Sauternes bottled in the year you were born or your anniversary.

Hippest cocktail hour: Le Bar at Plaza Athénée, 25 Ave Montaigne (M: Franklin D Roosevelt) 53.67.66.00. Wear black. Modern, clean décor. Order sushi and relax.

Jet-set Club: La Suite, 40 Ave George V (M: George V) 53.57.49.49. On the second floor windowed space is divided into restaurant and Sweet Bar with everyone from J. Lo to Robert DeNiro. Owner is Cathy Guetta, diva doyenne.

Largest outdoor terrace in Paris: Chez Francis, 7887 Pl de l'Alma (M: Alma-Marceau) 47.20.86.83. Lunch and dinner. Reservations for dinner recommended because of terrific view of Eiffel Tower.

Lipsmacking Lunch: Casa dell'Estelle, 14 Rue de Castellane (M: Madeleine) 42.65.41.56. Chef Ferrari creates Italian dishes under €15, such as arugula-topped pizza. Heated sidewalk terrace. Closed Sunday.

8

8e. Elysée, Champs Elysées

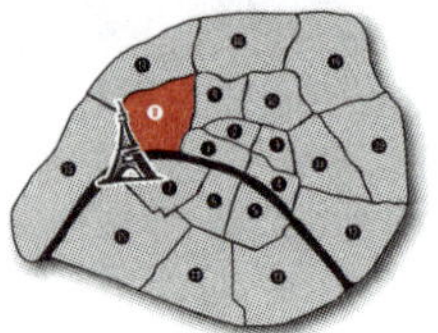

Macaroons: Laduree, 75 Ave des Champs Elysées (M: Franklin D Roosevelt) 40.75.08.75. A FAVORITE.

Most "Côstes wannabee": Hôtel Pershing Hall, 49 Rue Pierre Charron (M: Franklin D Roosevelt) Renovations have improved setting, service still varies.

Most beautiful toilettes: Place de la Madeleine, outside the church, East, next to Flower Market, go down the stairs to this art nouveau public washroom, where each toilet has stain glass windows (M: Madeleine).

Most crowded bakery: Boulangerie St-Philippe, 73 Ave Franklin D Roosevelt (M: St-Phillippe-du-Roule) 43.59.78.76. Luncheonette. Delectable eclairs and apple tarts.

Most renowned Stamp Dealer: Edouard Berck, 6 Pl de la Madeleine (M: Madeleine) 42.60.34.26. Now run by his daughter, Elysabeth. Stamps from all over the world. Mon-Saturday.

8

Most Truffles: Terres de Truffes, 21 Rue Vignon (M: Madeleine) 53.43.80.44. Owned by truffle master Clement Bruno of Provence. Open all day. Sip at wine bar, dine in pleasant dining room. We enjoyed our 3 course truffle lunch. Closed Sunday.

Noisiest dining room: Market, 15 Ave Matignon (M: Champs-Elysées) See Gastronomique.

Oldest floral designer: Trousselier, 73 Blvd Haussmann (M: St-Lazare) 42.66.16.16. It's a tie with:

Oldest and most exquisite florist: Lachaume, 10 Rue Royale (M: Concorde) 42.60.59.74. Mon-Sat. Closed in August. Floral designs since 1845.

Oldest metro station: Franklin D. Roosevelt

Oldest silversmith: Odiot, 7 Pl de la Madeleine (M: Madeleine) 42.65.00.95.

Oldest stationers: Cassegrain, 422 Rue St-Honore (M: Concorde) 42.60.20.08.

Oldest toy store in Paris: Au Nain Bleu, See Shops.

Perfect powder puffs: Parfums Caron, 34 Ave Montaigne (M: Franklin D Roosevelt) 47.23.40.82. These make the perfect souvenir, for yourself or friends. $25. Choose from white, blue, yellow, fuchsia, pink, apricot, green, and lilac.

Snazziest clientele: Rue Balzac, 3-5 Rue Balzac (M: George V) 53.89.90.91. Trendy restaurant from Michel Rostang.

Steak Frites: La Mascotte, 270 Rue du Faubourg St-Honore (M: Ternes) 42.27.75.26.

Wine bar: Ma Bourgogne, 133 Blvd Haussmann (M: Miromesnil) 45.63.50.61. Great view + good food + wine. Need reservations for lunch because of big local crowd. Closed Sat/Sunday.

World famous Gourmet Store with caviar: Hediard, 21 Pl de la Madeleine (M: Madeleine) 43.12.88.77.

SHOPS:

Anna Lowe, 104 Rue du Faubourg St-Honore (M: Champs-Elysées-Clemenceau) 42.66.11.32. Designer discount haute couture.

Ariane Dandois, 92 Rue du Faubourg St-Honore (M: St-Philippe-du-Roule) 43.12.39.39. 18th and 19th century decorative arts.

Au Nain Bleu, 406-410 Rue St-Honore. (M: Concorde) 42.60.39.01. Oldest toy store in Paris. We have found some unusual music boxes, too!

Au Verger de la Madeleine, 4 Blvd Malesherbes (M: Madeleine) 42.65.51.99. 1937 Family-owned épicerie with rare wines. You will find old Sauternes bottled in the year you were born or for your anniversary.

Aveline, 94 Rue du Faubourg St-Honore (M: Champs-Elysées-Clemenceau) 42.66.60.29. Antique store. Jean-Marie Rossi is considered to be one of the best antique dealers in Paris.

Azzaro, Loris, 65 Rue du Faubourg St-Honore. (M: Concorde) 42.66.92.06. Stylish high fashions.

8

Baccarat, 11 Pl de la Madeleine (M: Madeleine) 42.65.36.26. Closed Sunday. 10a-7p.

Balenciaga, 10 Ave George V (M: George V) 47.20.21.11. Recently renovated with incredible accessories.

Balmain, 4 Rue Francois (M: Franklin D Roosevelt) 47.20.35.34. Haute couture. Call for appointment.

Be Boulangépicier, 73 Blvd de Courcelles (M: Villiers) 46.22.20.20. Sanwiches à la Alain Ducasse and Eric Kayser in a deli/take-out/bakery/grocery. Freshly baked bread.

Bernardaud, 11 Rue Royale (M: Madeleine) 47.42.82.66. Home décor. Elegant porcelain.

Bottega Venetta, 12 Ave Montaigne (M: Franklin D Roosevelt) 53.57.89.89. Shoes.

Boulangerie St-Philippe, 73 Ave Franklin D Roosevelt (M: St-Phillippe-du-Roule) 43.59.78.76. Luncheonette and great eclairs and apple tarts.

Burberry, 8 Blvd Malesherbes (M: Rennes) 40.07.77.77.

Calvin Klein, 53 Ave Montaigne (M: Franklin D Roosevelt) 56.88.12.12.

Camper shoes, 14 Rue du Faubourg St-Honore (M: Concorde) 42.68.13.65. Many different locations. This store has a very good selection.

Caron Parfums, 34 Ave Montaigne (M: Franklin D Roosevelt) 47.23.40.82. Perfumes. You will find the perfect souvenir, for yourself or friends. $25 Comes in white, blue, yellow, fuchsia, pink, apricot, green, and lilac. A FAVORITE. Another location is at 90 Rue Faubourg St-Honore. (M: Miromesnil) 42.68.25.68.

8e. Elysée, Champs Elysées

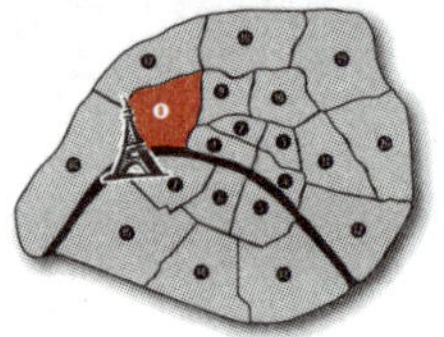

Cartier, 154 Ave des Champs Elysées (M: George V) 40.74.01.27. Another location is at 90 Rue Faubourg St-Honore (M: Miromesuil) 42.68.25.68. Flagship store, resembles apartment.

Cassegrain, 422 Rue St-Honore (M: Concorde) 42.60.20.08. Fine stationery since 1919. A FAVORITE.

Chanel, 42 Ave Montaigne (M: Franklin D Roosevelt) 47.23.74.12/fax 47.20.84.445. Haute couture. Call or fax to request a tour of Madame Chanel's private quarters upstairs.

Chloé, 44 Ave Montaigne (M: Franklin D Roosevelt) 47.23.00.08. Designer boutique.

Chopard, 72 Rue du Faubourg St-Honore (M: Concorde) 42.66.67.30. Fine jewelry

Christian Dior, 30 Ave Montaigne (M: Franklin D Roosevelt) 40.73.54.44. Haute couture.

Christian Lacroix, 73 Rue du Faubourg St-Honore (M: Concorde) 42.68.79.00. Boutique. Haute couture.

8

Claudine Dunoyer, 17 Rue Vignon (M: Madeleine) 47.42.00.65. Tiny store. Friendly "createur" of tops, skirts, accessories.

Comme des Garçons, 54 Rue du Faubourg St-Honore (M: Concorde) 53.30.27.27. Ladies and mens couture.

Courrèges, 40 Rue François I. (M: George V) 53.67.30.00. Haute couture.

D. Porthaut, 18 Ave Montaigne (M: Alma-Marceau) 47.20.75.25. Luxurious linens, hand-embroidered tablecloths, napkins.

Dalloyau, 99-101 Rue du Faubourg St-Honore (M: St-Philippe-du-Roule) Serving quality foods, similar to Fauchon, since 1802. Also voted Best Macaroons. Open Sunday.

Dior Joaillerie, 28 Ave Montaigne (M: Franklin D Roosevelt) 47.23.52.39. Exquisite jewelry.

Didier Aaron Galerie, 118 Rue du Faubourg St-Honore (M: St-Philippe-du-Roule) 47.42.47.34. Art and furniture from 18th and 19th centuries.

Dolce & Gabbana, 22 Ave Montaigne (M: Alma-Marceau) 42.25.68.78. Haute couture.

Dominique Sirop, 14 Rue du Faubourg St-Honore (M: Concorde) 42.66.60.57. Haute couture.

Edouard Berck, 6 Pl de la Madeleine (M: Madeleine) 42.60.34.26. Stamp dealer. See Superlatives.

Emmanuel Ungaro, 2 Ave Montaigne (M: Franklin D Roosevelt) 53.57.00.00. Couture.

Ercuis à Graveur, Galerie Royale, 9 Rue Royale (M: Concorde) 42.66.59.21. Exquisite collection of flatware with semiprecious stones.

Eres, 2 Rue Tronchet (M: Havre-Caumartin) 47.42.28.82. Lingerie and swimwear. Several locations.

Eve Cazes, 20 Rue de Miromesnil (M: Miromesnil) 42.65.95.44. Unique antique and secondhand jewelry, designer pieces.

Evisu, 54 Rue du Faubourg St-Honore (M: Concorde) 42.65.07.44. Clothing for men. Jeans.

Façonnable, 9 Rue du Faubourg St-Honore (M: Concorde) 47.42.72.60. Classic French men's store along with new women's line.

Fauchon, 24 -30 pl de la Madeleine (M: Madeleine) 47.42.60.11. Shops open Mon-Sat 9:30a-7p and Tea-room open 8a-7p. They now have satellite shops throughout Paris in 1st, 4th, and 7th arrondissements.

Fendi, 36 Rue François 1st (M: George V) 49.52.84.52. Designer boutique.

Franck Namani, 4 Rue Marbeauf (M: Alma-Marceau) 49.52.86.95. Menswear. The store located at 54 Rue Faubourg St-Honore (M: Concorde) 44.51.19.19. has ladies fashions. Original cashmere.

Frette, 49 Rue du Faubourg St-Honore (M: Concorde) 42.66.47.70. Exquisite bed and bath linens, tablecloths.

Galerie Ariane Dandois, 92 Rue du Faubourg St-Honore (M: Miromesnil) 43.12.39.39. Three-story space decorated with rare Greek marble, specializing in European and Asian antiques. Closed Sun/Monday.

Galerie Bertin Toublanc, 35 Ave Matignon (M: Miromesnil) 44.71.06.27. Specializing in contemporary international art and photography. Closed Sun/Mon.

Galerie Daniel Malingue, 26 Ave Matignon (M: Franklin D Roosevelt) 42.66.60.33. Selection of Impressionists, Masters, Modern works and sculptures by Chagall, Dufy, Magritte, Matisse, Picasso, Renoir. Closed Sun/Monday morning.

Glen, 18 Rue de l'Arcade (M: Madeleine) 42.66.52.32. French country charm in traditional faïence. The "Joli Paris" series features Paris street scenes.€44 set of canapé plates.

Giorgio Armani, 41 Ave George V (M: George V) 56.89.06.50. Haute couture.

Givenchy, 3 Ave George V (M: Alma-Marceau) 44.31.51.25. Haute couture.

Grande Herboristerie, 87 Rue Amsterdam (M: St-Lazare) 48.74.83.32. Apothecary since 1880 specializes in plants, herbs, natural remedies.

Griff' Troc, 119 Blvd Malesherbes (M: Madeleine) 45.61.19.47. Consignment with Chanel, Versace, Hermès, Prada.

Gucci, 21 Rue Royale (M: Madeleine) 44.94.14.70. Couture.

8e. Elysée, Champs Elysées

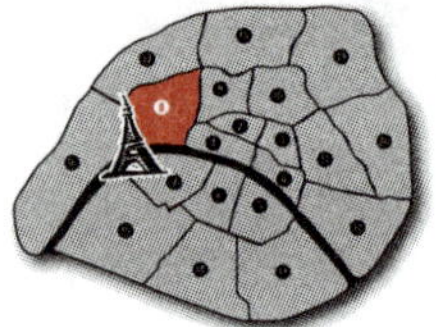

Guerlain, 68 Ave des Champs Elysées (M: Franklin D Roosevelt) 45.62.52.57. Three-story cosmetic boutique with chandelier, a "fountain" of their most popular fragrances. Beauty salon and spa are on the third floor: 45.62.11.21.

Hanae Mori, 5 Pl de l'Alma (M: Alma-Marceau) 47.23.52.03. Haute couture.

Harry Winston, 29 Ave Montaigne (M: Franklin D Roosevelt) 47.20.03.09.Famous jeweler.

Haviland, 25 Rue Royale, Village Royal (M: Madeleine) 42.66.36.36. Since 1842, Limoges china, tableware.

Hediard, 21 Pl de la Madeleine (M: Madeleine) 43.12.88.77. Gourmet foods, caviar.

Helmut Lang, 219 Rue St-Honore (M: Concorde) 58.62.53.20. Modern designer boutique for high-end men and womens fashion. Two stories with accessories and perfume, too.

Hermès, 24 Rue du Faubourg St-Honore (M: Concorde) 40.17.47.17. The ultimate Paris experience! A FAVORITE. Closed Sunday.

8

Ines de la Fressange, 31 Ave Franklin D Roosevelt (M: Franklin D Roosevelt) 56.88.34.00. Elegant designer.

Jadis et Gourmande, 49 bis Ave Franklin D Roosevelt (M: Franklin D Roosevelt) 42.25.06.04. Chocolate candies, chocolate Bordeaux bottles, and chocolate letters to create your own gift or souvenir.

Jean-Paul Gaultier, 44 Ave George V (M: George V) 44.43.00.44. Haute couture.

Jean-Pierre Cohier, 270 Rue du Faubourg St-Honore (M: Ternes) 42.27.45.26. Fabulous bakery and baguettes.

Kirk & Rosie Rich, 9 Rue de la Tremoille (M: Alma-Marceau) 47.23.81.00. Trendy, eclectic shop.

La Maison du Miel, 24 Rue Vignon (M: Madeleine) 47.42.26.70. Honey from around the world plus "all the products of the hive".

Lachaume, 10 Rue Royale (M: Concorde) 42.60.59.74. Mon-Sat. Floral designs since 1845. Closed in August.

Lacoste, 95 Ave des Champs Elysées (M: George V) 47.23.39.26. The "alligator."

Ladurée, 75 Ave des Champs Elysées (M: Franklin D Roosevelt) 40.75.08.75. Macaroons, Pastries.

Lalique, 11 Rue Royale (M: Madeleine) 53.05.12.12. Crystal.

Lancel, 4 Rond-Point des Champs Elysées (M: Franklin D Roosevelt) 42.25.18.35. Quality handbags.

Lanvin, 15 Rue Faubourg St-Honore (M: Concorde) 44.71.33.33. Newer lines, haute couture.

Le Drugstore Publicis, 133 Ave des Champs Elysées (M: George V) 47.20.78.00. This complex seems like an airport and has boutiques and cinema. Marcel is private restaurant.

Les Cristalleries de Saint-Louis, 13 Rue Royale (M: Concorde) 40.17.01.74.

Louis Vuitton, 101 Ave des Champs Elysées. (M: George V) 53.57.24.60. Global flagship store. Extraordinary design showcases artistic fashions. Multi-levels offer selections at the Bag Bar, luggage lounge. Closed Sundays.

Louis Vuitton Galerie, enter Rue Bassano, around the corner, and an elevator will take you up to an exhibition space that holds revolving shows.

Maison de la Truffe, 19 Pl de la Madeleine (M: Madeleine) 42.65.53.22. French delicatessen serving truffles, caviar and smoked fish. Squeezed in among the shelves are 12 mini tables for 3-course prix fixe lunch which features truffles in each course. Reservations recommended. A FAVORITE. €65. Closed Sunday.

Makassar - France, 19 Ave Matignon (M: Franklin D Roosevelt) 53.96.95.85. Art Deco antiques, paintings, sculptures.

Marquise de Sévigné, 32 Pl de la Madeleine (M: Madeleine) 42.65.19.47. Some of the best chocolates. A FAVORITE.

Mauboussin, 66 Ave des Champs Elysées (M: George V) 42.56.03.42. Prestigious jeweler with elegant and exclusive diamond designs. Also in 1e.

Max Mara, 31 Ave Montaigne (M: Franklin D Roosevelt) 47.20.61.13. Women's fashions.

Mercedes Benz, 118 Ave des Champs Elysées (M: George V) 53.83.00.53. Accessories with/without logo for €37-€135.

Miss Griffes, 19 Rue de Penthièvre (M: Miromesnil) 42.65.10.00. Discount store offering designer clothing.

Montaigne Market, 57 Ave Montaigne (M: Franklin D Roosevelt) 42.56.02.82. On this avenue, expect pricey, but in the back of this high-style boutique you will find "vintage" labels at discounts.

Nina Ricci, 39 Ave Montaigne (M: Franklin D Roosevelt) 40.88.67.60. Beautiful lingerie, scarves, parfume, jewelry. Closed Sunday.

Nouez-Moi, 8 Rue Clément Marot (M: Alma-Marceau) 47.20.60.26. Extraordinary linens. Ask them to embroider your initials. Another location in 16e.

Obrey, 13 Rue Tronchet, near Pl Madeleine (M: Havre-Caumartin) 42.66.69.73 Expensive jewelry.

Odiot, 7 Pl de la Madeleine (M: Madeleine) 42.65.00.95. Silversmiths.

Parfumerie Generale, 6 Rue Robert-Estienne) (M: Franklin D Roosevelt) 43.59.10.62. New little cosmetic shop has rare brands.

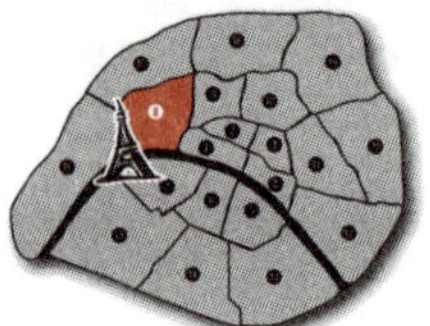

Parfums Caron, 34 Ave Montaigne (M: Franklin D Roosevelt) 47.23.40.82. Their powder puffs make the perfect souvenir, for yourself or friends. $25. Another location is at 90 Rue Faubourg St-Honore (M: Miromesnil) Choose from white, blue, yellow, fuchsia, pink, apricot, green, and lilac. A FAVORITE.

Perrin Antiquaires, 98 Rue du Faubourg St-Honore (M: St-Philippe-du-Roule) 42.65.01.38. High-end antique dealer, furniture, decorative objects from 17th and 18th centuries.

Petit Bateau, 116 Ave des Champs Elysées (M: George V) 40.74.02.03. Childrens clothes with tees 'that many women like to wear.

Pierre Balmain, 44 Rue François 1er (M: Franklin D Roosevelt) 47.20.35.34. Haute couture.

Prada, 10 Ave Montaigne (M: Franklin D Roosevelt) 53.23.99.40. Haute couture.

Prunier, 15 Pl de la Madeleine (M: Madeleine) 47.42.98.98. You will find a food shop, curing room, and a seafood bar serving caviar-based degustation creations.

Pucci, 36 Ave Montaigne (M: Franklin D Roosevelt) 47.20.04.45. High fashion.

Puiforcat, 2 Ave Matignon (M: Champs Elysées-Clemenceau) 45.63.10.10. Baby spoons vases, accessories.

Ralph Lauren, 2 Pl Madeleine (M: Madeleine) 44.77.53.50. Haute couture showroom.

Résonances, 3 Blvd Malesherbes (M: Madeleine) 44.51.63.70. Paris version of Restoration Hardware.

Roger Vivier, 29 Rue du Faubourg (M: Concorde) 53.43.00.85. Shoes ... fabulous shoes.

Scarlett, 10 Rue Clement-Marot (M: Alma-Marceau) 56.89.03.00. Vintage Chanel, Hermès, Louis Vuitton. Has Private warehouse with special collections of Dior, Balenciaga, that you may ask about at the main boutique and call for appointment.

Sephora, 70 Ave des Champs Elysées (M: George V) 53.93.22.50. Cosmetics and perfume. Several locations in Paris.

Sonia Rykiel, 70 Rue Faubourg St-Honore (M: Concorde) 42.65.20.81. Fashions. Several locations in Paris.

Ste. Benneton Graveur, 75 Blvd Malesherbes (M: Miromesnil) 43.87.57.39. Since 1880, exceptional family-owned stationers.

Territoire, 30 Rue Boissy d'Anglais (M: Concorde) 42.66.22.13. Gardeners' delight.

Torrente, 1 rond-point des Champs Elysées (M: Franklin D Roosevelt) 40.74.04.75. Haute couture.

Trousselier, 73 Blvd Haussmann (M: St-Lazare) 42.66.16.16. Florist.

Valentino, 17-19 Ave Montaigne (M: Franklin D Roosevelt) 47.23.64.61. Closed Sunday.

Valombreuse, 108 Rue du Faubourg St-Honore (M: Champs-Elysées-Clemenceau) 47.42.79.19. Luxurious hand-embroidered linen, organdy, silk, cotton tablecloths, placemats, pillows.

Vicente de Oro, 27 Rue Jean Mermoz (M: Franklin D Roosevelt) 42.66.63.42. Jewelry, fine watches.

Virgin Records Mégastore, 52 Ave des Champs Elysées (M: Franklin D Roosevelt) 49.53.50.00. Also has in-store café.

VJW Boutique, 60 Rue Francois 1er (M: George V) 42.25.15.41. Designer of fine jewelry and watches.

Wolford, 18 Rue Marbeuf (M: Franklin D Roosevelt) 40.70.06.06. Several locations

Yves Saint Laurent, 38 Rue Faubourg St-Honore (M: Concorde) 42.65.74.59. A FAVORITE.

Zadig & Voltaire, 18-20 Rue Francois Premier (M: Franklin D Roosevelt) 40.70.97.89. Trendy style-conscious lines.

RESTAURANTS: LES PLATS DU JOUR:

1728, 8 Rue d'Anjou (M: Madeleine) 40.17.04.77. Swanky sushi. Designer desserts. Lunch requires reservations. Expensive.

A l'Affiche, 48 Rue de Moscou (M: Rome) 45.22.02.20. Modern French cooking. Fresh blackboard menu. Closed Sunday.

Al Diwan, 30 Ave George V (M: George V) 47.23.45.45. Lebanese. Open Sunday.

Au Clou de la Girafe, 7 Rue Paul Baudry (M: Franklin D Roosevelt) 56.88.29.55. Chef Frederic Claudel serves wonderful, light traditional meals. €50 dinner. Closed Sat lunch/Sunday.

Bath's, 9 Rue de la Tremoille (M: Alma-Marceau) 40.70.01.09. Michelin one-star. Try the tasting menu. Closed Sat/Sunday.

Bert's, 4 Ave du President Wilson (M: Alma-Marceau) 47.23.43.37. Good for light sandwiches, soups, crowded for lunch.

Brasserie Lorraine, 2 Pl Ternes (M: Ternes) 56.21.22.00. Freres-Blanc classic bistro chain. Fun terrace, consistent food.

Buddha Bar, 8 Rue Boissy-d'Anglais (M: Concorde) 53.05.90.00. Trendy Asian. Hip DJ and popular wine bar and scene. A FAVORITE.

Café Lenotre, 10 Ave Champs Elysées (M: Concorde) 42.65.85.10. Casual dining in garden.

Casa dell'Estelle, 14 Rue de Castellane (M: Madeleine) 42.65.41.56. Chef Ferrari creates Italian dishes under €15, such as arugula-topped pizza. Heated sidewalk terrace. Closed Sunday.

8e. Elysée, Champs Elysées

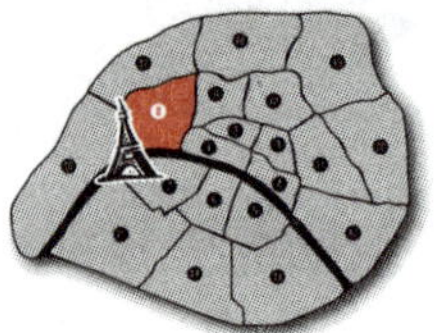

Caviar Kaspa, 17 Pl de Madeleine (M: Madeleine) 42.65.33.52. We always have fun here. Elegant and decadent. Caviar and vodka. A FAVORITE.

Chez Catherine, 3 Rue Berryer (M: George V) 40.76.01.40. Creative French style dishes. Reserve for a memorable evening of food, wine, service, and décor. Friendly.

Chez Francis, 7887 Pl de l'Alma (M: Alma-Marceau) 47.20.86.83. Lunch and dinner. Reservations for dinner recommended because of terrific view of Eiffel Tower from terrace.

Chez Savy, 23 Rue Bayard (M: Champs-Elysées) 47.23.46.98. Art deco setting. Good bistro food, mostly meat. Good value on wines. Closed Sunday.

Chiberta, 3 Rue Arsène Houssaye (M: Charles-de-Gaulle-Etoile) 53.53.42.00. Modern French by Guy Savoy. Fun menu and good service. Closed Saturday lunch and Sunday.

8

Citrus Etoile, 6 Rue Arsène Houssaye (M: Charles-de-Gaulle-Etoile) 42.89.15.51. Elizabeth Epié warmly greets you with a smile, as you enter this inviting bi-level restaurant with wine cave. Giles, her husband and chef, presents provocatively simple and sublime menu items. Good wine list too. A FAVORITE. €100 for two. Closed Saturday lunch/Sunday.

De Vèz, 5 Pl de l'Alma (M: Alma-Marceau) 53.67.97.53. Chef/owner Christian Valette owns a ranch, so meat is his specialty. Tapas are good, too. Modern décor. Terrace. Good wine list. €90 for 2.

Dominique Bouchet, 11 Rue Treilhard (M: Miromesnil) 45.61.09.46. Legion d'Honneur chef serves French with Japanese influence. Clean décor, small space. Reservations necessary because he gets almost perfect scores. €100 for two, before wine. Closed Sat/Sun.

Fouquet's, 99 Ave des Champs-Elysées. (M: George V) 47.23.70.60. Opened in 1899. Famous for traditional French meals. Big outdoor terrace and trademark red awning for great people-watching. Expensive. Open Sunday.

Garnier, 111 Rue St-Lazare (M: St-Lazare) 43.87.50.40. Lots of seafood at this popular brasserie. Reserve window table upstairs. Open Sunday.

L'Angle du Faubourg, 195 Rue du Faubourg St-Honoré (M: Ternes) 40.74.20.20. New, opened by Taillevent, with lighter ingredients and prices! Has wonderful wine list, too.

L'Appart, 9 Rue du Colisée (M: Franklin D Roosevelt) 53.75.42.00. Decorated à la Parisian apartment. Meals and service are inconsistent.

L'Astor, 11 Rue D'Astorg (M: St-Augustin) 53.05.05.20. Hôtel Astor. Good reviews. Joel Robuchon oversees restaurant.

L'Avenue, 1 Ave Montaigne (M: Franklin D Roosevelt) 40.70.14.91. Simple, chic, trendy. Côstes brothers formula. A FAVORITE. Open Sunday.

L'Envue, 39 Rue Boissy-d'Anglais (M: Concorde) 42.65.10.49. New, from chef Patrice Cannac, previously of Hotel Côstes. Closed Sunday.

L'Obelisque Hotel de Crillon, 10 Pl de la Concorde (M: Concorde) 44.71.15.15. The "other" less formal restaurant.

La Cour Jardin, in the courtyard at Plaza Athénée, 25 Ave Montaigne (M: George V) 53.67.65.00. Wonderful salads and light meals in beautiful garden. Open 7/7.

La Farnesina, 9 Rue Boissy d'Anglais (M: Concorde) 42.66.65.57. Fresh buffalo mozzarella is flown in from Naples on Mondays. Try the risotto with shaved truffles.

La Ferme des Mathurins, 17 Rue Vignon (M: Madeleine) 42.66.46.39. International cuisine at moderate prices. Closed Sat lunch/Sunday.

La Fermette Marbeuf, 5 Rue Marbeuf. (M: Franklin D Roosevelt) 53.23.08.00. Tourists like the Belle Epoque setting. Busy after 9pm. Reservations advised. Open Sunday.

La Maison de l'Aubrac, 37 Rue Marbeuf (M: Franklin D Roosevelt) 43.59.05.14. Beef around the clock. Paris chefs come here when their restaurants close. Hundreds of wines.

8

La Mascotte, 270 Rue du Faubourg St-Honore (M: Ternes) 42.27.75.26. Classic bistro, friendly service - all at good prices. Several locations in Paris.

Le Berkeley, 7 Ave Matignon (M: Franklin D Roosevelt) 42.25.72.25. Classic Côstes, Oysters and champagne. Breakfast, lunch, and dinner until 2am. Terrace. Open Sunday.

Le Bistrot du Sommelier, 97 Blvd Haussmann. (M: Miromesnil/St-Augustin) 42.65.24.85. The prix fixe menu paired with wine is not as good as selecting your own wine from their extensive wine list. White linen tablecloths. Closed Sat/Sun.

Le Carre, 12 Pl St-Augustin (M: St-Augustin) 44.69.00.22. New French fare.

Le Cou de la Girafe, 7 Rue Paul Bandry (M: St-Philippe-du-Roule) 56.88.29.55. Chic décor, wonderful dinners at €90 for two and good wine list. Closed Sunday/Monday lunch.

Le Jardin, Hotel Royal Monceau, 37 Ave Hoche (M: Ternes) 42.99.98.70. Perfect Paris setting in garden, glass-enclosed pavilion. New French cuisine and good selection of southern French wines. Closed Sunday.

Le Sarladais, 2 Rue de Vienne (M: St-Augustin) 45.22.23.62. Southwestern specialties and several selections of foie gras make this a great value. Friendly service, too. Closed Sunday.

Les Gourmets des Ternes, 87 Blvd de Courcelles (M: Villiers) 42.27.43.04. Jack Nicholson's favorite for tender steaks. True bistro food.

Les Saveurs de Flora, 36 Ave George V (M: George V) 40.70.10.49. Flavorful meals. Informal elegance. Closed Sunday.

8e. Elysée, Champs Elysées

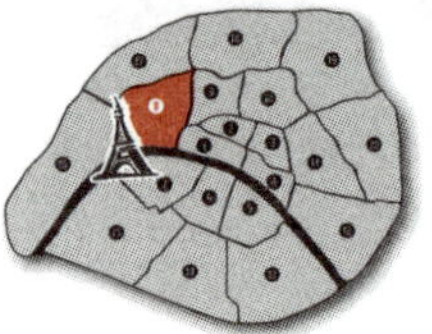

Libre Sens, 33 Rue Marbeuf (M: Franklin D Roosevelt) 53.96.00.72. Young crowd in modern fashionably lit room. Mixed light menu.

Lo Sushi, 8 Rue de Berri (M: George V) 45.62.01.00. Long exotic sushi bar. Self-service.

Ma Bourgogne, 133 Blvd Haussmann (M: Miromesnil) 45.63.50.61. Good food and wine. Reputable wine bar. Steak tartare and classics. Cash only. Reserve. Closed Sunday.

Man Ray, 34 Rue Marbeuf (M: Franklin D Roosevelt) 56.88.36.36. Trendy, well known bar, restaurant, nightclub. Mediocre meals, good scene.

Marcel, in Drugstore Publicis, 199 Ave des Champs Elysées (M: Charles-de-Gaulle-Etoile) 47.20.78.00. Alain Ducasse presides over this restaurant/private club.

Marius et Janette, 4 Ave George V (M: Alma-Marceau) 47.23.84.36. Seafood. Terrace with great view of Eiffel Tower.

Maxims, 3 Rue Royale (M: Concorde) 42.65.27.94. Enjoy lunch and visit the museum for good selection of belle époque period collectibles. 2p-5:30 except Mon/Tues.

Minims de Paris, 7 Rue Royale (M: Concorde) 42.65.91.77. The little baby of Maxims, more affordable. Beautiful setting. Banquettes Parisian-style. A FAVORITE.

Music Hall, 63 Ave Franklin D Roosevelt (M: St-Philippe-du-Roule) 45.61.03.63. Chef Nepple serves fashionable contemporary dishes, €30 entrees, amid hip décor. Lounge and bar. Open 24 hours. House music. Ultra chic.

Pomze, 109 Blvd Haussmann (M: St-Philippe-du-Roule) 42.65.65.83. Apple-icious. Small plates.

Prunier, 15 Pl de la Madeleine (M: Madeleine) 47.42.98.98. You will find a food shop, curing room, and a seafood bar serving caviar-based degustation creations.

Rue Balzac, 3-5 Rue Balzac. (M: George V) 53.89.90.91. Trendy restaurant from Michel Rostang. Terrace.

Saveurs et Salon, 3 Rue Castellane (M: Madeleine) 40.06.97.97. Wines "match" the delicious food. Hip Crowd. Modern and comfy décor. Upstairs preferred. A FAVORITE.

Sébillon, 66 Rue Pierre Charron (M: Franklin D Roosevelt) 43.59.28.15. House specialty is leg of lamb.

Sens, 23 Rue de Ponthieu (M: Franklin D Roosevelt) 42.25.95.00. Duplex by the Pourcel twins, modern and stylish. Upstairs is a pool parlor, wide-screen TV and live jazz in décor of soft grey and neon red. Downstairs, enjoy tasty meals and a wonderfully priced wine list from the Languedoc region. €25 3-course lunch includes glass of wine. Dinners at €60. Closed Sat. lunch/Sunday.

Senso, 16 Rue de la Tremoille (M: Alma-Marceau) 56.52.14.14. Call ahead for this new one by Sir Terence Conran. Bar offers "tastes."

Spicy Restaurant, 8 Ave Franklin D Roosevelt (M: Franklin D Roosevelt) 56.59.62.59. Fusion and fashion. Reasonably priced. Open Sunday.

Spoon, Food, and Wine, 14 Rue de Marignan (M: Franklin D Roosevelt) 40.76.34.44. Alain Ducasse. Mediocre reviews. Closed Sat-Sunday.

Stella Maris, 4 Rue Arsene-Houssaye (M: Charles-de-Gaulle-Etoile) 42.89.16.22 Chef/owner Yoshino trained with Robuchon for a unique blend of Japanese to classic French cooking.

Tante Louise, 41 Rue Boissy d'Anglas (M: Concorde) 42.65.06.85. Traditional 1930's bistro. Closed Sat-Sunday.

Terres de Truffes, 21 Rue Vignon (M: Madeleine) 53.43.80.44. Owned by truffle-master Clement Bruno, of Provence. Sip at the wine bar or dine in the pleasant dining room, or take-away. Closed Sunday. A FAVORITE.

Tong Yen, 1 bis, Rue Jean Mermoz (M: Franklin D Roosevelt) 42.25.04.23. Exotic Southeast Asian cuisine. Fashionable place to be seen.

Villa Mauresque, 5-7 Rue Commandant-Rivière (M: St-Philip-du-Roule) 42.25.16.69. French Moroccan menu and contemporary dining room. Flavorful meat dishes. €90.

Village d'Ung et Li Lam, 10 Rue Jean Mermoz (M: Franklin D Roosevelt) 42.25.99.79. six ton aquarium on the ceiling of this Chinese-Champs Elysées Thai menu.

Visconti, 4 Rue de l'Arcade (M: Madeleine) 42.65.53.13. Cozy décor upstairs and downstairs. Roberto offers fresh Italian meals with a friendly smile. Open 7/7.

Yvan, 1 bis, Rue Jean Mermoz (M: Franklin D Roosevelt) 43.59.18.40. Well-liked by many. Belgian influences.

RESTAURANTS: GASTRONOMIQUE:

Alaine Ducasse, 25 Ave Montaigne (M: Franklin D Roosevelt) 53.67.65.00. Gastronomique. Alain Ducasse. Dinner for two over €400. Spectacular In every way. A FAVORITE. Must reserve.

Apicius, 20 Rue D'Artois (M: St-Phillppe-du-Roule) 43.80.19.66. Chef Jean-Pierre Vigato creates nouvelle masterpieces. Plan to spend at least €200 for two, before wine. €130 Prix fixe menu. Closed Sat/Sunday.

La Maison Blanche, 15 Ave Montaigne (M: Franklin D Roosevelt) top of Théâtre Champs-Elysées. 47.23.55.99. Awarded three stars by Michelin. Service may be pompous. We give it mixed reviews for our money.

La Table du Lancaster, Hotel Lancaster, 7 Rue de Berri (M: George V) 40.76.40.18. Michel Troisgros arranges themed menus. €130 prix fixe menu.

Lasserre, 17 Ave Franklin D Roosevelt (M: Champs-Elysées) 43.59.02.13. New chef. Romantic historic building with painted ceiling that opens to let the stars shine. Live piano music. Nadine is one of first female sommelier in Paris. Jacket/tie required for men. A FAVORITE.

8e. Elysée, Champs Elysées

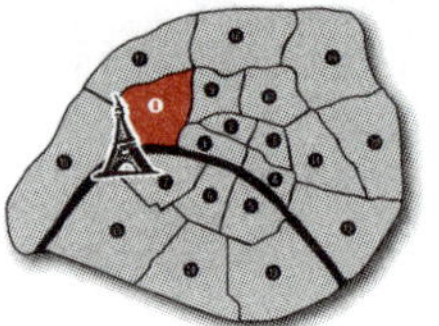

Laurent, 41 Ave Gabriel (M: Champs-Elysées-Clemenceau) 42.25.00.39. New chef, Alain Pegouret, trained with Christian Constant. Classic French. Garden patio.

Le Bristol, 112 Rue du Faubourg St-Honore (M: Miromesnil) 53.43.43.00. Chef Eric Frechon prepares sublime meals to enjoy inside or in the garden.

Le Cinq, 31 av George V, (M: George V) 49.52.71.54. Almost perfect. Chef Philippe Legendre, formally with Taillevent, serves up superb menu. Exceptional dining experience with superlative wine list.

Le Maxan, 37 Rue de Miromesnil (M: Miromesnil) 42.65.78.60. Chef Laurent Zajac prepares haute cuisine for clientele dressed in haute couture.

Le Stresa, 7 Rue Chambiges (M: Alma-Marceau) 47.23.51.62. Italian. Hip. Pricey. Supermodels and movie stars make getting a table a challenge.

Ledoyen, 1 av Dutuit (M: Champs-Elysées-Clemenceau) 53.05.10.01 Gastronomic and romantic. Closed Sat-Sunday.

Les Ambassadeurs, 10 pl de la Concorde, in Hôtel Crillon (M: Concorde) 44.71.16.16. Gastronomic. Superlative meals from master Chef Piège who moved from Plaza Athenée. Enjoy cocktails in the Bar du Crillon before dinner. Dinner for two $400+.

Les Elysées du Vernet, 25 Rue Vernet in Hôtel Vernet (M: George V) 44.31.98.98. Beautiful setting of stained-glass dome with Chef Eric Briffard serving wonderful soups and French cuisine. Closed Sunday.

Market, 15 Ave Matignon (M: Champs Elysées) 56.43.30.90. (Chef Jean-Georges Vongerichten's name means high superb quality and prices. Open Sunday.

Nobu, 15 Rue Marbeuf (M: Franklin D Roosevelt) 56.89.53.53. Japanese haute cuisine. Same standards as New York City. Open Sunday.

Pierre Gagnaire, 6 Rue Balzac, Hotel Balzac (M: George V) 58.36.12.50. One of the best. Short wine list. Open Sunday.

Restaurant de L'Astor, in the Sofitel Westin Demeure. 11 Rue d'Astorg (M: St-Augustin) 53.05.05.20. Chef Eric le Cerf is a protégé of Joel Robuchon and delights diners. The glass ceiling adds elegance. Wine list is limited. Reservations recommended.

Senderens, 9 Pl de la Madeleine (M: Madeleine) 42.65.22.90. Alain Senderens tries to present a perfect wine-and-food dining experience. We were disappointed in our lunch at €150 for 2. Upstairs tapas bar. Service was friendly and attentive.

Taillevent, 15 Rue Lamennais (M: George V) 44.95.15.01. Voted Number One among many. Reservations required. Mon-Sat. Our prix fixe lunch €130 for six courses was wonderful. 3 sommeliers assist in wine selection from their private cellar. Clean modern décor. Note: cigars and cigarettes allowed. Closed Sunday.

W Restaurant, Hotel Warwick, 5 Rue de Berri (M: George V) 45.61.82.08. Chef Franck Charpentier presides over dining room offering Provencal haute cuisine and excellent service.

BONNE SOIREE: PARIS AT NIGHT:

Atelier Renault, 53 Ave des Champs Elysées (M: Franklin D Roosevelt) 49.53.70.00. Has Thursday DJ.

Bar de l'Hotel Crillon, 10 Pl de la Concorde (M: Tuileries) 44.71.15.36. Jazz piano.

Bar due Bristol Hotel, 112 Rue du Faubourg St-Honore (M: Champs-Elysées) 53.43.43.00.

Black Calvados, 40 Ave Pierre -1er de Serbie (M: George V) 47.20.77.77. Popular with the club set.

Bound, 49 Ave George V (M: George V) 53.67.84.60. Long pink bar, rock music and light show. Grazing menu with sushi, pasta, cheeseburgers.

Buddha Bar, 8 Rue Boissy d'Anglas (M: Concorde) 53.05.90.00. Both a cocktail bar, restaurant, and nightclub. DJ.

Charlie Birdy, 124 Rue La Boétie (M: Franklin D Roosevelt) 42.25.18.06. Restaurant. Concerts by rising rock and R & B artists along with big names. Call ahead for schedule, 42.25.13.28.

Crazy Horse, 12 Ave George V (M: George V) 47.23.32.32. Famous strip show.

Culture Bière, 65 Ave des Champs Elysées (M: Franklin D Roosevelt) 42.56.88.88. Sleek and modern beer boutique with restaurant upstairs.

Drugstore Publicis, 133 Ave des Champs Elysées (M: George V) 44.43.79.00. Midnight omelets.

Keur Samba, 79 Rue La Boétie (M: St-Philippe-du-Roule) 43.59.03.10. Nightclub that really starts to rock at 2 am. Cover. Midnight-7am. Actors, models, musicians of all sorts. Risqué.

La Cantine du Faubourg, 105 Rue du Faubourg St-Honore (M: Champs-Elysées-Clemenceau) 42.56.22.22. All-night restaurant, bar. Trendy art gallery or night club.

La Suite, 40 Ave George V (M: George V) 53.57.49.49. See Superlatives. Late night Sweet Bar, til 5 am.

Le Bar du Plaza, 25 Ave Montaigne (M: Franklin D Roosevelt) 53.67.66.65. Hotel Plaza Athénée is the perfect place to end the evening. A FAVORITE.

Le Marcel, 133 Ave des Champs Elysées (M: George V) 44.43.66.66. Private club in Drugstore Publicis. Managed by Alain Ducasse. Star-studded clientele.

Le Petit Yvan, 1 bis Rue Jean Mermoz (M: Franklin D Roosevelt) 42.89.49.65. Dancing.

Lido, 116 Ave des Champs Elysées (M: George V) 40.76.56.10. Two shows nightly.

Man Ray, 34 Rue Marbeuf (M: Franklin D Roosevelt) 56.88.36.36. Trendy restaurant/club owned by Johnny Depp and Sean Penn. Chef Marchand, ex- Meurice. Live jazz. Mon-Thu. Call.

8e. Elysée, Champs Elysées

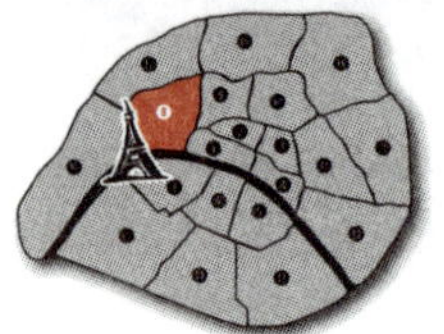

Mathis Bar, 3 Rue de Ponthieu (M: Franklin D Roosevelt) 53.76.01.62. Located in 1920's-era Matignon hôtel and is another hip bar to see and be seen.

Maxims, 5 Rue Royale (M: Concorde) 42.65.27.94. Art Nouveau nightclub. No cover.

Monkey Club, 65-67 Rue Pierre Charron (M: Franklin D Roosevelt) 58.56.20.50. Street level dining, downstairs disco/dancing.

Music Hall, 63 Ave Franklin D Roosevelt (M: St-Philippe-du-Roule) 45.61.03.63. Lounge, Bar, restaurant. Open 24 hours. House music. Ultra chic.

Neo, 23 Rue Ponthieu (M: Franklin D Roosevelt) 42.25.87.14. Popular with party set, proprieter Nick Bast (his name, honest!) caters to Bruce Willis and others.

Pink Paradise, 23 Rue Ponthieu (M: Franklin D Roosevelt) 58.36.19.20. Upscale strip club. Pole dancing lessons for €25.

Regines, 49-51 Rue de Ponthieu (M: Franklin D Roosevelt) 43.59.21.60.

8

Royce, 3 Rue Saussaies (M: Miromesnil) 43.12.82.00. Sporty set populates this bar owned by soccer star Claude Makelele.

Theatre des Champs-Elysées, 15 Ave Montaigne (M: Alma-Marceau) 49.52.50.50. Call for concerts. Box office Mon-Sat. No performances July 1st - September 7th.

Theatre du Rond-Point, 2 bis Ave Franklin D Roosevelt (M: Champs-Elysées-Clemenceau) 44.95.98.00. Modern French theatre. Call box office.

Villa d'Este, 4 Rue Arsène-Houssaye (M: Charles-de-Gaulle-Etoile) 42.56.14.65. Dinner and show and dancing. Call.

VIP Room, 76 Ave des Champs-Elysées (M: Franklin D Roosevelt) 56.69.16.66. Snazzy night club with living room ambiance.

My Special Travel Notes

8

My Special Travel Notes

8

9e. Opéra

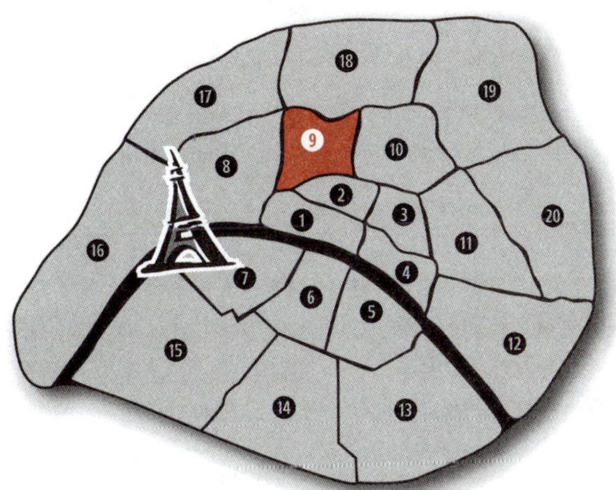

Marvel at the ornate interior of **L'Opéra Garnier.**

Sample some of Paris' Best chocolate at **L'Etoile d'Or** and say Bonjour to Denise Acabo.

Shopaholics will fill their day at **Galeries Lafayette** and **Le Printemps.**

The newest show at **Folies Bergere** will dazzle you with great evening entertainment.

MAJOR METROS:

- MADELEINE
- OPÉRA
- HAVRE-CAUMARTIN
- ST-LAZARE
- TRINITÉ
- CADET
- GRANDS BOULEVARDS
- LE PELETIER

9e. Opéra

FAMOUS SIGHTS:

Musée Gustave Moreau (Musée National), 14 Rue la Rochefoucault (M: Trinité) 48.74.38.50. Voted one of the best museums. €4. Townhouse and studio of artist Gustave Moreau has over 4,800 drawings, sculptures, watercolors. We enjoy! Closed Tuesday.

Opéra Garnier, (M: Opéra) 92.69.78.68. Built during Napoleon III's reign. Restored façade is amazing. Beautiful, ornate interior is open10a-4:30p except during matinees. A FAVORITE. The Grand staircase and foyers are extravagant and the West Pavilion holds a library-museum. Box office Mon-Sat 11a-6:30p. The purest honey is made from the rooftop.

DIVERSIONS:

Bliss Spa in **Galeries Lafayette.** See "Shops"

Concerts (free) on Thursdays at 12:45p at Paroisse de la Sainte-Trinité, Pl d'Estienne d'Orves (M: Trinité).

9

Drouot Richelieu - principal auction house of Paris, 9 Rue Drouot (M: Drouot Richelieu) 48.00.20.20. Sixteen exhibition rooms. On Fridays, buy Gazette de l'Hôtel Drouot to find out about auctions. Pre-auction viewing Mon.-Sat.

Fashion shows at Galeries Lafayette, 40 Blvd Haussmann (M: Chaussee d'Antin) 42.82.30.25. Fashion shows: Reserve in advance. 48.74.02.30. at Welcome Desk on ground floor in SW corner of main store. Shows are on Tuesdays at 11:00am and Fridays (April - October) at 2:30p on the 7th floor. Refreshments are served. You can also see the Fashion Shows at Printemps at 10:00 on Tuesdays. Free.

Fragonard Musée du Parfum, 39 Blvd des Capucines. (M: Opéra) 47.42.04.55. Enter through a courtyard and go upstairs to see collection of perfume bottles from 17th to 20th century. Free. Mon-Sat 9a - 5p.

Gallery: L'Oeil du Huit, 8 Rue Milton (M: Notre Dame de Lorette) 40.23.02.92. Exhibitions, New artists.

Musée de la Parfumerie, 9 Rue Scribe (M: Opéra) 47.42.04.56. Free. Mon-Sat.

Musée Grévin, 10 Blvd Montmartre (M: Grands Boulevards) 47.70.85.05. Wax works. French history, sports figures, film stars. 10a-6:30p .€17 adults/€10 ages 6-14/€9 5 and under. Two shows throughout the day, one with a magician.

Musée de la Vie Romantique, 16 Rue Chaptal (M: St-Georges) 8.74.95.38. Open 10a-5:30p €4.50, free admission to permanent exhibitions. Visit the town house in a little park, with garden café, owned by painter Ary Scheffer who entertained George Sand, Frederic Chopin. Closed Mon.

Rooftop views from the top of **Printemps** and **Galeries Lafayette.**

WALK: Rue Notre-Dame de Lorette to Pl St George, south, to Square d'Orléans where #5 Chopin lived, #2 George Sand lived, then on to Rue de la Victoire to Rue LaFayette, Rue du Faubourg Montmartre.

Passages Jouffroy/Verdeau, 10-11 Blvd Montmartre, between (M: Richelieu Drouot) and (M: Grands Boulevards). A passage back in time with old bookstores, antique postcard stores. Til 9:30p.

Spa Phytomer, 99 Rue de Provence (M: Havre-Caumartin) 44.63.04.88. Day spa for men. Galeries Lafayette Homme.

SUPERLATIVES:

Best Bread: Daniel Dupuy, 13 Rue Cadet (M: Cadet) 48.24.54.26. Sample the "rochetor".

Best Brunch: Rose Bakery, 46 Rue des Martyrs (M: Notre Dame de Lorette) 42.88.12.80.

Best Candy: A la Mère de Famille, 35 Rue du Faubourg Montmartre (M: Peletier) 47.70.83.69. Several locations in Paris.

Best Chocolatier: Denise Acabo's L'Etoile d'Or, 30 Rue Fontaine (M: Blanche) 48.74.59.55. We really think everything is delicious here! A FAVORITE.

Best Ice Cream (to some, better than Berthillon): Baggi, 29 Rue de Mogador (M: Trinité) Try a mokaline cone: coffee, caramel and chocolate bits.

Hippest Fast Food: Cojean, 4 Rue de Sèze (M: Madeleine) 40.06.80.80. Salmon tortillas, trendy milk shakes.

Landmark Café: le Café Zephyr, 12 Blvd Montmartre (M: Grands Boulevards) 47.70.80.14.

SHOPS:

Annexe des Créateurs, 19 Rue Godot de Mauroy (M: Madeleine) 42.65.46.40. One store for daytime wear and another store for evening wear. Discount prices up to 70%-designer brands for men and women.

Anouschka, 6 Ave Coq (M: Havre-Caumartin) 48.74.37.00. Vintage designs.

Beryl Bijoux Artisanat, 80 Rue de Provence (M: Havre Caumartin/Opéra) 40.16.99.60. Pendants, brooches, cocktail rings.

Detaille, 10 Rue St Lazare (M: Notre Dame de Lorette) 48.78.68.50. Beauty company founded in 1905.

Et Puis C'est Tout, 72 Rue des Martyrs (M: Notre Dame de Lorette) 40.23.94.02. Vintage, modern & retro.

Fouquet, 36 Rue Laffitte (M: Le Peletier) 47.70.75.00. Sublime candies, caramel, truffles. Also in 8e.

Galeries Lafayette, 40 Blvd Haussmann (M: Chausee-d'Antin) 42.82.34.56. Make sure you go to Welcome desk on ground floor for a card authorizing 10% discount in addition to the VAT if you spend $175 in one day. Has dining such as La Terrasse for drinks on the roof with a great view of Paris.

9e. Opéra

Galeries Lafayette Homme, for men.

Judith Lacroix, 3 Rue Henri-Monnier (M: St-Georges) 48.78.22.37. Another location for irresistible children's clothes from designer Lacroix.

Printemps, 64 Blvd Haussmann - next door to Galeries Lafayette (M: Havre Caumartin) 42.82.50.00. Make sure you get card for 10% discount from Welcome Desk on ground floor. Fashion shows every Tues. at 10am. Panoramic view of Paris from top floor.

Printemps Beauté et Maison has 2 floors of cosmetics and body lotions and 7 floors of home décor.

L'Etoile d'Or, 30 Rue Fontaine (M: Blanche) 48.74.59.55. Chocolate! We really think everything is delicious here! Denise Acabo takes special care.

Mango, 6 Blvd des Capucines (M: Opéra) 53.30.82.70. Clothing chain from Spain.

Mia Zia, 4 Rue de Caumartin (M: Havre-Caumartin) 44.51.94.54. North African and Indian designs by Valerie Barkowski.

Old England, 12 Blvd des Capucines (M: Opéra) 47.42.81.99. Very popular.

Pain d'Epice, 29 Passage Jouffroy (M: Richelieu-Drouot) 47.70.08.68 Toy store with collectors' items.

RESTAURANTS: LES PLATS DU JOUR:

I Golosi, 6 Rue de la Grange-Bateliere (M: Richelieu-Drouot) 48.24.16.63. Italian. Fresh. Huge wine list. A FAVORITE. Closed Sunday.

16 Haussmann, in Hôtel Ambassador, (M: Havre-Caumartin) 44.83.40.58. Philippe Starck furniture. Sunday brunch. Set menus.

Auberge et Cie, 23 Rue Clauzel (M: St-Georges) 48.78.74.40. Southwestern menu in cozy setting. Seafood and lighter fare, too. Closed Sunday.

Autour d'un Verre, 21 Rue de Trévise (M: Cadet) 48.24.43.74. Small wine store and bar du vin, showcasing "bio" wines. Charcuterie, salads, plats. Lunch M-F/dinner M-Sat. Closed Sunday.

Bar Rouge, in Galeries Lafayette Gourmet, 97 Rue de Provence (M: Opéra) 40.23.52.59. A wine library with tapas and small bites. Closed Sunday.

Bistro des Deux Theatres, 18 Rue Blanche (M: Trinite-d'Estienne) 45.26.41.43. One of six Willy Dorr restaurants. All serve a complete 3-course meal with Kir Royale and wine for €32.

Café de la Paix, 2 Rue Scribe (M: Opéra) 40.07.36.36. Inside the Le Grand Intercontinental Hotel. Enjoy the seasonal menu by Chef Laurent Delarbe. Contemporary traditional French preparations. €55 Dinner.

Carte Blanche, 6 Rue Lamartine (M: Notre Dame de Lorette) 48.78.12.20. Asian influences, organic veggies, palette-challenging combinations, at times. Modern French. €35. Closed Sat. lunch and Sundays.

Casa Olympe, 48 Rue St George (M: St-Georges) 42.85.26.01. Chef Dominique Versini highly recommended. Two floors. Cozy décor. A FAVORITE. Closed Sat/Sunday.

Charlot le Roi des Coquillages, 81 Blvd de Clichy (M: Pl de Clichy) 53.20.48.00. King of seafood.

Chez Jean, 8 Rue St-Lazare (M: Notre Dame de Lorette) 48.78.62.73. Jean Frederic Guidoni owns this newer restaurant with young chef serving inventive haute cuisine. Meat is his specialty, so try the rack of rabbit. Closed Sunday.

Dell Orto, 45 Rue St-Georges (M: St-Georges) 48.78.40.30. Pasta comes with high price in Tuscan-style dining room. Dinner only. Closed Sunday.

L'Alsaco, 10 Rue Condorcet (M: Anvers) 45.26.44.31. Hearty Alsatian.

L'Auberge du Clou, 30 Ave Trudaine (M: Anvers) 48.78.22.48. Modern French with eclectic dishes. Fireplace on second floor is comfy in winter. No credit cards.

L'Oenothèque, 20 Rue St-Lazare (M: Notre Dame de Lorette) 48.78.08.76. Friendly owner offers good wines, reasonably priced by-the-glass + so-so food. Closed Sunday.

La Cloche d'Or, 3 Rue Mansart (M: Blanche) 48.74.48.88. Steak tartare at 3 am.

9

Le Ch'Ti Catalan, 4 Rue de Navarin (M: Pigale) 44.63.04.33. Delicious and ample servings. Closed Sunday.

Le Général La Fayette, 52 Rue La Fayette (M: Cadet) 47.70.59.08. 10a – 4a Brasserie. Convertible sidewalk terrace on sunny days.

Le Laffitte, 43 Rue Laffitte (M: Le Peletier) 42.80.07.66. Olivier and his wife preside over this small delicious café where the wine is freely poured. Closed Sat/Sunday.

Les Bacchantes, 21 Rue de Caumartin (M: Havre-Caumartin) 42.65.25.35. Friendly bistro à vins gets crowded during lunch because of location near Opéra and department stores. Traditional menu changes daily. Moderate prices. Closed Sunday.

Les Comediens, 7 Rue Blanche (M: Trinité) 40.82.95.95. Fills up with après-theatre goers, actors for mediocre food with a lively ambiance. Closed Sunday.

Les Vivres, 28 Rue Pétrelle, (M: Barbès-Roch) 42.80.26.10. Wine bar and grocery annex. Lamb €20. Open daily for lunch and dinner on Fridays.

Momoka, 5 Rue Jean-Baptiste (M: Pigale) 40.16.19.09. Must reserve because this is very tiny and only serves dinner. Three set menus each evening. Fabulous desserts. Fresh ginger lemonade, limited wine list.

Pétrelle, 34 Rue Pétrelle (M: Barbès-Roch) 42.82.11.02. Chef Jean-Luc André prepares seasonal menus. Moderate prices.

Radis Roses Restaurant, 68 Rue Rodier (M: Anvers) 48.78.03.20. Entirely non-smoking. Tiny, trendy, new French that has a New York feeling. Closed Sunday.

9e. Opéra

Restaurant Chartier, 7 Rue du Faubourg Montmartre (M: Grands Boulevards) 47.70.86.29. Classic French cuisine at low price. Open Sunday.

Rose Bakery, 46 Rue des Martyrs (M: Notre Dame de Lorette) 42.88.12.80. Good brunch.

Velly, 52 Rue Lamartine (M: Notre Dame de Lorette) 48.78.60.05. Talented young chef, Alain Brigant serves good classic food at low prices. Chalkboard menu. Two dining rooms.

RESTAURANTS: GASTRONOMIQUE:

Table d'Anvers, 2 Pl d'Anvers (M: Anvers) 48.78.35.21. Chef Philippe Colin offers superb traditional French prix fixe dinners. Attentive service. Closed Sunday.

BONNE SOIREE! PARIS AT NIGHT:

Barramundi, 3 Rue Taitbourg (M: Richelieu-Drouot) 47.70.21.21. Regular soirées on weekends. World music, weeknights. Expensive, eclectic menu. Closed Sun.

Casino de Paris, 16 Rue de Clichy (M: Pl-Clichy or Lieges) 49.95.99.99.

Folies Bergere, 32 Rue Richer (M: Cadet) 44.79.98.98. Famous club and entertaining show. A FAVORITE. Call for show schedule.

Hamman Club, 94 Rue d'Amsterdam. (M: Pl-Clichy) 55.07.80.05. Very late at night it starts to get "hot". Dance floor.

Hotel Amour, 8 Rue Navarin (M: St-Georges) 48.78.31.80. Book one of the 20 rooms upstairs that are available by the hour. Oh-so-trendy!

Le Limonaire, 21 Rue Bergère (M: Grands Boulevards) 45.23.33.33. Cabaret, dinner show, wine bar. Mix of young/old chansonniers.

L'Olympia, 28 Blvd des Capucines (M: Opéra) 55.27.10.00. Celebrated concert hall. Call ahead for entertainment listings.

Theatre Edouard VII, 10 Pl Edouard VII (M: Opéra) 47.42.59.92. Enjoy dinner at Café Guitry inside before the play Filled with theatre posters, and serves traditional, moderately-priced meals.

My Special Travel Notes

9

My Special Travel Notes

9

10e. Canal St. Martin, Magenta

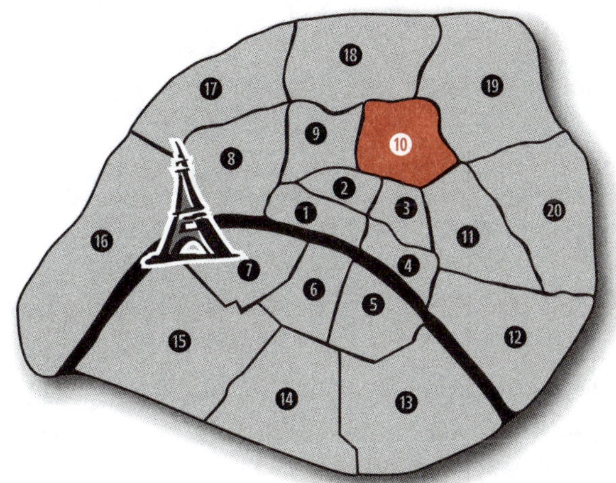

Visit **Pinacothèque de Paris** exhibit space.

Walk the **Quai de Valmy,** along the **Canal St. Martin.** Shop at **Antoine et Lili.**

Enjoy two classics: **Brasserie Flo** and **Brasserie Julien.** And one modern: **Chez Prune.**

MAJOR METROS:

- GARE DU NORD
- GARE DE L'EST
- STRASBOURG ST-DENIS
- CHATEAU D'EAU
- POISSONNIERE
- LOUIS BLANC

10e. Canal St. Martin, Magenta

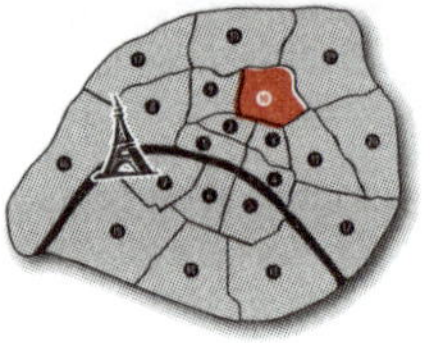

DIVERSIONS:

Pinacothèque de Paris, 30 bis, Rue de Paradis (M: Château d'Eau or Gare de L'Est) 47.70.64.30. M-F. Private exhibition space showing eclectic series of international artists from privately owned collections, housed in the former Baccarat Crystal Muséum. Call. Admission €12/ €4.50 for English audio guides. Museum restaurant under the direction of famous chef Alain Ducasse.

Canal St. Martin - Walk along Quai de Valmy (M: Jaures). A FAVORITE. Walk south to Port d l'Arsenal in 4e.

Couvent des Récollets, 148 Rue du Faubourg St-Martin (M: Gare de L'Est) Arts and architecture center with garden and café. Half the space is international artists and the other is bookstore specializing in architecture and photography. 11a-7p (2p-7p on weekends.) Closed Monday.

Fondation Icar, 159 Quai de Valmy (M: Jaures) 53.26.36.61. Institute for Co-Opéra-tion of Arts & Research. Call for events.

Gare du Nord and **Gare de l'Est:** Major RER and train terminals.

Passage Industrie: This is an area where you can find any imaginable hair salon product- especially low-priced products not available in U.S. It runs east and west, between Rue du Faubourg and Blvd de Strasbourg, near (M: Château d'Eau).

10

Square St. Laurent (near Gare de l'Est) and **Jardin Villemin** enter from Rue des Recollets, which continues east to Canal St. Martin.

SUPERLATIVES:

Classic dining: Chez Michel, 10 Rue de Belzunce (M: Gare du Nord) 44.53.06.20. Chef Thierry Breton makes sublime contemporary food. Closed Sunday.

Hippest "troquet": Le Martel, 3 Rue Martel (M: Château d'Eau) 47.70.67.56. French and North African cuisine enjoyed by a cosmopolitan crowd.

Music: New Morning, 7-9 Rue des Petites Ecuries (M: Château d'Eau) 45.23.51.41. Intimate club and well-known in Paris for live music. Call for schedule. Shows usually begin at 9pm.

Paris' Oldest Disco, Le Java, 105 Rue du Faubourg du Temple (M: Belleville) 42.02.20.52. Has global music, call for schedule.

SHOPS:

Antoine et Lili, 95 Quai de Valmy (M: Jacques Bonsergent) 40.37.41.55. Mod mix of hip fashion, jewelry, lots of fun and funky stuff. Pink fashion boutique, chartreuse garden store and yellow café serves light, ever-changing menu.

Creations Delphine, 206 Rue La Fayette (M: Louis Blanc) 40.35.36.30. Fine leather creations from Delphine Pariente.

Futurware Lab, 29 Rue Petites Ecuries (M: Château d'Eau) 42.23.66.08. Boutique. A FAVORITE.

GingerLyly, 33 Rue Bequrepaire (M: Jacques Bonsergent) 42.06.07.73. Local designers, with mix of vintage.

Jamin Puech, 61 Rue d'Hauteville (M: Poissonnière) 40.22.08.32. Handbag designers. Closed Sunday.

Le Verre Vole, 67 Rue Lancry (M: Jacques Bonsergent) 48.03.17.34. Bio-friendly wine bar and store. Another location in 11e.

Maison de la Porcelaine, 21 Rue de Paradis (M: Château d'Eau) 47.70.22.80.

OBA, 83 Quai de Valmy (M: Jacques Bonsergent) 42.40.39.91. Brazilian art and crafts.

OFR, 30 Rue Beaurepaire (M: République) 42.45.72.88. Avant-garde books.

Purple Institut, 9 Rue Pierre Dupont (M: Louis Blanc) 40.34.14.21. Founded by Purple magazine.

Stella Cadente, 93 Quai de Valmy (M: Jacques Bonsergent) 42.09.28.00. Pop art designer boutique

Zôa, 55 Rue de Lancry (M: Jacques Bonsergent) 44.52.01.67. Owner Alexandre Fiess offers one-of-a-kind, hardly-ever-worn vintage clothes for children, up to 12 years old. Antique baby clothes, retro furniture, antique toys.

RESTAURANTS: LES PLATS DU JOUR:

Auberge Pyrénèes-Cevennes, 106 Rue de la Folie Méricourt (M: Goncourt) 43.57.33.78. Good, classics like cassoulet and foie gras. $30. Closed Sunday.

Aux Deux Canards, 8 Rue Faubourg-Poissonniere (M: Bonne Nouvelle) 47.70.03.23. Owner Gerard Faesch serves exceptional regional meals with the freshest ingredients. €60. Friendly service.

Brasserie Flo, 7 Cour des Petites-Ecuries (M: Château d'Eau) 47.70.13.59. Classic trays of fresh seafood. Lively atmosphere.

Brasserie Julien, 16 Rue du Faubourg (M: Strasbourg St-Denis) 47.70.12.06. Art nouveau brasserie.

Café L'Atmosphere, 49 Rue Lucien-Sampaix (M: Jacques Bonsergent) 40.38.09.21. Reasonably priced wine. Outdoor tables. Call for music schedule on Sundays.

Chez Casimir, 6 Rue de Belzunce (M: Gare du Nord) 48.78.28.80. More casual annex of Chez Michel. Affordable wine list.

Chez Michel, 10 Rue de Belzunce (M: Gare du Nord) 44.53.06.20. Chef trained at Ritz and presents modern twists. Seafood is specialty. Good service. A FAVORITE. Closed Sunday.

10e. Canal St. Martin, Magenta

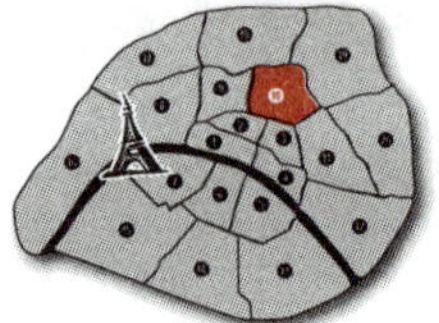

Chez Prune, 71 Quai de Valmy (M: Jacques Bonsergent) 42.41.30.47. Hip, relaxed bistro. Mixed eclectic menu. We enjoyed our lunch here. Open Sunday.

L'Ile Enchantée, 65 Blvd de la Villette (M: Belleville) 42.01.67.99. Newly renovated bar and bistro.

La Boca, 12 Rue de la Fidélité (M: Gare de l'Est) 53.24.69.70. Trendy.

La Grille, 80 Rue du Faubourg Poissoniere (M: Poissonniere) 47.70.89.73. Some say "the best Turbot" in all of Paris. Small, probably less than 20 tables. Closed Sunday.

La Madonnina, 10 Rue Marie et Louise (M: Goncourt) 42.01.25.26. Italian. Tables outside get filled in nice weather.

La Marine, 55 bis Quai de Valmy (M: Jacques Bonsergent) 42.39.69.81. Canal-side, unpretentious dining and café bar.

Le Martel, 3 Rue Martel (M: Château d'Eau) 47.70.67.56. French and North African cuisine. Cosmopolitan crowd.

Le Verre Vole, 67 Rue Lancry (M: Jacques Bonsergent) 48.03.17.34. Wine bar and store. Unsulphured, unfiltered wines. Charcuterie with €12 plat du jour. Closed Monday lunch.

10

BONNE SOIREE! PARIS AT NIGHT:

De La Ville Café, 34 Blvd Bonne Nouvelle (M: Bonne Nouvelle) 48.24.48.09. Trendy DJ's set the mood and tempo on the dance floor.

Hotel du Nord, 102 Quai Jemmapes (M: Gare de l'Est) 40.40.78.78. French fusion cuisine in trendy restaurant and nightclub.

La Fontaine, 20 Rue de la Grange aux Belle (M: Goncourt) 42.45.36.27. Jazz every night. Local crowd.

Le Java, 105 Rue du Faubourg de Temple (M: Belleville) 42.02.20.52. Disco.

New Morning, 7 & 9 Rue des Petites Ecuries (M: Château d'Eau) 45.23.51.41. Call for entertainment and show times. Live music.

Point Ephémère, 200 Quai de Valmy (M: Jaures) 40.34.02.48. Warehouse for concerts, exhibitions, dance studio – all create an eclectic atmosphere. Monthly ART DINNERS with guest speakers. Call to find out what's happening.

My Special Travel Notes

10

My Special Travel Notes

10

11e. Bastille, Republique et Voltaire

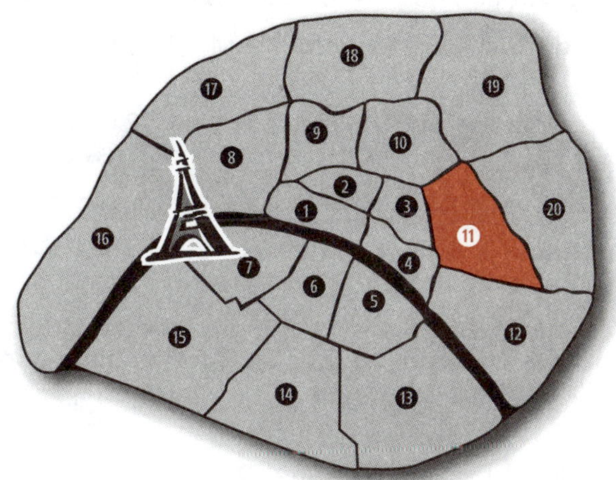

Hip, fun, historical and artsy. People-watch at **Pause Café Bastille.**

Marché Bastille is one of the best outdoor markets in Paris. On Saturdays, it becomes **Marché de la creation.**

Dine at **Blue Elephant** for the best Thai food, or go to **Mansouria** for the best couscous.

MAJOR METROS:

- BASTILLE
- BRÉGUET-SABIN
- RICHARD LENOIR
- VOLTAIRE
- CHARONNE
- RÉPUBLIQUE
- OBERKAMPF
- PARMENTIER

11e. Bastille, Republique et Voltaire

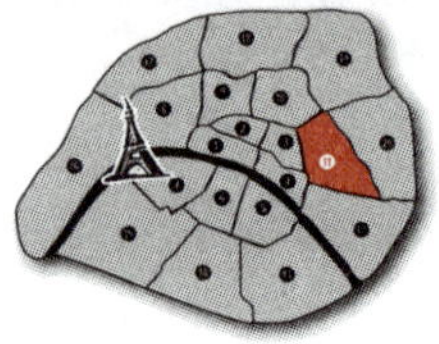

DIVERSIONS:

This "hip" arrondissement is always fun to walk.

Antique and Arts district: walk Rue de la Roquette, Rue du Lappe, Rue de Charonne, Rue Keller, Rue Faubourg St-Antoine (M: Bastille or M: Ledru-Rollin).

Cirque d'Hiver, 110 Rue Amelot (M: Filles du Calvaire) 47.00.28.81. Famous "**clown bar**".

Chocolate Factory: La Petite Fabrique, 12 Rue St-Sabin (M: Bréguet-Sabin) 48.05.82.02. 40 kinds of chocolate bars. Tues-Sat.

Gymnase Club, 9 Rue de Malte (M: République) 47.00.80.95. $23 Day pass.

Hip streets: Rue de Charonne (M: Charonne) and Ave de la République (M: République) Rue Moret (M: Couronnes) for vintage clothes and accessories.

Musée Edith Piaf, 5 Rue Crespin du Gast (M: Ménilmontant) 43.55.52.72. Life-sized model of this famous "swallow". Mon-Thu afternoons.

O Château, 100 Rue de la Folie Méricourt (M: Goncourt) 44.73.97.80. Olivier Magny offers intimate and entertaining wine classes and tastings on French wines, in English. Call to reserve and find out where your tasting will be held because locations vary throughout Paris. Sample tastings: Plaisirs du Vin is €50 per person, two hours and the French Wine Discovery is €40 per person for 1 € hours. "For pleasure, not pressure."

11

Richard Lenoir Market also known **Marché Bastille** (M: Bastille) A FAVORITE. Outdoors market Thur/ Sunday. 9a - 1p. **Place de la Bastille** to Rue St-Sabin. On Saturdays 9:30a-7p it becomes **Marché de la Creation,** an artists' market filled with painters, photographers, sculptors, via Rue St-Sabin. and more.

Theâtre de la Bastille, 76 Rue de la Roquette (M: Bastille) 43.57.42.14. Inventive contemporary dance and theatre. Get tickets 30 minutes before performances via Box Office by Phone only. M-F.

SUPERLATIVES:

Best Algerian patisserie: La Bague de Kenza, 106 Rue St-Maur (M: Rue St-Maur) 43.14.93.15. Almond paste, honey and pistachio desserts, among others. Tea room.

Another best patisserie: Les Noces d'Or, 59 Ave Philippe August (M: Philippe August) 48.50.74.77.

Best wine list: Café du Passage, 12 Rue de Charonne (M: Bastille) 49.29.97.64. Over 300 choices for wine. Good charcuterie and salads. Taped jazz. Popular.

Best Café East of Café Flore: Pause Café Bastille, 41 Rue de Charonne (M: Ledru-Rollin or Charonne) 48.06.80.33.

Best couscous: Mansouria, 11 Rue Faidherbe (M: Faidherbe Chaligny) 43.71.00.16. Ms Fatéma Hal wrote the book on couscous! Elegant. Try the mourouzia lamb dish. €70.

Best Thai: Blue Elephant, decorated like a Thai village. See Restaurants.

Best oysters in Paris: L'Ecailler du Bistrot, See Restaurants.

Best "night" beauty bar: Viseart Beauty Bar, 72 bis, Rue Jean Pierre Timbaud (M: Courennes) 43.55.43.54. Cosmetics and beauty-by-night. 8p - 11p.

Most filmed cobblestone street in Paris: Cour Damoye, (M: Bastille) Between Pl Bastille and Rue Daval, it is lined with art galleries, gift shops, and even a wine cave. Closed to the general public at night. 9a-8p.

More hard-to-find wines: Les Domaines Qui Montent, 136 Blvd Voltaire (M: Voltaire) 43.56.89.15. Wine bar and plats du jour.

SHOPS:

44 degrees, 59 Rue Jean-Pierre Timbaud (M: Couronnes) 56.98.18.44. Boutique.

Anne Willi, 13 Rue Keller (M: Ledru-Rollin) 48.06.74.06. Trendy fashion boutique.

Come On Eline, 16 Rue des Taillandiers (M: Ledru-Rollin) 43.38.12.11. Three floors vintage clothes, accessories. Moderate prices for Dior, YSL. 11:30a-8:30p M-F. 4p-8p Sunday.

Des Petits Hauts, 5 Rue Keller (M: Ledru-Rollin) 43.38.14.39. "Some little tops."

FNAC, 4 Pl de la Bastille (M: Bastille) 43.48.30.90.Music cds, videos. Huge international selection.

Franck Sorbier, 6 Rue Jean-Pierre Timboud (M: Couronnes) 43.38.02.15. Haute couture.

Gaëlle Barre, 17 Rue Keller (M: Ledru-Rollin) 43.14.68.87. Ladieswear.

Galerie Liliane et Michel Durand-Dessert, 28 Rue de Lappe (M: Bastille) 48.06.92.23. Art gallery. Tues-Sat.

Galerie Patrick Seguin, 5 Rue Taillandiers (M: Ledru-Rollin) 47.00.32.35. Antiques and art.

Grand Monde Galerie, Cour Damoye, 12 Pl de la Bastille (M: Bastille) 48.05.51.30. Contemporary posters featuring fashion and advertising. Call for shop hours.

Habitat, 10 Pl de la Replublique (M: Republique) 48.07.13.14. Contemporary furniture.

Ingrek-Be, 17 Rue Keller (M: Bastille) 43.14.78.78. Limited editions from avant-garde young designers.

Isabel Marant, 16 Rue de Charonne (M: Ledru-Rollin) 49.29.71.55. Drapey and flattering designs that are hard to find in U.S.

La Bague de Kenza, 106 Rue St-Maur (M: Rue St-Maur) 43.14.93.15. Patisserie. Almond paste, honey and pistachio desserts, among others. Tea room.

11e. Bastille, Republique et Voltaire

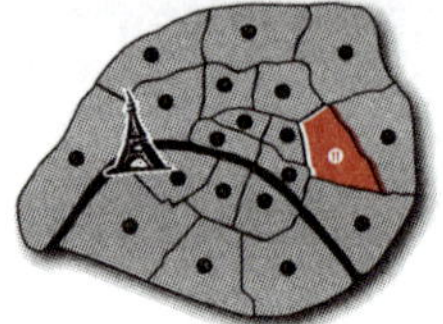

La Cave de L'Insolité, 50 Rue de la Folie-Mericourt (M: Bréguet-Sabin) 53.36.08.33. Bio-wines, glassware collection.

La Petite Fabrique, 12 Rue St-Sabin (M: Bréguet-Sabin) 48.05.82.02. 40 kinds of chocolate bars. Open Tues-Sat.

Le 18, 18 Rue Keller (M: Bastille) 48.05.55.62. Fashion "themes" change monthly, according to what's hot and trendy.

Le Verre Volé, 38 Rue Oberkampf (M: Oberkampf) 43.14.99.46. Organic wines and spirits. Another location in 10e.

Les Fées d'Herbe, 23 Rue Faidherbe (M: Faidherbe-Chaligny) 43.70.14.76. Whimsical flower shop.

Les Noces d'Or, 59 Ave Philippe August (M: Philippe August) 48.50.74.77. Delicious pastries.

Librairie Amzallag, 78 Rue de la Roquette (M: Philippe Auguste) 47.00.85.96. Great selection of art books.

Louison, 20 Rue St. Nicholas (M: Ledru-Rollin) 43.44.02.62. Handbags, travel accessories from designer who used to work for Hogan bags.

Marhaba, 30 Rue Faidherbe (M: Faidherbe-Chaligny) 43.70.59.44. Owner-designer Soraya Lolli presents Moroccan tunics, slippers, soaps, tea sets.

Metal Pointus, 9 Rue Charonne (M: Bastille) 47.00.81.60. Costume jewelry.

Michel Cousin's L'Autre Boulange, 43 Rue de Montreuil (M: Faidherbe-Chaligny) 43.72.86.04. Cousin bakes organic breads in wood-fired oven.

Mixing Club, 42 Rue de la Folie-Mericourt (M: Breguet Sabin) 43.55.02.74. Decorators. Household accessories.

Nuits de Satin, 9 Rue Oberkampf (M: Filles du Calvaire) 43.57.65.05. Classic lingerie.

Onze, 11 Rue Oberkampf (M: Filles du Calvaire) 43.55.32.11. Youngish Indie clothing labels.

Papeterie Saint Sabin, 16 Rue St-Sabin (M: Bréguet-Sabin) 47.00.78.63. Elegant stationery, fine French papers.

Yves Gratas, 9 Rue Oberkampf (M: Filles du Calvaire) 49.29.00.53. His jewelry designs can be found at Agnes B. and Marithe et Francois Girbaud. Closed Sun/Monday.

RESTAURANTS: LES PLATS DU JOUR:

A l'Ami Pierre, 5 Rue de la Main d'Or (M: Ledru-Rollin) 47.00.17.35. This friendly bistro takes you back in time and serves big helpings of classic Southwestern French fare. The ultimate cheese plate. Closed Sunday.

Au Vieux Chene, 7 Rue du Dahomey (M: Faidherbe-Chaligny) 43.71.67.69. Chef Stephane Chavassus offers fresh menu daily in bright dining room and zinc bar. Reserve. Closed Sunday.

Bistrot Paul Bert, 18 Rue Paul-Bert (M: Faidherbe-Chaligny) 43.72.24.01. Blackboard menu. Good traditional fare. Get the frites (French fries)!

Blue Elephant, 43-45 Rue de la Roquette (M: Bastille) 47.00.42.00. Tasty Thai. Decorated like a Thai village. Higher prices. Open Sunday.

Café Charbon, 109 Rue Oberkampf. (M: Parmentier) 43.57.55.13. Original hangout of the artsy crowd. Traditional menu. Serves brunch. Open Sunday.

Café de l'Industrie, 16 Rue St Sabin (M: Bréguet-Sabin) 47.00.13.53. Look at celebrities' pix on wall. Convivial bistro fare.

Cartet, 62 Rue de Malte (M: République) 48.05.17.65. Recent good reports. Priced right, the faded décor is deceiving. Good food, good service, friendly. No credit cards. Closed Sunday.

Casa Hidalgo, 17 Rue de la Forge Royale (M: Faidherbe-Chaligny) 40.24.10.54. Spanish restaurant, tapas, paella at low prices.

Casa Vigata, 44 Rue Leon Frot (M: Charonne) 43.56.38.66. Sicilian food from chef/owner Roberta who prepares various fresh pasta sauces in cozy space. Open Sunday.

Chardenoux, 1 Rue Jules Valles (M: Charonne) 43.71.49.52. Bistro built in 1900 with zinc bar and engraved glass partitions. New owners and new chef this year. Generous portions. Closed Sat./Sunday.

Chez Imogene, 25 Rue Jean Pierre Timbaud (M: Oberkampf) 48.07.14.59. Cute creperie.

Chez Paul, 13 Rue de Charonne (M: Bastille/Ledru-Rollin) 47.00.34.57. Classic seasonal bistro dishes.

Chez Philippe, 106 Rue de la Folie-Mericort (M: St Ambroise) 43.57.33.78. Cozy, with beamed ceilings. Menu includes paella and cassoulet. $30. Reserve. Closed Sat/Sunday.

Chez Ramulaud, 269 Rue du Faubourg-St-Antoine (M: Nation) 43.72.23.29. Popular wine bar/bistro with live music, Sunday brunch. Highly-rated €28 dinner. Reserve.

Jacques Melac/Bistrot a Vins Melac, 42 Rue Leon-Frot (M: Charonne) 43.70.59.27. Tiny neighborhood wine bar and restaurant. Friendly. A FAVORITE.

Khun Akorn, 8 Ave de Taillebourg (M: Avron) 43.56.20.03. Delicate Thai cuisine in spacious setting.

L'Aiguière, 37 bis, Rue de Montreuil (M: Faidherbe-Chaligny) 43.72.42.32. Traditional French in cozy and romantic dining room. Extensive wine list. Closed Sunday.

11e. Bastille, Republique et Voltaire

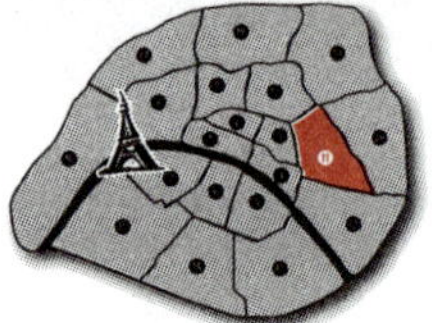

L'Assiette du Purple, 35 Rue de Faidherbe (M: Charonne) 43.71.65.30. Since 1923. Stylish, contemporary French. Closed Sunday.

L'Autre Café, 62 Rue Jean Pierre Timbaud (M: Parmentier) 40.21.03.07. Neighborhood café, snacks.

L'Ecailler du Bistrot, 22 Rue Paul-Bert (M: Faidherbe-Chaligny)43.72.76.77. Seafood. Reasonable prices. Friendly.

La Fabrique, 3 Rue du Faubourg St Antoine (M: Bastille/ St-Paul) 43.07.67.07. Reservations advised after 10:30 M-Sat.

La Main d'Or, 133 Rue du Faubourg St-Antoine (M: Faidherbe-Chaligny) 44.68.04.68. Traditional Corsican food and wine. Renovated with air purifiers and simple décor. Closed Sunday.

La Muse Vin, 101 Rue de Charonne (M: Charonne) Wine shop and tiny bistro with small dishes and daily dinner specials. Sample wines from smaller vineyards.

Le C'Amelot, 50 Rue Amelot (M: Chemin Vert) 43.55.54.04. Chef Varnier offers innovative meals. Pre-fixe no-choice dinners. Cozy.

Le Marsangy, 73 Ave Parmentier (M: Parmentier) 47.00.94.25. Small and comfortable with 3-course dinners for under $40. Affordable wine list, too. Closed Sunday.

Le Passage des Carmagnoles, 18 Passage de la Bonne Graine (M: Ledru-Rollin) 47.00.73.30. Good food, warm welcome. Closed Sunday.

11

Le Petit Keller, 13 bis, Rue Keller (M: Bastille) 47.00.12.97. Unbeatable prices.

Le Réfectoire, 80 Blvd Richard Lenoir (M: St Ambroisie) 48.06.44.85. Lunch and dinner 7/7. Locals play boules in park across the street.

Le Repaire de Cartouche, 99 Rue Amelot (M: St-Sebastian Froissart) 47.00.25.86. Classic bistro, great value. Regional menu.

Le Temps au Temps, 13 Rue Paul-Bert (M: Faidherbe-Chaligny) 43.79.63.40. Young Sylvain Endra and his wife welcome diners at precisely 8 pm to enjoy Lyonnaise cooking with a twist. Set menu, €30. Closed Sunday.

Le Villaret, 13, Rue Ternaux (M: Parmentier) 43.57.89.76. Inventive twists on classic French. Good wine list, too. Great value. A FAVORITE.

Le Vin de Zinc, 25 Rue Oberkampf (M: Oberkampf) 48.06.28.23. Wine bar showcasing small producers. Prix fixe lunch €12 and dinner for two €60. Closed Sun/Mon.

Les Amognes, 243 Rue du Faubourg St-Antoine (M: Faidherbe-Chaligny) 43.72.73.05. Inventive meals, fun, friendly, and affordable. Closed Sunday. A FAVORITE.

Les Domaines Qui Montent, 136 Blvd Voltaire (M: Voltaire) 43.56.89.15. Wine bar and plats du jour.

Les Funambules, 12 Rue Faidherbe (M: Faidherbe-Chaligny) 43.70.83.70. Chef Tony Delsuc, from Plaza Athenée serves seafood.

Les Jumeaux, 73 Rue Amelot (M: Chemin Vert) 43.14.27.00. Shake hands with the twins who are the cook and maitre d' who offer delightful service and combine Asian and French flavors.

Mansouria, 11 Rue Faidherbe (M: Faidherbe-Chaligny) 43.71.00.16. Ms Fatéma Hal wrote the book on couscous! Elegant. Try the mourouzia lamb dish. €70.

Paris Main d'Or, 133 Rue du Faubourg-St-Antoine (M: Ledru-Rollin) 44.68.04.68. Convivial Corsican. Closed Sunday.

Pause Cafe Bastille, 41 Rue de Charonne (M: Charonne) 48.06.80.33. Ordinary food, not-so-ordinary ambiance.

Restaurant Astier, 44 Rue Jean Pierre Timbaud (M: Couronnes) 43.57.16.35. Frederic also owns Café Moderne. The chef trained with Yannick Alléno of the Meurice and prepares classic seasonal French food and the sommelier offers a diverse wine list.

BONNE SOIREE: PARIS AT NIGHT:

Boteca, 131 Rue Oberkampf (M: Ménilmontant) 43.57.15.47. Club. Has food, too.

Chez Raymonde, 119 Ave Parmentier (M: Parmentier/Goncourt) 43.55.26.27. A truly French soirée where everyone joins the dinner-dancing. Prix fixe up to €38 on weekends. 7p-1am. Closed Sunday.

Favela Chic, 18 Rue du Faubourg du Temple (M: République) 40.21.38.14. Tapas and music bar.

La Casbah, 18 Rue de la Forge Royale (M: Ledru-Rollin) 43.71.71.89. DJ / live local music.

Le Balajo dance hall at 9 Rue de Lappe. (M: Bastille) 47.00.07.87.

Le Mecano, 99 Rue Oberkampf (M: Parmentier) 40.21.35.28. Nostalgic bar, shabby-chic décor, young bobo crowd who love the scene under the chandeliers. 9-2a.

Le Nouveau Casino, 10 Rue Oberkampf (M: Oberkampf) 43.57.57.40. Club annex of popular Café Charbon has live music.

Le Réservoir, 16 Rue de la Forge Royale (M: Ledru-Rollin) 43.56.39.60 Popular nightspot w/ music. Jazz brunch Sunday. 12:30p.

Le Sans-sanz, 49 Rue du Faubourg St-Antoine (M: Ledru-Rollin) 44.75.78.78. Food upstairs. Open til 2 am, DJ spins, club scene.

Le Scherkhan, 144 Rue Oberkampf (M: Filles du Calvaire) 43.57.29.34. Also has food. Popular hangout among fashionistas.

11e. Bastille, Republique et Voltaire

Megalo Bar, 6 Rue de Lappe (M: Bastille) 48.05.05.12. The bouncer smiles back at you and super loud music appeals to the crowd. 6p-2a.

Satellit, 44 Rue de la Folie Mericourt (M: Oberkampf) 47.00.48.87. Live music, concerts. World music bar/club. Call first.

the bottle shop, 5 Rue Trousseau (M: Ledru-Rollin) 43.14.28.04. Same owners as Lizard Lounge.

Wax, 15 Rue Daval (M: Bréquet-Sabin) 40.21.16.16. After 9 pm.

My Special Travel Notes

11

My Special Travel Notes

11

12e. Bercy

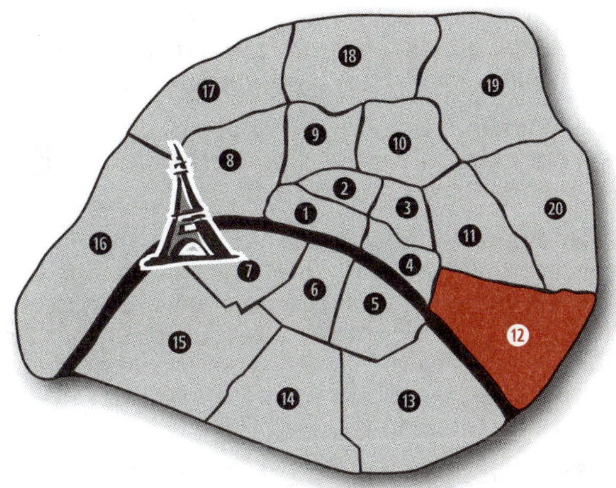

See filmmaking history at **Cinémathèque Francaise.** This stunning building was designed by Frank Gehry.

Visit a typical Paris market such as **Pucés d'Aligre.**

Enjoy the plats du Jour at **Chai 33** or **Le Train Bleu.**

MAJOR METROS:

- RÉPUBLIQUE
- GARE DU LYON
- LEDRU-ROLLIN
- BERCY
- REUILLY
- PORTE DE CHARENTON
- PORTE DE VINCENNES

12e. Bercy

DIVERSIONS:

Bercy Village (M: Cour Saint-Emilion) Stone warehouses rehabbed into shops and restaurants, Also known as **Cour Saint Emilion. Parc de Bercy,** (M: Bercy) has fountains, lawns, garden plots, plus cobblestone streets named after wine regions with shops and cafés.

Bois de Vincennes (M: Porte-Doree) **Château de Vincennes** 44.75.20.10. (M: Château Vincennes) Grand park.

Casse-Croute à L'Opéra, Studio Bastille, 120 Rue de Lyon (M: Bastille) 40.10.17.89. Enjoy light snacks/sandwiches and free concerts from 1p-2p performed by Opéra National de Paris, on Thursdays.

Cinémathèque Française, 51 Rue Bercy (M: Bercy) 71.19.33.33. Cutting-edge and sleek Frank Gehry building with giant nude males etched in the windows along the entrance gives you a sense of what's inside. Exhibitions on the 2nd and 7th floors. A must for cinema lovers, you will see an Oscar award, a gown that Vivien Leigh wore in Gone With The Wind, movie clips, set designs, and more. Four movie theatres show film classics. France's Film Library is also housed here. 12p - 7p. $4. A FAVORITE. Closed Tues.

La Maison Rouge has opened **L'Intime,** 10 Blvd de la Bastille (M: Bastille) 40.01.08.81. Private art space in 15 rooms. Call for exhibitions.

Parc Floral de Paris, Esplanade du Château de Vincennes. (M: Château Vincennes).

Passarelle Simone-de-Beauvoir is the 37th and newest bridge in Paris. It connects Parc de Bercy and Bibliothèque Nationale de France Mitterrand. Pedestrians use the upper arched level and cyclists use lower pathway.

Pucés d' Aligre (M: Ledru-Rollin) Tues-Sunday. 8a-1p. Antique flea market and food market. Stroll along Rue de Cotte.

Viaduc des Arts/Promenade Plantée is a raised walkway above Ave Daumesnil.

SUPERLATIVES:

Best décor: Le Train Bleu, See Restaurants.

Best frites (fries): A-I Biche au Bois, 45 Ave Ledru-Rollin (M: Ledru-Rollin) 43.43.34.38

Best organic bread: Boulangerie Bio, 5 Pl d'Aligre (M: Ledru-Rollin) 43.45.46.60.

SHOPS:

Arom, 73 Ave Ledru-Rollin (M: Ledru-Rollin) 43.46.82.59. Poetic flower shop.

Bookstorming, 10 bis Blvd Bastille (M: Bastille) 43.43.02.76. Bookshop.

Boulangerie Bio, 5 Pl d'Aligre (M: Ledru-Rollin) 43.45.46.60. Popular organic bakery.

Maison du la RATP, 54 Quai de la Râpée (M: Qaui de la Râpée) Rail transport.

Nathalie Dumeix, 10 Rue Theophile Roussel (M: Ledru-Rollin) 43.46.00.22. Dressmaker. Haute couture.

Serge Amoruso Design, 13 Rue Abel (M: Gare de Lyon) 43.45.14.10. Fine leather and travel goods. You can watch them at work.

Surcouf, 139 Ave Daumesnil (M: Dugommier) 53.33.20.00. Computer supplies. Closed Mondays.

RESTAURANTS: LES PLATS DU JOUR:

A la Biche En Bois, 45 Ave Ledru-Rollin (M: Gare de Lyon) 43.43.34.38. Mostly meat, seasonal game. Gets crowded, so make reservations. Closed Sunday.

Au Trou Gascon, 40 Rue Taine (M: Daumesnil) 43.44.34.26. Great meals from chef Alain Dutournier. Cassoulet, foie gras. €100 for two. A FAVORITE. Closed Sunday.

Chai 33, 33 Cour Saint-Emilion (M: Cour St-Emilion) 53.44.01.01. New wine bar/restaurant from Thierry Beguet of Buddha Bar.

Comme Cochons, 135 Rue de Charenton (M: Reuilly-Diderot) 43.42.43.36. Inventive, original meals, prix fixe. Closed Sunday

L'Ebauchoir, 43 Rue de Céteaux (M: Ledru-Rollin) 43.42.49.31. Popular with artsy crowd. Traditional French food. Warm, artsy, atmosphere. Reserve. Closed Sunday.

L'Oulette, 15 Pl Lachambeaudie (M: Cour St-Emilion) 40.02.02.12. Good cassoulet from chef Marcel Baudis. Pleasant and warm welcome. Expensive. Closed Sunday.

La Gazetta, 29 Rue de Cotte (M: Ledru-Rollin) 43.47.47.05. Mediterranean flavors.

La Saint Amarante, 4 Rue Biscornet (M: Bastille) 43.43.00.08. Christophe Dupire trained at Ritz and serves traditional French fare. Somewhat drab decor. Closed Sat/Sunday.

Le Duc de Richelieu, 5 Rue Parrot (M: Gare de Lyon) 43.43.05.64. Convenient location near train station. Traditional meals by the former manager of Le Gavroche. Closed Sunday.

Le Square Trousseau, 1 Rue Antoine-Vollon (M: Ledru-Rollin) 43.43.06.00. Belle époque bistro. Popular with fashion crowd. Trendy and somewhat touristy.

Le Train Bleu, Gare de Lyon, Pl Louis Armand (M: Gare du Lyon) 43.43.09.06. Rococo design. New chef.

Les Grandes Marches, 6 Pl de la Bastille (M: Bastille) 43.42.90.32. Brasserie with striking décor and mixed menu, sometimes slow service.

Les Zygomates, 7 Rue de Capri (M: Daumesnil) 40.19.93.04. Friendy, affordable, freshly prepared traditional French. Popular. Closed Sunday.

Sardegna à Tavola, 1 Rue de Cotte (M: Ledru-Rollin) 44.75.03.28. Attracts a crowd with their Italian regional meals at good prices. A FAVORITE. Reserve. Closed Sunday.

Viaduc Café, 43 Ave Daumesnil (M: Gare du Lyon) 44.74.70.70. Jazz brunch gets crowded on Sundays. Service til 4pm. $80 for two with wine.

RESTAURANTS: GASTRONOMIQUE:

Au Pressoir, 257 Ave Daumesnil (M: Michel-Bizot) 43.44.38.21. Gastronomic feasts. Impressive wine list. Closed Sunday.

BONNE SOIREE! PARIS AT NIGHT:

Barrio Latino, 46 Rue du Faubourg St-Antoine (M: Ledru-Rollin) 55.78.84.75. Same owners as Buddha Bar. Late night dancing and tapas.

China Club, 50 Rue de Charenton (M: Ledru-Rollin) 43.43.82.02. Three level night-club with Chinese restaurant.

Opéra Bastille, 120 Rue de Lyon, Pl de la Bastille (M: Bastille) 40.01.17.89. Show time is 7:30p with 3p matinees. €5 standing-room-only tickets go on sale 45 minutes before show times. A FAVORITE.

My Special Travel Notes

12

My Special Travel Notes

12

13e. Place d'Italie

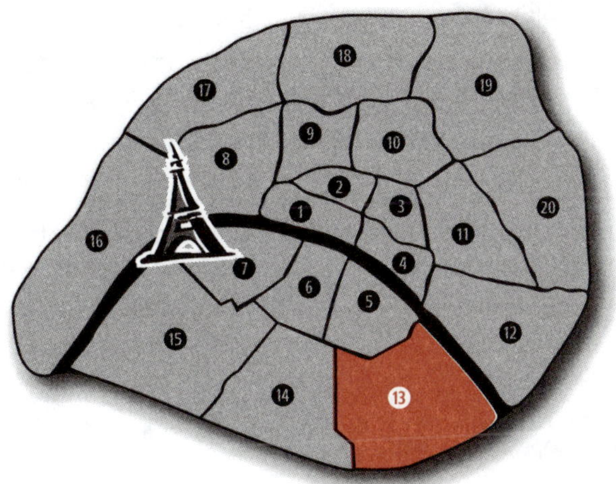

Rue Louise-Weiss and **La Butte aux Cailles** are two neighborhoods to explore.

Spend time at the exhibitions at **Bibliothèque Nationale de France Mitterand.**

Dance along the Seine and mingle with Parisians on a restored barge boat, **Batofar Quai Mauriac** or **Guingette Pirate.**

MAJOR METROS:

- NATIONALE
- QUAI DE LA GARE
- PORTE D'IVRY
- GOBELINS
- PLACE D'ITALIE
- CORVISART
- GLACIÈRE

13

13e. Place d'Italie

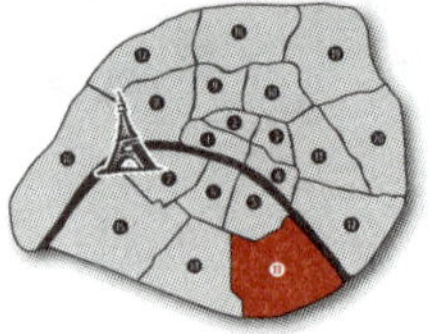

FAMOUS SIGHTS:

Bibliothèque Nationale de France Mitterrand, 11 Quai François Mauriac (M: Quai de la Gare) 53.79.53.79. Closed Monday. The National Library, call for exhibitions. €3.30. Closed Sat. morning/Sunday/Monday.

DIVERSIONS:

Rue Louise-Weiss is another "trendy neighborhood" to discover local artists, galleries, collectors.

Walk La Butte-aux-Cailles neighborhood (M: Corvisart) Re-emerging area. Rue Bobillot, Rue de la Butte aux Cailles, Rue Alphand, Rue Barrault, Place Paul Verlaine. Many shops and cafes are closed on Sundays. Also, near Place d'Italie, where Rue de la Butte-aux-Cailles intersects with Rue des Cinq Diamants, you will see a "leaning building" and Rue Pere Guerain is fun. A FAVORITE.

Cité Floral area is where the streets are all named for flowers (eg. Rue des Orchides) It's near Pl de Rung, where Rue Brillat-Savarin intersects with Rue Auguste-Lancon (M: Cité Universitaire).

Enjoy Art Deco and Moderniste houses, including Le Corbusier, Villa Planeix, 24 boulevard Massena (M: Porte d'Ivry).

Part of this arrondissement includes Paris' **Chinatown.**

SUPERLATIVES:

Largest organic food restaurant: BIO Art. See Restaurants.

More bread: Le Grenier á Pain, 52 Ave d'Italie (M: Place d'Italie) 45.80.16.36. Traditional French baker.

SHOPS:

Agatha, 30 Pl Italie (M: Pl d'Italie) 45.80.05.29. Costume jewelry. Popular. Several locations in Paris.

Air de Paris, 32 Rue Louise-Weiss (M: Bibliothèque) 44.23.02.77. Gallery.

Kateo, 70 Rue Javelot (M: Tolbiac) 45.70.78.20. Young designer fashions.

Kreo, 11 Rue Louise-Weiss (M: Chevaleret). 53.60.18.42. Retro inspired furniture design. Look for other galleries along Rue Louise-Weiss, known as Association Scène Est, among them is Air de Paris and Jennifer Flay galleries.

Les Abeilles, 21 Rue de la Butte-aux-Cailles (M: Corvisart) 45.81.43.48. Honey! Tues-Sat. 11a-7p.

Printemps - Italie, 30 Ave d'Italie (M: Place d'Italie) 40.78.17.17. Department store.

RESTAURANTS: LES PLATS DU JOUR:

Anacréon, 53 Blvd St Marcel (M: Les Gobelins) 43.31.71.18. Good value. Closed Sunday.

Au Petit Marguery, 9 Blvd de Port-Royal (M: Les Gobelins) 43.31.58.59. Veteran waiters, new ownership. Bistro classics. Make sure you order soufflé for dessert.

BIO Art, 3 Quai Francois Mauriac (M: Bibliothèque Francois Mitterand) 45.85.66.88. Health-conscious crowd enjoys modern preparations of organic food. Closed Sunday.

Chez Gladines, 30 Rue des Cinq Diamante (M: Corvisart) 45.80.70.10. Younger crowd enjoys their Basque specialties, such as potatoes oozing with melted cheese.

Chez Paul, 22 Rue de la Butte aux Cailles (M: Corvisart) 45.89.22.11. Best restaurant for pot-au-feu.

Djoon, 22 Blvd Vinvent Auriol (M: Quai de la Gare) 45.70.83.49. Ultra modern and hip with polished cement floors. Classic French with twists. Moderate. Closed Sunday.

L'Aimant du Sud, 40 Blvd Arago (M: Glacière/Les Gobelins) 47.07.33.57. Mediterranean food. Good Southwest wine. Large terrace makes reservations necessary in summer. Closed Sunday.

L'Avant Gout, 26 Rue Bobillot (M: Corvisart) 53.80.24.00. Good. Chef Christophe Beaufort presents delicious meals at bargain prices. Reserve in advance. A FAVORITE. Closed Sun.

L'Ourcine, 92 Rue Broca (M: Gobelins) 47.07.13.65. Simple, modern bistro with regional Basque meals at moderate prices. Closed Sunday.

La Pince à Sucre, 57 Rue Corvisart (M: Corvisart) 43.31.81.73. Simple, small, good. Closed Sunday.

Le Terroir, 11 Blvd Arago (M: Les Gobelins) 47.07.36.99. Good hearty and tasty meals served with regional wines and a smile. Moderately-high prices. Closed Sunday.

Les Cailloux, 58 Rue des Cinq Diamants (M: Corvisart) 45.80.15.80. Popular and inexpensive so gets noisy. Generous portions of pasta. Closed Sunday.

O'Jules, 2 Rue Bobillot (M: Pl d'Italie) 45.80.60.33. Trendy Coste-like atmosphere with good terrace and people watching on Place d'Italie.

Pearl, 53 bis Blvd Arago (M: Les Gobelins) 47.07.58.57. Trendy, trying for ultra chic in both the décor and meals, mostly global.

Tandem, 10 Rue de la Butte aux Cailles (M: Corvisart) 45.80.38.69. Philippe and his brother own this small bar a vins specializing in au naturelle – no sulphites and artisanal selections. A FAVORITE. Closed Sunday.

13e. Place d'Italie

Temps des Cerises, 18-20 Rue de la Butte aux Cailles (M: Corvisart) 45.89.69.48. True neighborhood restaurant with chalkboard menu.

BONNE SOIREE! PARIS AT NIGHT:

Batofar, 11 Porte de la Gare. Opposite 11 Quai Francois Mauriac.(M: Bibliothèque Nationale) 56.29.10.00. Call for music/dancing schedule. No credit cards. Popular barge boat, completely restored with solid sound system. 4am on weekends.

Guinguette Pirate, Porte de la Gare, facing 11 Quai Mauriac. 56. 29.10.20. Call to confirm music schedule. Take Metro to Madeleine (8e) and then board the meteor metro #14 line for 12 minutes to Quai de la Gare for great summer evenings along the Seine to mingle with Parisians, dancing/nightlife:

Guinguette Pirate, Quai de la Gare. 44.24.89.89 for local listings.

La Folie en Tete, 33 Rue de la Butte-aux-Cailles (M: Corvisart) 45.80.65.99. Popular with students. DJ and live music. Call.

Oya, 25 Rue de la Reine Blanche (M: Les Gobelins) 47.07.59.59. Over 200 board games.

13

My Special Travel Notes

13

My Special Travel Notes

13

14e. Montparnasse

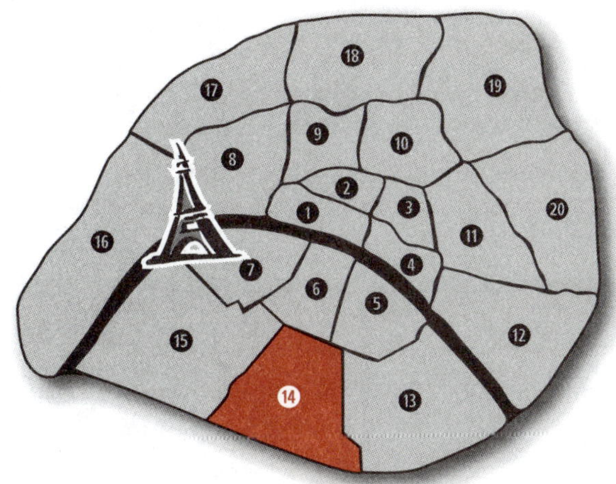

We like the **Pucés de Vanves** flea market.

Sit at **Le Select** and watch all the tourists and Parisians stroll by.

Call to attend a wine class at **Decouverte du Vin.** Or, relax in the wild garden after enjoying the exhibition at **Fondation Cartier.**

Dine at **La Cerisaie** for excellent "Sud Ouest" meals or at **Le Duc** for fine seafood.

MAJOR METROS:
- MONTPARNASSE
- EDGAR QUINET
- VAVIN
- DENFERT-ROCHEREAU
- ALÉSIA
- PORTE D'ORLÉANS
- PORTE DE VANVES

14e. Montparnasse

DIVERSIONS:

Boulevard du Montparnasse, (M: Vavin) Sit at Le Select (across from La Coupole restaurant) and people-watch! A FAVORITE.

Cimetière du Montparnasse, 3 Blvd Edgar-Quinet. (M: Raspail) 44.10.86.50. Cemetery where Baudelaire, Jean Seberg, Jean-Paul Sartre, Simone de Beauvoir. You will find "the Kiss" gravestone in the corner. Purchase map. 9a-6p.

Club Energym, 6 Rue Lalande (M: Denfert-Rochereau) 43.22.12.02. Classes and Sauna.

Decouverte du Vin, Centre d'Information de Documentation et de Dégustation, 30 Rue de la Sabliere (M: Mouton-Duvenet) 45.45.32.20. Call for class schedules covering wine basics to Grand Cru.

Fondation Cartier, 261 Blvd Raspail (M: Raspail) 42.18.56.50. Center for contemporary art. Tues.-Sunday. Noon - 8p, Thursdays til 10p. Call for exhibitions. €4.57. Enjoy the wonderful wild garden.

Gymnase Club, 28 Ave General-Leclerc (M: Mouton-Duvernet) 45.42.50.57. Day passes.

Les Bains d'Odessa, 5 Rue d'Odessa (M: Montparnasse) 43.20.73.32. Parisian baths with spa, hamman baths.

Les Catacombes, 1 Pl Denfert-Rochereau (M: Denfert-Rochereau) 43. 22. 47. 63. Closed Mon. Open 9a- 4p. Network of limestone quarries containing neat piles of skulls and bones taken from Parisian graveyards.

Marché de la Creation, Sundays 10a-6p. Walk up the Metro exit: Edgar Quinet.

Parc Montsouris, Blvd Jourdan (M: Cité Universitaire) Open dawn to dusk.

Pucés de Vanves, flea market. See Superlatives.

SUPERLATIVES:

Best Baguette: La Fournée d'Augustine, 96 Rue Raymond Losserand (M: Pernety) 45.43.42.45. Pierre Thilloux awarded grand prize 2005.

Best Cheese: Fromagerie Pierre Boursault, 71 Ave de Général le Clerc (M: Mouton Duvernet) 43.27.93.30. Ask for Bleu de Termignon.

Best croissants: Le Palais d'Or, 71 Rue de la Tombe-Issoire (M: Alésia) 43.27.66.26. Pastry shop.

Best Flea Market: Pucés de Vanves, Flea market at Ave Marc Sangnier and Georges-Lafenestre. (M: Porte de Vanves) Look for antique pastis bottles. 7:30a-7p Sat/Sunday. From the Metro, walk across the street and 1 block East. A FAVORITE.

Best Wine Bar: Les Caves Solignac, 9 Rue Decres (M: Plaisance) 45.45.58.59. Closed Sat/Sun. 7:30a-7p. Best from 8a-1p.

Oldest Observatory still in operation: Observatoire de Paris, 61 Ave de l'Observatoire (M: Denfert-Rochereau) 40.51.22.21. By-appointment-only on the first Saturday of each month.

Outdoor tables: Le Pavillon Montsouris. See Restaurants.

Robert Doisneau's favorite bistro: Vin des Rues, 21 Rue Boulard (M: Denfert-Rochereau) 43.21.82.60. Closed Sun/Mon.

Oldest neighborhood wine bar: Cave Peret, 6 Rue Daguerre (M: Denfert-Rochereau) 43.22.08.64. Art Nouveau décor and stocks over 150 wines.

SHOPS:

Alias, 21 Rue Boulard (M: Denfert-Rochereau) 43.21.29.82. Neighborhood's oldest bookstore. A FAVORITE.

Cave Peret, 6 Rue Daguerre (M: Denfert-Rochereau) 43.22.08.64. Art Nouveau décor and stocks over 150 wines.

Fromagerie Pierre Boursault, 71 Ave de Général le Clerc (M: Mouton Duvernet) 43.27.93.30. Fromagerie with good selection of cheeses. Ask for Bleu de Termignon.

Galeries Lafayette Montparnasse, 22 Rue Départ (M: Montparnasse) 45.38.52.87. Department Store.

La Fournée d'Augustine, 96 Rue Raymond Losserand (M: Pernety) 45.43.42.45. Pierre Thilloux awarded grand prize for baguettes in 2005.

Le Palais d'Or, 71 Rue de la Tombe-Issoire (M: Alésia) 43.27.66.26. Pastry shop.

Puzzle Michèle Wilson, 116 Rue du Chateau (M: Gaité) 43.22.28.73. Founded in 1975 by Michèle Wilson and now owned by Mrs. Ollée-Laprune, where you will find hand-cut art reproduction jigsaw puzzles.

SR Store, 64/112 Rue d'Alesia (M: Alésia) 43.95.06.13. Sonia Rykiel clothing outlet. A FAVORITE.

14

RESTAURANTS: LES PLATS DU JOUR:

Apollo, 3 Pl Denfert-Rochereau (M: Denfert-Rochereau) 45.38.76.77. Dine in former train station. Summer terrace. Mixed reviews.

Au Moulin Vert, 34 bis, Rue des Plantes (M: Alésia) 45.39.31.31. Highly recommended. Traditional meals. Pretty décor.

Au Vin des Rues, 21 Rue Boulard (M: Denfert-Rochereau) 43.21.82.60. Intimate, rustic, authentic wine bar. Good reviews. See Superlatives.

De Bouche A Oreille, 34 Rue Gassendi (M: Denfert-Rochereau) 43.27.73.14. Modern bistro dishes in simple dining room. Talented chef is gaining popularity. Cosed Sunday.

14e. Montparnasse

L'Amuse Bouche, 186 Rue du Château (M: Mouton-Duvernet) 43.35.31.61. Cozy, casual, good wine cellar. Romantic. Closed Sunday.

L'Opportun, 84 Blvd Edgar Quinet (M: Edgar Quinet) 43.20.26.89. Freshly prepared, authentic Lyonnais meals. Tiny, friendly, reasonable and smoky. Closed Sunday.

La Cagouille, 10 Pl Constantin Brancusi (M: Gaité) 43.22.09.01. Grilled mussels and fresh seafood. Casual. Terrace. €42 prix fixe seafood. Non-smoking area.Open Sunday.

La Contre Allée, 83 Ave Denfert-Rochereau (M: Denfert-Rochereau) 43.54.99.86. Casual and cozy, contemporary French meals with foie gras and artichokes and Muscat wine jelly as a staple. Non-smoking is a plus. €35. Closed Sunday.

La Coupole, 102 Blvd Montparnasse (M: Vavin) 43.20.14.20. 1930's landmark. Best bet is seafood platter.

La Cerisaie, 70 Blvd Edgar-Quinet (M: Raspail) 43.20.98.98. Husband/chef won best chef under age 30 and his wife own this tiny 21-seat bistro with daily blackboard menu specializing in Sud Oeust (southwest) preparations. Not fancy. We enjoy these fresh simple meals. Lunch and dinner. €32 for 3 courses. Closed Sat./Sun. No smoking. A FAVORITE.

La Maison Courtine, 157 Ave du Maine (M: Mouton-Duvernet) 45.48.08.04. Southwestern French at modest prices and good wine list. Closed Sunday.

La Régalade, 49 Ave Jean Moulin (M: Alésia) 45.45.68.58. Set menu. We think it's very over-rated, but has affordable wines, generous terrines of homemade country pate, hearty plates. Closed Sunday.

Le Dome, 108 Blvd du Montparnesse (M: Vavin) 43.35.25.81. Seafood is specialty. Lively crowd. €100 for two. Open Sunday.

Le Bistrot de L'Echanson, 20 Rue Gaité (M: Gaité) 43.22.86.46. Traditional menu. Good selection of Cotes du Rhone wines. Closed Sun./Monday.

Le Pavillon Montsouris, 20 Rue Gazan (M: Cité Universitaire) 43.13.29.00. Greenhouse overlooking the park. Classic French meals.

Le Plomb du Cantal, 3 Rue du Gaité (M: Edgar Quinet) 43.36.16.92. Terrace. Friendly service. The best slice of rhubarb pie in my life!

Les Fils de la Ferme, 5 Rue Mouton Duvernet (M: Mouton Duvernet) 45.39.39.61. Inexpensive neighborhood restaurant.

Natasha, 17 bis. Rue Campagne Première (M: Raspail) 43.20.79.27. Alain Cirelli offers comfort food in comfy-cozy setting.

SUNDAY DINNERS at Jim Haynes, 83 Rue de la Tombe-Issoire (M: St Jacques) 43.27.17.67. Jim_Haynes@wanadoo.fr. Different chefs help Jim prepare meals each Sunday. €20-25. Expect 50 – 75 to attend.

RESTAURANTS: GASTRONOMIQUE:

Le Duc, 243 Blvd Raspail (M: Raspail) 43.20.96.30. Ranked #1 for seafood at very expensive prices. The sole is superb. Dining experience is not affected by décor, which needs improvement. Closed Sunday.

BONNE SOIREE! PARIS AT NIGHT:

Bobino, 20 Rue de la Taite (M: Gaite) 43.27.75.75. Cabaret.

La Coupole, 102 Blvd du Montparnasse (M: Vavin) See Restaurants for dining. Downstairs, dancing and salsa nights on Tuesdays.

Petit Journal, 13 Rue du Commandant Mouchotte (M: Montparnasse Bienvenue) 43.21.56.70. Live music. Call for schedule. A FAVORITE.

Rosebud, 11 bis, Rue Delambre (M: Edgar-Quinet) 43.20.44.13 or 43.35.38.54. Relaxing and cozy cocktail bar, piped-in jazz. Attracts crowd that is over 35 years.

Theatre d'Edgar, 58 Blvd Edgar Quinet (M: Edgar-Quinet) 42.79.97.97. Chansonniers. Call ahead.

Utopia Café Concert, 79 Rue de l'Ouest (M: Gaité) 43.22.79.66 Live music. Call ahead.

My Special Travel Notes

14

15e. Vaugirard, Tour Montparnasse

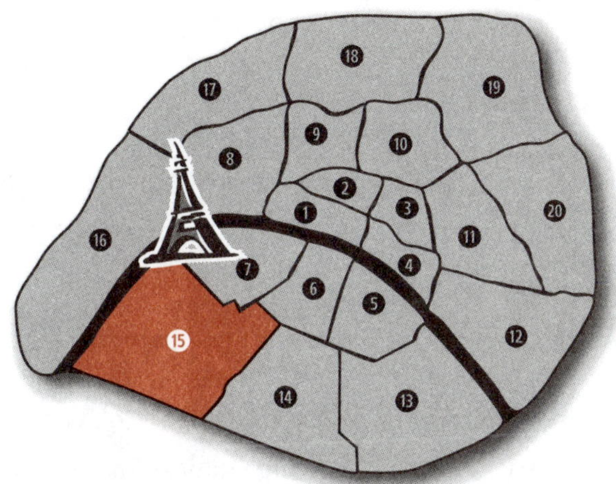

Go to the 59th floor of **Tour Montparnasse** and enjoy a panoramic view of Paris.

Buy personalized French stamps as souvenirs at **Musée de la Poste.**

Dine at one of our favorite restaurants, **L'Os à Moelle.**

MAJOR METROS:

- FALGUIÈRE
- PASTEUR
- LE MOTTE PICQUET
- SÉGUR
- VAUGIRARD
- BIR HAKEIM

15e. Vaugirard, Tour Montparnasse

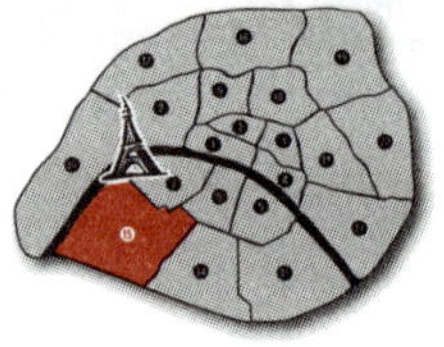

FAMOUS SIGHTS:

Musée Antoine Bourdelle, 16-18 Rue Antoine Bourdelle (M: Falguière) 49.54.73.73. Tues-Sat: 10a-5p. Sculpture gardens. Free. Very nice in good weather.

Tour Montparnasse, 33 Ave du Maine (M: Montparnasse-Bienvenue) From 56th and 59th floors you get a complete view of Paris. Open air rooftop terrace, shops, 10a-9p. €7.60.

DIVERSIONS:

Allée des Cygnes (M: Passy) is across from Bir Hakeim Bridge where you will find a walking path offering great views of both banks of the Seine.

Eutelsat Balloons, Parc Andre Citroen, Rue Balard (M: Javel) 9a-9p. €5-10. Weather permitting.

Parc André Citroen, Rue Balard (M: Javel) This is a contemporary park with urban landscaping, canals, fountains. Stroll around rows of floral, herbal, and Oriental gardens. Greenhouses. Open 9a-7p.

Gym Pour Tous, 211 bis, Rue Croix Nivert (M: Cambronne) 45.30.19.68

La Ruche (beehive) 2 Passage Dantzig (M: Convention) Artists' studios.

Musée de la Poste, 34 Blvd Vaugirard (M: Montparnasse or Pasteur) 42.79.24.24. You can buy personalized French stamps for $9/sheet of 10.

Restaurant du Marché, 59 Rue de Dantzig (M: Porte de Versailles) 48.28.31.55. Good country-style cuisine and cozy red banquettes. Saturday morning cooking classes by chef-owner Francis Levèque.

SUPERLATIVES:

Best creperie: Ty Breiz, 55 Blvd de Vaugirard (M: Tour Montparnasse) 43.20.83.72.

Best lunch deal: Le Troquet, 21 Rue François Bonvin (M: Sèvres-Lecourbe) 45.66.89.00. See Restaurants.

Bread: Moulin de la Vierge, 166 Ave de Suffren (M: Sèvres-Lecourbe) 47.83.45.55. Special milled, organic flours.

Classic traditional: L'Os a Moelle, Ever-changing blackboard menu. A FAVORITE. See Restaurants.

SHOPS:

Poilane Bakery, 49 Blvd de Grenelle (M: Bir Hakeim) 45.79.11.49. Confectioner, bakery since 1932.

Puzzle Michèle Wilson, 116 Rue du Chateau (M: Gaité) 43.22.28.73. Founded in 1975 by Michèle Wilson and now owned by Mrs. Ollée-Laprune, where you will find hand-cut art reproduction jigsaw puzzles. You can watch the cutters at their work.

Village Suisse, Marché antiquities, Mon/Thursday, 78 Ave de Suffren intersects with 54 Ave de la Motte Piquet (M: Le Motte-Piquet) Antique dealers and shops.

RESTAURANTS: LES PLATS DU JOUR:

Au Roi du Café, 59 Rue Lecourbe (M: Sèvres Lecourbe) 47.34.48.50. Classic, original zinc counter. Cozy terrace. Plats du jour for under €20. 9a-2a.

Bistro d'Hubert, 41 Blvd Pasteur (M: Pasteur) 47.34.15.50. Cute bistro. Good portions of simple, good food. Cozy. Open Sunday. Reserve.

L'Ami Marcel, 33 Rue Georges-Pitard (M: Plaisance) 48.56.62.06. Chef from the Ritz prepares exquisite meals. Lunch formula €24. Closed Sunday.

L'Os a Moelle, 3 Rue Vasco de Gama (M: Lourmel) 45.57.27.27. Inventive dishes by chef/owner Thierry Faucher. Great value. Go out of your way to find this "hole in the wall." A FAVORITE. Closed Sun/Monday.

La Dînée, 85 Rue Leblanc (M: Balard) 45.54.20.49. Chef Christophe Chabanet produces innovative dishes.

La Grande Rue, 117 Rue de Vaugirard (M: Falguiere) 47.34.96.12. Old-fashioned neighborhood bistro. Classic French meals from chef who trained with Ducasse. Closed Sun/Monday.

La Petite Auberge, 13 Rue du Hameau (M: Porte de Versailles) 45.32.75.71. Patés Riviera-style, frites maison, plats du jour. €25.

La Villa Corse, 164 Blvd Grenelle (M: Cambronne) 53.86.70.81. Delicious Corsican-style meals in a cozy atmosphere. Closed Sunday.

Le Banyan, 24 Pl Etienne Pernet (M: Felix Faure) 40.60.09.31. Former chef at Blue Elephant serves Thai and Asian influenced meals in pleasant interior. Closed Sunday.

Le Baribal, 186 Rue de Vaugirard (M: Volontaires) 47.34.15.32. Warm welcome and good Southwest-style meals.

Le Bec Rouge, 46 bis, Blvd Montparnasse (M: Falguire) 42.22.45.54. Wine bar, traditional rotisserie, good rhubarb struedel.

Le Beurre Noisette, 68 Rue Vasco de Gama (M: Lourmel) 48. 56. 82. 49. Popular Market menu, low price. Good service. Closed Sunday/Monday.

Le Bistrot d'en Face, 1 Rue Sextius Michel (M: Duplex) 45.77.14.59. Reasonable food. Reasonable prices.

Le Ciel de Paris, Tour Maine Montparnasse, 33 Ave du Maine (M: Montparnasse) 40.64.77.64. €50 dinner. Revolving restaurant provides a great view of Paris.

Le Clos Morillons, 50 Rue des Morillons (M: Porte de Vanves) 48.28.04.37. Has new décor and new chef. Moderate prices. Closed Sunday.

15e. Vaugirard, Tour Montparnasse

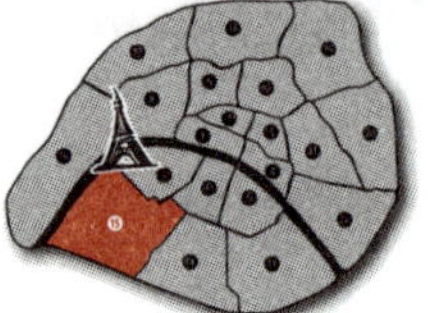

Le Dix Vins, 57 Rue Falquière (M: Pasteur) 43.20.91.77. Jean-Philippe and Hervé serve good humor, seasonal cuisine, and good house wines. €20 menu du jour.

Le Gastroquet, 10 Rue Desnouettes (M: Porte de Versailles) 48.28.60.91. Chef-owner presents solid meals and good service. Save room for dessert.

Le Quinzième, 14 Rue Cauchy (M: Javel) 45.54.43.43. Chef Cyril Lignac presents inventive market-fresh Mediterranean French meals and extraordinary desserts. Modern décor, Open kitchen. Extensive wine list. Tasting menu is €80.

Le Père Claude, 51 Ave de la Motte-Picquet (M: La Motte-Picquet) 47.34.03.05. Classic French from Perraudin family bistro. Moderate prices.

Le Tire-Bouchon, 62 Rue des Entrepreneurs (M: Charles Michels) 40.59.09.27. The name means corkscrew, so naturally they offer good wine list and tasting menu. Husband and wife, friendly. Closed Sunday.

Le Triporteur, 4 Rue de Dantzig (M: Convention) 45.32.82.40. Neighborhood brasserie offers popular Basque blackboard menu and good service. Reservations needed. Closed Sun.

Le Troquet, 21 Rue François Bonvin (M: Sèvres Lecourbe) 45.66.89.00. Great, affordable dining. Popular. 4-course prix fixe. A FAVORITE. Closed Sunday.

R, 8 Rue de la Cavalerie (M: La Motte-Piquet) 45.67.06.85. Penthouse with great view of the Eiffel Tower. Terrace.

Restaurant du Marché, 59 Rue de Dantzig (M: Porte de Versailles) 48.28.31.55. Good country-style cuisine and cozy red banquettes. Saturday morning cooking classes by chef-owner Francis Levèque.

RESTAURANTS: GASTRONOMIQUE:

Thierry Burlot, 8 Rue Nicolas Charlet (M: Pasteur) 42.19.08.59. Chef from Crillon creates inventive dishes in casual elegance. Expensive. Closed Sunday.

My Special Travel Notes

15

My Special Travel Notes

15

16e. Passy, Trocadero

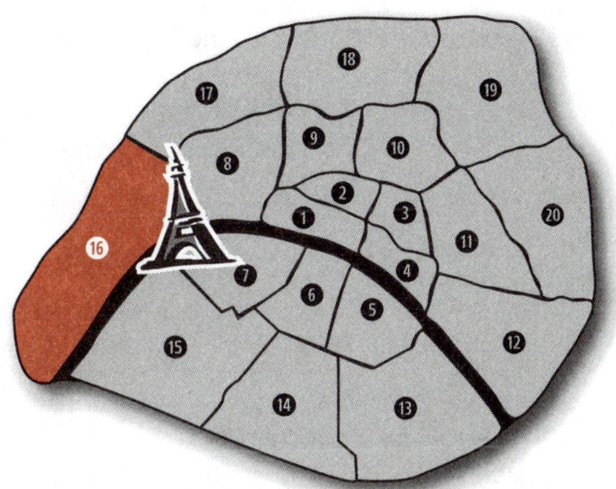

One of our favorite museums is **Musée Marmotton.**

Maison Baccarat has a stunning crystal display as well as "the best table in Paris."

Make reservations at the popular wine bar **Cotes Vignes.**

Hiramatsu and **Table de Joel Robuchon** are two fabulous gastronomique dining events for big splurges.

MAJOR METROS:

- KLÉBER
- IÉNA,
- TROCADÉRO
- VICTOR HUGO
- PORTE DAUPHINE
- PORTE MOLITOR
- RUE DE LA POMPE
- PORTE DE LA MUETTE

16e. Passy, Trocadero

FAMOUS SIGHTS:

Maison Baccarat, 11 Pl des Etats-Unis (M: Boissière) 40.22.11.00. 1902 mansion, with interior designed by Philippe Starck. It's a crystal palace. In the small museum, €7, you'll see crystal that was designed for Josephine Baker, Aristotle Onassis, and Coco Chanel. Dine in the Cristal Room Baccarat. See, below, for the "Best Table in Paris." Closed Tuesday. 10a-7p museum and 8:30a - 10:30p for Restaurant.

Musée Marmottan, 2 Rue Louis Boilly (M: La Muette) 42.2407.02. A FAVORITE. Admission €6.50. 10a-6p. Monet and Impressionists. Closed Mon. (If you like Balzac, you are near Maison Balzac, see Diversions, below).

DIVERSIONS:

Bois de Boulogne - Huge park. Walk the paths or sit on a park bench to people-watch. For bike rentals enter by (M: Ave Foch) and look for **Paris Cycles** 47.47.22.37. For rowboats enter by (M: Ave Henri Martin) **Parc de Bagatelle** - Absolutely beautiful **rose gardens.** Also, **Jardin d'Acclimation** is great for children with an outdoor circus, train, puppet theatre. **Pré Catalan** in Bois de Boulogne, Route de Suresnes (M: Porte Dauphine) 44.14.41.41. A very expensive lunch or dinner in a beautiful location in the park.

Cimetière de Passy, 2 Rue du Comandant-Schloesing (M: Trocadéro) Cemetery. The concierge at gate can point out famous grave sites.

Fondation Pierre Bergé YSL, 3 Rue Leonce Reynoud (M: Alma Marceau) 44.31.64.00. Museum exhibition honoring Yves Saint Laurent - his couture and personal art collection. Call for exhibitions. 9:30a-1p and 2:30p - 7p. Closed Monday.

Hair salon: Alexandre Zouari, 1 Ave de Président Wilson (M: Alma Marceau) 47.23.79.00. Voted one of bests by W magazine. He also creates elegant jewelry designs with diamonds.

Hair Salon: Capon Coiffure, 2 Rue Largillière (M: La Muette) 42.30.98.34. Where Dior jewelry designer, Victoire de Castellane has her hair styled.

Jardins du Trocadéro, (M: Trocadéro) Botanical garden.

La Belle Ecole, 7 Rue Scheffer (M: Rue de la Pompe) 47.04.50.20/fax 47.04.50.21. Camille and Constance manage this French finishing school in the arts de vivre. Call to reserve place in classes held in changing venues. Makeup sessions and floral arts take place at Hotel Crillon, pastry-making and Chocolate Tasting (fills up quickly) at the Atelier des Arts Culinaire. Specify English.

Maison Boissier, 184 Victor Hugo (M: Victor Hugo) 45.03.50.77.Tea room with Chef Christian Vautier.

Musée d'Art Moderne de le Ville de Paris, 11 Ave Président Wilson. (M: Iéna) 53.67.40.00. 10a-5:45 p. Admission. Permanent and temporary exhibitions of modern art. Call for exhibitions. Closed Mondays.

Musée de la Marine, In Palais de Chaillot (M: Trocadéro) 53.65.69.69. Good for children. €7 adults/€4 kids. Closed Tues.

Musée de l'Homme, In Palais de Chaillot (M: Trocadéro) 44.05.72.72. Human history dislayed by anthropological, archaelogical and ethnological displays. Closed Tues.

Musée de la Mode et du Costume, Palais Galliera, 10 Ave Pierre 1 er de Serbie (M: lèna) 56.52.86.00. Over 200 years of haute couture in a beautiful palace.

Musée de Radio-France, 116 Ave du President Kennedy (M: Ranelagh) 56.40.15.16. By appointment only. Guided tour, and history, of French radio and TV.

Musée du Vin, 5-7 Square Dickens (M: Passy) 45.25.63.26. 10-6p. Cellars built by monks. Caves may seem musty. Admission €6.50. Closed Mon. Call Monique Jossee, 01.64.09.44.80. for classes on some Saturdays throughout the year.

Musée Galliera, 10 Ave Pierre (M: léna) 56.52.86.00. Closed Mondays. Various exhibitions.

Musée Guimet, 6 Pl d'léna (M: léna) 56.52.53.00. Newly renovated. Extensive Asian art collection. Closed Tues. $4 Once-a-week they conduct a workshop for children ages 7-12. Puppet-making, kimono creations, calligraphy lessons. 56.52.53.00. €7. 2-6p, Wednesdays. **Enjoy a discreet picnic at Guimet's annex,** 17 Ave d'léna, a beautiful Japanese garden. Open 1p, free admission to garden and annex.

Outdoor Market on Ave President Wilson, across from Pl d'Iena (M: léna) on Wed and Sat mornings. A FAVORITE. Fun to hunt down cashmere scarves and fine foie gras.

Palais de Tokyo Contemporary Muséum, 13 Ave Présidont Wilson (M: léna) 47.23.38.86. Closed Mon. Huge space with modern contemporary art, Exhibition space is on the left. On the right you will find satellite activities: bookstore, self-service café, BlackBlock boutique for trendy trinkets, TokyoEat restaurant/bar with modern (of course!) décor and light meals.

Palais de Chaillot, Pl du Trocadéro-et-du 11-Novembre (M: Trocadéro) 53.65.69.69. View the Eiffel Tower from its terrace or **Le Café de l'Homme,** 44.05.30.15. Two wings and gardens, pools, theatre, library and restaurant. Left wing renovated to include **Cité de l'Architecture** and **Musée du Cinéma Henri Langlois.** Right wing has **Musée de la Marine** and **Musée de l'Homme** (above) Beneath the terrace is **Théâtre National de Chaillot.** 53.61.31.00. Seats 1,200 with mainstream European film classics and musicals.

Parc Sevres d'Auteuil, 3 Ave de la Porte d'Auteuil and 1 Ave Gordon Bennett (M: Porte d'Auteuil) Botanical garden and hothouses.

Tennis lovers can visit the **Stade Roland-Garres,** 2 Ave Gordon Bennet (M: Porte d'Auteuil) 47.43.48.00. See the Tenniseum, a multi-media museum. Closed Mon.

16e. Passy, Trocadero

SUPERLATIVES:

Best croissants: Béchu, 118 Ave Victor-Hugo (M: Victor-Hugo) 47.27.97.79.

Best poached eggs: Le Brandevin, 29 Rue du Dr Blanche (M: Jasmin) 42.24.19.33.

Best crepes suzettes: Paul Chêne. See Restaurants.

Best dépots-ventes (vintage store): Réciproque, #88,89,92,93-101 Rue de la Pompe (M: Pompe) 47.04.30.28 or 47.27.93.52. A FAVORITE.

Best gazpacho: Passiflore, See Restaurants.

Best view: Hôtel Raphael's roof top restaurant, 17 Ave Kléber (M: Kléber) 53.64.32.00. A FAVORITE.

Best Table in Paris: Cristal Room Baccarat, in Maison Baccarat, 11 Pl des Etats-Unis (M: Boissiére) 40.22.11.10. Request the "little dining room" for a party of 8 - has its own private terrace and a black Baccarat crystal chandelier. Must be booked months in advance.

Best meal served in a private mansion: Chez Alain Bourgade. Call 06.77.79.16.71 to reserve, up to 12 people. He will prepare your meal in his beautiful private mansion. His garden is sublime in good weather.

Finest Orchids: Au Nom de l'Orchidée, Vanessa Elia sells the best in town. See Shops.

Most élégant bar: Dokhan's champagne bar, 117 Rue de Lauriston (M: Trocadéro) 53.65.66.99. Tastings on Thursdays. Open til 3am.

Trés chic bar: English Bar in Hôtel Raphaël, 17 Ave Kléber (M: Kléber) 53.64.42.00.

Most romantic: Bar l'Hôtel Saint James Club, 5 Pl due Chancelier Adenauer (M: Porte Dauphine) 44.05.81.81. Relax in leather chairs and a garden terrace.

Widest Avenue in Paris: Avenue Foch off of Pl Charles-De-Gaulle. Twelve avenues begin here, forming a star.

Winner Grand Prix Chocolate: Patrice Chapon, 52 Ave Mozart (M: La Muette) 42.24.05.05. Delicious chocolates. A FAVORITE.

16 **World-class paella: Rosimar,** 26 Rue Poussin (M: Michel-Ange-Auteuil) 45.27.74.91. Must order when you reserve. See Restaurants.

SHOPS:

Au Nom de l'Orchidée, 67 Ave Paul Doumer (M: La Muette) 40.50.08.08. Absolutely gorgeous orchids.

Franck & Fils, 80 Rue de Passy (M: La Muette) 42.15.00.37. Elegant, with classic selections. Closed Sunday.

Christofle Paris, 95 Rue de Passy (M: La Muette) 46.47.51.27. Fine tableware.

Gilles Didier Affiches, 38 Rue Boileau (M: Michel-Ange-Molitor) 40.71.04.41. By appointment. Original Cappiello posters and more.

Nouez-Moi, 27 Rue Sablons (M: Trocadero) 47.27.69.88. Extraordinary linens. Ask them to embroider your initials. A FAVORITE. Another location in 8e.

Patrice Chapon, 52 Ave Mozart (M: La Muette) 42.24.05.05. Winner Grand Prix Chocolate. Delicious chocolates.

Réciproque, #88,89,92,93-101 Rue de la Pompe (M: Pompe) 47.04.30.28 or 47.27.93.52. Vintage at its best.

Renoma boutique, 129 bis Rue de la Pompe (M: Victor Hugo) 44.25.38.25. High fashion. Accessories are at another location at 118 Rue Longchamp (M: Victor Hugo) 44.05.38.33.

Regis, 89 Rue de Passy (M: La Muette) 45.27.70.00. Chocolatier for 50 years. Fluffy chocolate cakes.

Roy Chocolatier, 27 Rue de Longchamp (M: Kléber) 47.27.34.36. Fine chocolates since 1948.

Talma, 61 Ave Mozart (M: Jasmin) 42.88.20.20. Owner Alain-Paul Ruzé stocks wide assortment of stationery, china, frames.

Zouari Diamonds, 1 Ave Président Wilson (M: Alma Marceau) 47.23.79.00. Hair salon, voted one of bests by W magazine. He also creates elegant jewelry designs with diamonds. His collections are called: Flowers, Oriental, Square and Love.

RESTAURANTS: LES PLATS DU JOUR:

6 New York, 6 Ave de New York (M: Passy) 40.70.03.30. Chef Jean-Pierre Vigato from Apicius runs modern restaurant. Good view of Eiffel Tower. Expensive. Closed Sunday.

59 Poincaré, 59 Ave Raymond Poincaré (M: Trocadéro) 47.27.59.59. Alain Ducasse used to be here. Vegetarian.

A & M Bistro, 136 Blvd Murat (M: Port du St-Cloud) 45.27.39.60. New, stylish, traditional food. Good value for wines. Closed Sunday.

Au Rendez-vous des Chauffeurs, 11 Rue des Portes-Blanches (M: Marcadet) 42.64.04.17. Huge portions of dependably decent food and tasty French fries. Very affordable. Closed Sunday.

Bistrot de L'Etoile Lauriston, 19 Rue Lauriston (M: Charles-de-Gaulle-Etoile) 40.67.11.16. Popular with locals and tourists alike. Modern classic preparation. Closed Sunday.

Boissier, 184 Ave de Victor Hugo (M: Victor Hugo) 45.03.59.11. Lunch, tea room, melt-in-your-mouth chocolate mousse cake. Circa 1827.

16e. Passy, Trocadero

Bon, 25 Rue de la Pompe (M: Passy) 40.72.70.00. Mixed menu in Phillippe Starck-designed restaurant. Good vegetarian selection. Expensive. Open Sunday.

Carette, 4 Pl du Trocadero (M: Trocadéro) 47.27.88.56. Elegant, old-fashioned café.

Cote Vignes, 16 Rue Lauriston.(M: Charles-de-Gaulle-Etoile) 45.00.27.45. Popular wine bar, so reservations are necessary. Closed Sat. lunch/Sundays.

La Butte Chaillot, 110 bis, Ave Kléber (M: Trocadéro) 47.27.88.88. Trendy Guy Savoy bistro. Mix of classics and new dishes. €90 for two.

La Gare, 19 Chaussée de la Muette (M: La Muette) 42.15.15.31.Chef prepares both classic and nouveau dishes. The pistachio crème brulée was superb. €35 3-course meal. Modern décor with skylight. Terrace. Late night crowd. Owners of two other restaurants in Paris. Close to Metro and taxi stand. A FAVORITE. Open Sunday.

La Grande Armée, 3 Ave de la Grande Armée (M: Charles-de-Gaulle-Etoile) 45.00.24.77. Côstes brothers formula restaurant.

La Maison des Arts et Metiers, in Hotel Particular, 9 bis, Ave d'Iéna (M: Iéna) 40.69.27.53. Five course dinners prepared by ex-Crillon/Ritz chef Thierry Chevalier. €80 + wine.

La Salle à Manger, in Hôtel Raphaël, 17 Ave Kléber (M: Kléber) 53.64.32.11. Evenings are an event by chef Philippe Delahaye.

La Table du Lauriston, 129 Rue Lauriston (M: Trocadéro) 47.27.00.07. Fresh and simple preparations. Comfortable décor.

La Terrasse Mirabeau, 5 Pl de Barcelona (M: Javel) 42.24.41.51. Creative contemporary cooking in comfortable room with bay windows. Closed Sunday.

Le Bigorneau, 71 Ave Paul Doumer (M: La Muette) 45.04.12.81. Seafood presented from talented previous owner of Marius et Jeanette. Catch-of-the day specials.

Le Brandevin, 29 Rue du Docteur Blanche (M: Jasmin) 42.24.19.33. Friendly neighborhood bistrot.

Le Café de l'Homme, in Palais Chaillot, Pl du Trocadero (M: Trocadero) 44.05.30.15. Dine in the terrace for a spectacular view of the Eiffel Tower.

16 **Le Pavillon des Princes,** 69 Ave de la Porte d'Auteuil (M: Porte d'Auteuil) 47.43.15.15. New chef.

Le Petit Rétro, 5 Rue Mesnil (M: Victor Hugo) 44.05.06.05. A real bargain at $60 for two.

Le Scheffer, 22 Rue Scheffer. (M: Trocadéro) 47.27.81.11. Good neighborhood bistro with fresh cooking. Gets crowded. Smoking permitted.

Le Vin dans Les Voiles, 8 Rue Chapon (M: Exelmans) 46.47.83.98. Good selection of wines complimenting the seasonal blackboard menu. Good value and small space. Closed Sunday.

Le Vinci, 23 Rue Paul Valéry (M: Victor Hugo) 45.01.68.18. Fine fresh Italian food prepared by chef who trained with Joel Robuchon. Closed Sunday. A FAVORITE.

Noura, 21 Ave Marceau (M: Alma Marceau) 47.20.33.33. Middle Eastern specialties. Very fresh Lebanese dishes. €30. A FAVORITE.

Oum el Banine, 16 bis, Rue Dufrenov (M: Porte Dauphine) 45.04.91.22. Cozy space. Serves couscous and other Moroccan meals. They deliver. Closed Sunday.

Passiflore, 33 Rue de Longchamp (M: Iéna) 47.04.96.81. Chef Roland Durand's fusion menu and spacious décor gets good dining reviews. Closed Sunday.

Paul Chêne, 123 Rue Lauriston (M: Victor Hugo) 47.27.63.17. Ask for Poule au pot, an old-time classic French dish. Friendly, €100 for two. Closed Sunday.

Rosimar, 26 Rue Poussin (M: Michel-Ange-Auteuil) 45.27.74.91. Paella is their specialty and you must order when you reserve. Authentic Catalan cooking. Closed Sunday.

Stella, 133 Ave Victor Hugo (M: Victor Hugo) 56.90.56.00. Every day til 1am. Traditional French. Shellfish trays. Reasonably priced.

Thé Cool, 10 Rue Jean Balogne (M: Passy) 42.24.69.13. Tea room. The best low-fat cheesecake.

RESTAURANTS: GASTRONOMIQUE:

Cristal Room Baccarat, in Maison Baccarat, 11 Pl des Etats-Unis (M: Boissiére) 40.22.11.10. If you are a party of 6 - 8, ask for the "little dining room" with its own private terrace and a black Baccarat crystal chandelier. Check out the bathrooms. Must be booked months in advance.

Hiramatsu, 52 Rue de Longchamps (M: Trocadéro) 56.81.08.80. Superb blend of French and Japanese styles with impressive wine list. Reserve. Closed Sat/Sunday.

L'Astrance, 4 Rue Beethoven (M: Passy) 40.50.84.40. Chef Pascal Barbot trained at L'Arpége and has one seating for set menu. Closed Mon. Must reserve exactly one month in advance.

La Grande Cascade in Bois de Boulogne, 45.27.33.51. Worth the long taxi ride. Traditional gastronomique French with Ducasse-trained staff. Plan to spend long evening. Enjoy the French fromage carte après dinner. LOTS OF $$$. Open Sunday.

Le Pergolese, 40 Rue Pergolese (M: Porte Maillot) 45.00.21.40. Chef Gaborieau was awarded a Michelin star for southern France style cooking. The dining room has very few windows and may seem cramped to some. Closed Sat/Sunday.

Le Relais d'Auteuil, 31, Blvd Murat (M: Michel-Ange-Molitor) 46.51.09.54. Well worth the ride. Chef Patrick Pignol and his wife offer warm welcome and superb food. €195 pp. Very small, so reserve in advance. A FAVORITE. Closed Sunday.

16e. Passy, Trocadero

Maison Prunier, 16 Ave Victor Hugo (M: Charles de Gaulle-Etoile) 44.17.35.85. Re-opened as caviar house and can get Joe's Stone Crabs from Florida. Closed Sunday.

Pré Catalan in Bois de Boulogne, Route de Suresnes (M: Porte Dauphine) 44.14.41.41. Lunch and dinner, must reserve. A perfect park setting with terrace and fireplace for chilly winter nights. Haute cuisine presented at its finest. Very expensive. Closed Sunday.

Table de Joel Robuchon, 16 Ave Bugeaud (M: Victor Hugo) 56.28.16.16. Joel Robuchon restaurant offering excellent cuisine along with award-winning wine list by Wine Spectator magazine. Totally non-smoking. A FAVORITE.

BONNE SOIREE! PARIS AT NIGHT:

L'Etoile, 12 Rue de Presbourg (M: Charles-de-Gaulle-Etiole) 45.00.78.70. Late night piano bar and chic restaurant. A FAVORITE.

Le Duplex, 8 Ave Foch (M: Charles-de-Gaulle-Etoile) 45.00.45.00. Restaurant and disco Bistro food and good view of Arc de Triomphe.

Mange Disque, 58 Rue Fontaine au Roi (M: Goncourt/Couronnes) 58.30.87.07. Record bar, dance floor, jazz & techno concerts, pub food.

My Special Travel Notes

16

My Special Travel Notes

16

17e. Batignolles, Ternes

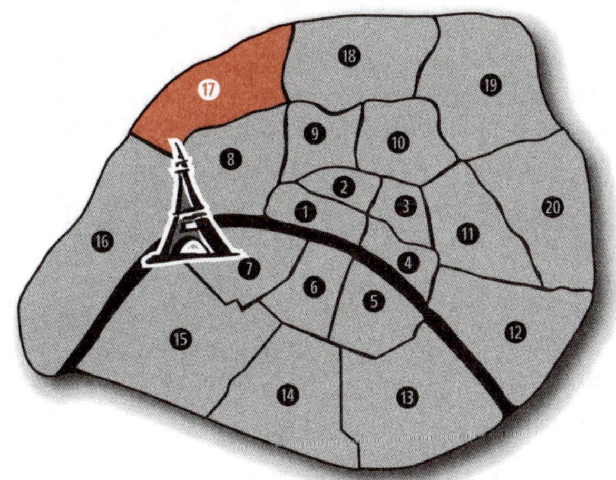

Taste the Best Baguettes in Paris at **Laurent Connan.**

Visit **Batignolles Biologigue Market** on Saturdays. All organic.

A perfect romantic evening might be dinner at **L'Ampère** or **Sormani** and then live music at **Meridian Jazz Club Lionel Hampton.**

MAJOR METROS:

- TERNES
- WAGRAM
- MALESHERBES
- VILLIERS
- CLICHY
- PORTE DE ST. OUEN

17e. Batignolles, Ternes

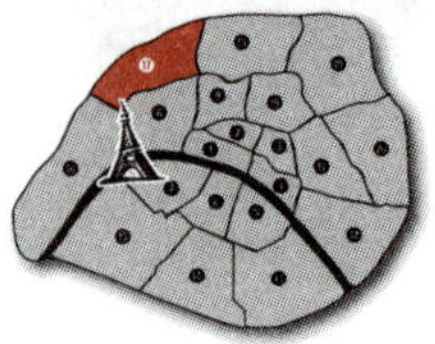

DIVERSIONS:

Batignolles Biologique Market, Blvd de Batignolles (M: Rome) Saturdays. All organic, an open-air "Whole Foods market" ambiance.

Cimetière Parisien des Batignolles (M: Porte de Clichy) Old cemetery.

Place des Ternes, just north of Arc de Triomphe, has Parisian neighborhood flair. Stroll Ave des Ternes, Ave Wagram, Rue du Faubourg St-Honore – some wonderful streets. Another walk is down Rue Courcelles, beginning at Pl de la République de l'Equateur (M: Courcelles) to Square Albert Bernard.

SUPERLATIVES:

Best Baguette of 2003: Laurent Connan, 38 Rue des Batignolles (M: Rome) 45.22.45.04.

Best Fromagerie: Alleosse, 13 Rue Poncelet (M: Ternes) 46.22.50.45. A FAVORITE. Closed Monday.

Priciest Italian: Sormani, See Gastronomique Restaurants.

SHOPS:

Agatha, 2 Ave Ternes (M: Ternes) 42.67.18.00. Designer costume jewelry. Several locations.

Alleosse, 13 Rue Poncelet (M: Ternes) 46.22.50.45. Superb cheeses. Closed Monday.

Androuet, 23 Rue Terrasse (M: Villiers) 47.64.39.20. Fromagerie.

Confectioner Charpentier, 87 Rue de Courcelles (M: Courcelles) 47.63.93.05. House specialty is La Rivoirine: almond paste, raisins, rum, all covered with milk chocolate and powdered sugar.

Dépot Vente 17th Consignment Shop, 109 Rue de Courcelles (M: Courcelles) 40.53.80.82. Up to 50% discount on designers such as Hermes, Chanel, Gucci, Dior, Vuitton, Prada.

French Touche, 1 Rue Jacquemont (M: La Fourche) 42.63.31.36. You will find almost anything here.

17

L'Esprit et le Vin, 81 Ave des Ternes (M: Chemin Vert) 45.74.80.99. 18th century corkscrews, oenological items, gadgets, gifts. 10a-7p. A FAVORITE. Closed Sunday.

Planet Bio, Organic supermarket. 47 Rue Guerrant (M: Porte de Champeret) 44.09.74.64.

Raoul Maeder, 158 Blvd Berthier (M: Porte de Clichy) 46.22.50.73. Baker. Good baguettes. He lost to Laurent Connan in 2002-03.

RESTAURANTS: LES PLATS DU JOUR:

Atelier Gourmand, 20 Rue de Tocqueville (M: Villiers) 42.27.03.71. Husband and wife offer daily menu and good service. Closed Sunday.

Baptiste, 51 Rue Jouffroy D'Abbans (M: Wagram) 42.27.20.18. Young new team. Inexpensive prices right now. Romantic, red and gold décor. Closed Sunday.

Bistral, 80 Rue Lemercier (M: Brochant) 42.63.59.61. Our friends in Paris call it magic! Food, wines, mosaic tables. Daily menu - carte €30. Closed Sun/Mon.

Bistrot à Coté, 16 Ave de Villiers (M: Villiers) 47.63.25.61. Rostang bistro offers fresh salads and 3 course €40 menu.

Bistrot des Dames, Hotel El Dorado, 18 Rue des Dames (M: Place de Clichy) 45.22.13.42. Small Mediterranean bistro with good wine list. Garden Open Sunday.

Café Lateral, 4 Ave Mac-Mahon (M: Charles de Gaulle-Etoile) 43.80.20.96. Excellent open-face tartine sandwiches.

Caïus, 6 Rue d'Armalille (M: Argentina) 42.27.19.20. New French from Chef Notelet, ex Le Troyon, presents great meals at modest prices. Closed Sunday

Caves Petrissans, 30 bis, Ave Neil (M: Charles de Gaulle-Etoile) 40.54.87.56. You can buy a bottle of wine in the shop and then eat good traditional food.

Chez Fred, 190 bis, Blvd Pereire (M: Porte Maillot) 45.74.20.48. Since 1945, a friendly, reasonably priced bistro. Closed Sunday.

Chez Leon, 32 Rue Legendre (M: Villiers) 42.27.06.82. New owners still provide classic regional meals at medium prices. Closed Sunday.

Groupil Le Bistro, 4 Rue Claude-Debussy (M: Porte de Champerret) 45.75.83.25. Young chef/owner presents simple seasonal French bistro fare at reasonable prices.

Kifune, 44 Rue St-Ferdinand (M: Argentine) 45.72.11.19. Japanese.

L'Abadache, 89 Rue Lemercier (M: La Fouche) 42.26.37.33. Cozy décor, good service, and fresh ingredients all come together at a price of €25.

L'Ampère, 1 Rue Ampère (M: Wagram) 47.63.72.05. Chef Philippe Detourbe, A FAVORITE, is now overseeing this popular neighborhood restaurant and brings his eclectic mix of fresh menu ideas. Closed Sun.

L 'Entredejeu, 83 Rue Laugier (M: Porte de Champerret) 40.54.97.24. Chef/owner Philippe Tredjeu and his wife offer a changing menu that's worth the trip. The prices will entice you to return. Closed Sunday

L'Impatient, 14 Passage Geffroy Didelot (M: Rome) 43.87.28.10. Flowers in bathtubs and patient waiters provide meals worth the wait and the trip here. Closed Sunday.

17e. Batignolles, Ternes

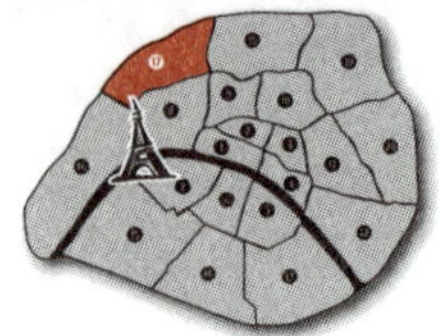

La Braisière, 54 Rue Cardinet (M: Malesherbes) 47.63.40.37. Very special neighborhood bistrot. Delicious new and old-style French flavors, friendly service, comfortable décor that keeps customers returning to this family-owned restaurant. Moderate prices.

La Cabane, 96 Rue Levis (M: Malesherbes) 46.22.51.50. Neighborhood restaurant that also delivers.

La Ruccola, 198 Blvd Malesherbes (M: Wagram) 44.40.04.50. Small Italian. Serves pasta made from freshest products. Closed Sunday.

La Soupière, 154 Ave de Wagram (M: Wagram) 46.22.80.10. Traditional French with a flair for wild mushrooms. Prix fixe at reasonable prices. Closed Sunday.

La Toque, 16 Rue de Tocqueville (M: Villiers) 42.27.97.75. Charming, small dining room with classic French dishes prepared by chef/owner Jacky Joubert. Not inexpensive. Closed Sunday.

Le Beudant, 97 Rue des Dames (M: Rome) 43.87.11.20. New owners and a good prix fixe lunch. Closed Sunday/Monday.

Le Clou, 132 Rue Cardinet (M: Malesherbes) 42.27.36.78. Chef/owner Christian LeClou, ex-Ledoyen, offers moderately priced gourmet food and good wine list.

Le Grain d'orge, 15 Rue de L'Arc-de-Triomphe (M: Charles de Gaulle-Etoile) 47.54.00.28. Cooking style is Northern France with Belgian influence. Flemish beer.

Le Jardin d'Isa, 1 Pl Charles-Fillion (M: Rome) 46.27.33.37. Quiet terrace. Savory Southern French with wine list to compliment. €50 for two.

Le Mont Liban, 42 Blvd des Batignoles (M: Rome) 45.22.35.01. Great Lebanese food as well as inexpensive fallafel sandwiches with native wine list.

Le Petit Colombier, 42 Rue des Acacias (M: Argentine) 43.80.28.54. Over- rated coq au vin. Good value at $105 for 2.

Le Va et Vient, 8 Rue des Batignolles (M: Rome) 45.22.54.22. Family-run bistro serving tasty generous portions of French and Alsatian meals. Closed Sunday.

Le Verre Bouteille, 85 Ave des Ternes (M: Porte Maillot) 45.74.01.02. Great for steak tartare. Open til 4:30 am.

17

Les Béatilles, 11 bis, Rue Villebois-Mareuil, (M: Charles de Gaulle-Etoile) 45.74.43.80. Chef Christian Bochaton and his wife serve meals with modern flavors. Expensive. Closed Sunday.

Meating, 122 Ave de Villiers (M: Pereire) 43.80.10.10. House specialty is meat. Same owners as La Gare.

Patrick Goldenberg, 69 Ave de Wagram (M: Ternes) 42.27.34.79. Traditional Jewish deli food.

Ripaille, 69 Rue Dames (M: Rome) 45.22.03.03. Cute, tiny. €30. Simple meals.

Soralena, 18 Rue Bayen (M: Ternes) 45.74.73.73. Chef who worked at Sormani now presents Mediterranean influenced well-prepared meals. Glamour crowd fills the tables regularly. Closed Sunday.

Taira, 10 Rue des Acacias (M: Argentine) 47.66.74.14. Small, modern. Good seafood à la French Japanese fusion. Three course prix fixe. A quiet secret. Closed Sunday.

Trendy's, 103 Rue de Prony (M: Pereire) 40.53.05.30. Fast food.

RESTAURANTS: GASTRONOMIQUE:

Guy Savoy, 18 Rue Troyon (M: Charles de Gaulle-Etoile) 43,80.40.61. Top Ten Chefs. Top five restaurants in Paris. Closed Sunday.

Michel Rostang, 20 Rue Rennequin (M: Ternes) 47.63.40.77. Gastronomic. One of the best tables in Paris, consistently ranks among the top restaurants. Grand cuisine and grand wine list. Expensive, but worth it. Closed Sunday.

Sormani, 4 Rue du Général Lanrezac (M: Charles de Gaulle-Etoile) 43.80.13.91. Upscale w/festive trompe-l'oeil mural. Goat cheese ravioli w/black truffles, tuna carpaccio, lobster risotto. A FAVORITE. Closed Sunday.

BONNE SOIREE! PARIS AT NIGHT:

L'Ane Rouge, 3 Rue Laugier (M: Ternes) 43.80.79.97. Dinner & 2-hour comedy show in French. Call.

Jazz Club Lionel Hampton, 81 Blvd Gouvion-St-Cyr (M: Porte Maillot) Le Méridien Hotel. 40.68.30.42. Cover. Call for music schedule. A FAVORITE.

Panoramique Bar on the top floor of Hotel Concorde Lafayette. 3 Pl du General-Koenig (M: Porte Maillot) 40.68.50.68. Piano bar with stunning view of Paris.

Pau Brasil, 32 Rue de Tilsitt (M: Charles de Gaulle-Etoile) 53.57.77.66. Nightly Brazilian-themed reviews @ 9:45p.

Palais des Congres, 2 Pl de la Porte Maillot (M: Porte Maillot) 40.68.00.05. Call for plays, musicals, concerts, comedy.

Stringfellows, 27 Ave des Ternes (M: Ternes) 47.66.45.00. Restaurant and Lap Dancing cabaret. 9p to 4am. Closed Sunday.

My Special Travel Notes

17

18e. Montmartre

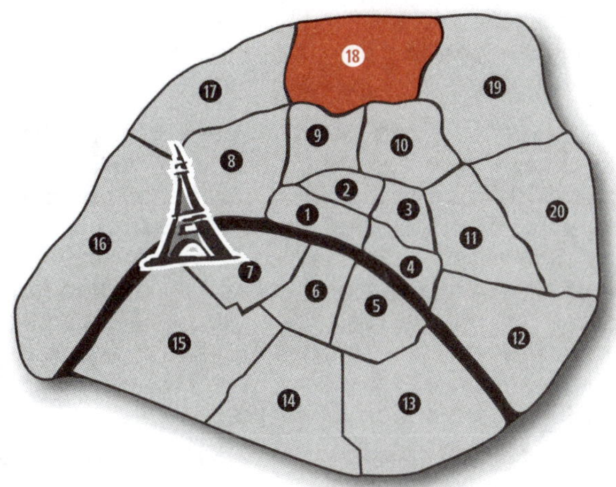

Visit the **I LOVE YOU WALL** in a lovely square.

After **Sacré Coeur Basilica,** take an afternoon stroll down to Rue St. Vincent. It's one of the Best **Places To Kiss in Paris.**

For evening entertainment, you can sing along at **L'Apin Agile** or enjoy the shows at **Moulin Rouge** or **Trianon Theatre.**

MAJOR METROS:

- ABBESSES
- LAMARCK-CAULAINCOURT
- PORTE DE CLIGNANCOURT
- GUY MOQUET
- ANVERS
- PIGALLE

18e. Montmartre

FAMOUS SIGHTS:

A good day to visit **Montmartre** is on Tuesday, when museums in the other arrondissements are closed.

Basilique Sacré Coeur - from the Parvis, Take the **Funicular** at Pl Suzanne-Valadon up to this famous church. (M: Anvers) It runs every 2 minutes and you can use a Metro ticket. The top station of the Funicular is at Pl Parvis-du-Sacré-Coeur. Fitness buffs can climb 100 meters of steps.

Stroll Montmartre from **Metro Abbesses** (**TIP!** take the elevator at this metro to avoid a very steep climb up the stairs) Walk across the street to **Square Jehan Rictus** and step into the garden with the **"I Love You" wall.** A FAVORITE. (See Diversions) Walk west on **Rue des Abbeses** - towards the cemetery. You will find a slight curve right on **Rue Lepic.** If it's lunchtime, you may consider having lunch with a view in the restaurant atop the **Terrasse Hotel.** Continue walking down Rue Lepic which then curves east. Take a left fork at **Pl JB Clement** and walk Rue Norvins to **Pl du Tertre,** filled with artists at easels, music, cafes. Or, after enjoying the I Love You wall, walk down Rue Yvonne Le Tac/Tardieu to get to the funicular at Pl Suzanne-Valadon to visit Sacré Coeur.

Exit **Sacré Coeur** and walk around to the back to **Rue de la Bonne** to **Rue St Vincent,** past **Au Lapin Agile** at 22 Rue des Saules- a famous nightclub of Paris' past, and **Rue Lepic,** where at #54 you'll find one of **Van Gogh's** former homes and #79 is the **Moulin de la Galette** (famous windmill).

Eglise St-Jean-de-Montmartre, 19 Rue des Abbesses (M: Abbesses) Church.

DIVERSIONS:

Chapelle du Martyr, 9 Rue Yvonne Le Tac (M: Abbesses) Crypt of original chapel which is built over the spot where St-Denis is said to have been martyred in 250 A.D.

Cimitière du Montmartre, 20 Ave Rachel (M: Pl de Clichy or Blanche) Open daily 8a -5 :30p. Well-landscaped cemetery where Alexendre Dumas, Edgar Degas, Leon Foucault, and Francois Truffaut are buried.

Cité Véron, Entrance at 92 Blvd de Clichy (M: Blanche) is the cul de sac to the left of Moulin Rouge and has a quirky mix of buildings. One of them is **Ophir, 8 Cité Veron,** (42.64.58.40.) a warehouse/store for the stage and theatre aficionado to find costumes, set designs, accessories.

Hair Salon: L'Abat-Jour, 19 Rue Yvonne-Le-Tac (M: Abbesses) 42.64.39.32. Patrick Rossignol and Chantal Juan run this unpretentious salon with good selection of natural products.

Marché aux Pucés Clignancourt/Pucés de St. Ouen, (M: Porte de Clignancourt) This is the end of Line 4. Walk north past the market stalls situated outside the Metro until you reach Rue de Rosiers. 5a-6p Sat/Sun/Mon. The **largest flea market in Europe,** has over 2,500 dealers and 10-15 main markets. **Vernaison,** at 99 Rue de Rosiers, is the oldest.

Metro Abbesses, (M: Abesses) is famous as one of the original metros. It is a long, steep climb up many stairs. There is also an elevator.

I LOVE YOU Wall inside Square Jehan Rictus is just across the street from M: Abbesses. Also called **Le Mur des je t'aime,** see I LOVE YOU written in every language in the world. Designed by Frederic Baron and Claire Kotis. A FAVORITE.

Musée de l'Erotisme, 72 Blvd de Clichy (M: Blanche) 42.58.28.73. Everything erotic: fertility idols, sculpture, paintings.

Musée du Vieux Montmartre, 12 Rue Cortot (M: Lamarck-Caulaincourt) 46.06.61.11. Eclectic collection of Toulouse-Lautrec paintings, André Gill caricatures. Closed Monday.

Paris Tonic Gym, 45 Rue Clignancourt (M: Chateau-Rouge) 42.23.40.33. Open daily.

Place du Tertre is filled with cafes, artists and easels, and other tourists!

Stroll along **Rue des Gardes** (M: Barbes-Roche) to find new ateliers and boutiques.

Salvadore Dali, Espace Montmartre, 9-11 Rue Poulbot (M: Abbesses) 42.64.40.10. Entrance €7. 10a-6p Open daily. Outstanding collection. A FAVORITE.

Square Suzanne-Buisson, bounded by Rue Girardon, Impasse Girardon, and Pl des Quatre-Freres-Casadesus (M: Lamarck-Caulaincourt) is great to sit and watch the petanque games, especially around mid-day.

Villa Léandre, off Ave Junot (M: Lamarck-Caulaincourt) Make a little detour down this lane to see eccentric homes owned by some creative types. At **11 Ave Junot,** open the gate to the "Artists Hamlet," **Hameau Des Artistes,** and you will glimpse a real artist community.

SUPERLATIVES:

Another **"best view" is Place Emile-Goudeau** (M: Abbesses)

Best place to kiss: 15 Rue St Vincent.

Best wine bar: Au Négociant, 27 Rue Lambert (M: Chateau-Rouge) 46.06.15.11.

Most eclectic bar: Kube bar in the Kube Hotel, 1-5 Passage Ruelle (M: La Chapelle) 42.05.20.00. Spend mega-Euros for one drink inside this bar made of ice. It's so cold they only allow you to stay for 30 minutes.

Most photographed steps: Rue Foyatier, between Pl Suzanne-Valadon and Rue Azais (M: Anvers).

18e. Montmartre

Only vineyard in Paris: Vignes Les Clos Montmartre, corner of Rue St. Vincent and Rue des Saules (near L'Apin Agile). (M: Lamarck-Caulaincourt) 1932. Closed to the public.

SHOPS:

Allison, 38 Rue des Abbesses (M: Abbesses) 42.62.37.28. Multi-chain boutique.

Antoine et Lili, 90 Rue Des Martyrs (M: Pigalle) 42.58.10.22. Stylish and trendy fashions. Several locations in Paris.

Doly'Doll, 41 Rue des Abbesses (M: Abbesses) 42.64.50.11. Funky boutique.

Emmanuelle Zysman, 81 Rue des Martyrs (M: Pigalle) 42.52.01.00. Handmade stylish bags and accessories.

Galerie Christine Diegoni, no. 47 ter, Rue d'Orsel (M: Anvers) 42.64.69.48. Art gallery.

Heaven, 83 Rue des Martyrs (M: Pigalle) 44.92.92.92. Young designers of feather lamps and fun clothes.

Kazana, 8 Rue Steinkerque (M: Anvers) 42.57.16.73. Scarves and accessories.

L'Oeil du Silence, 91 Rue des Martyrs (M: Abbesses) 42.64.45.40. Eclectic mix of books and music.

Ophir, at No. 8 in Cité Véron - see Diversions- for everything about stage, theatre, costumes. (M: Blanche) 42.64.58.40. Open M-Fri. 9a-1p. and also by appointment only.

Pamp'lune, 4 bus, Rue Piemontesi (M: Abbesses) 46.06.50.23. Upscale childrens store with hand-sewn, imaginative styles from Valerie Perrin and Evelyn Brunot. Infants – 10 year olds.

Spree, 116 Rue La Vieuville (M: Abbesses) 42.23.41.40. Clothing, jewelry, shoes, books and other one-of-a-kind collections. A FAVORITE.

Tissus Reine, 5 Pl St Pierre (M: Anvers) 46.06.02.31. Four floors of beautiful fabrics a la Project Runway.

RESTAURANTS: LES PLATS DU JOUR:

A La Mere Catherine, 7 Pl du Tertre (M: Abbesses) 46.06.32.69. Dine on terrace at Pl du Tetre or inside. Cote du Sud cooking style and wines.

A La Pomponette, 42 Rue Lepic (M: Blanche) 46.06.08.36. Old fashioned bistro since 1909. Music à la Paris, monthly. Call. Closed Sunday/lunch on Fri/Sat.

Au Bon Coin, 49 Rue des Cloys (M: Jules-Joffrin) 46.06.91.36. Good wine selections with friendly service and traditional fare. Several locations in Paris.

Au Negotiant, 27 Rue Lambert (M: L:amarck-Caulaincourt) 46.06.15.11. Wine bar that perfectly fits the neighborhood. Closed Sat/Sun.

Au Relais, 48 Rue Lamarck (M: Lamarck-Caulaincourt) 46.06.68.32. Warm and friendly atmosphere run by Christine and Carlos Martinez. Bistro fare, lots of ambiance and plenty of locals.

A. Beauvilliers, 52 Rue Lamarck (M: Lamarck-Caulaincourt) 42.54.54.42. Chef presents new French cuisine in redesigned setting. €45 lunch and dinner may get somewhat expensive.

Café Burq, 6 Rue Burq (M: Abbesses) 42.52.81.27. Fun bistro with contemporary fare and music and friendly atmosphere. Mix of young hip and locals. Closed Sunday.

Cafe del Gattopardo, 102 Rue Lepic (M: Abbesses) 42.58.06.22. Good Sicilian.

Chez Grisette, 14 Rue Houdon (M: Abbesses) 42.62.04.80. Tiny wine bistro in true Montmartre style.

L'Entr'acte Sonia et Carlos, 44 Rue d'Orsel (M: Anvers) 46.09.93.41. Simple food, full of paintings by local artists. Homestyle. Closed Sunday.

La Divette du Moulin, 98 rue Lepic (M: Abbesses) 46.06.34.84. Excellent traditional French meals and very accommodating service. A FAVORITE. Open Sunday.

La Famille, 41 Rue des Trois Freres (M: Abbesses) 42.52.11.12. Reservations suggested at this tiny restaurant. €30. Closed Sun.

La Fourmi Café, 74 Rue des Martyrs (M: Pigalle) 42.64.70.35. Simple neighborhood bistrot.

Le Moulin de la Galette, 83 Rue Lepic (M: Abbesses) 46.06.84.77. Renovated recently with new modern interior and patio. Romantic setting at reasonable prices. Open Sunday. A FAVORITE.

Le Poulbot Gourmet, 39 Rue Lamarck (M: Anvers) 46.06.86.00. French-style and good food makes this popular with the over-thirty locals. Ambiance and service add to the experience.

Le Restaurant, 32 Rue Veron (M: Abbesses) 42.23.06.22. Contemporary French with spicy flair by chef Yves Peledeau.

Le Square, 227 bis, Rue Marcardet (M: Guy Moquet) 53.11.08.41. Casual and classic French with inventive blackboard menu. Patio garden. Closed Sunday.

Soleil Gourmand, 10 Rue Ravignan (M: Abbesses) 42.51.00.50. Owned by two sisters. Provencale fare.

Terrasse Hotel, 12 Rue Joseph-du-Maitre (M: Blanche) 46.06.72.85. 7th floor roof garden restaurant and salon de tea.

Wepler, 14 Pl de Clichy (M:Clichy) 45.22.53.29. Late-night Parisian hangout for oysters & sauerkraut.

BONNE SOIREE! PARIS AT NIGHT:

Au Lapin Agile, 22 Rue des Saules (M: Lamarck-Caulaincourt) 46.06.85.87. Perfect picture of a French bohemian style sing-along. €24 Cover includes first drink.

Autour de Midi, 11 Rue Lepic (M: Blanche) 55.79.16.48. A Montmartre institution where you will find a good mix of jazz, ambiance, and hefty meals, along with friendly service. Call for music schedule. Closed Monday.

Aux Noctambules, 24 Blvd de Clichy (M: Pigalle) 46.06.16.38. Enjoy the house act, Pierre Carre, who sings French classics while playing accordion or keyboard. Open til the wee hours, where you can order champagne or a vodka slushie.

Chao Ba Café, 22 Blvd de Clichy (M: Pigalle) 46.06.72.90. Lounge, exotic drinks, funky music. 11a-2a Sun-Wed/til 4a on Thurs and 5a on Fri-Sat.

Elysée-Montmartre, 76 Blvd Rochechouart (M: Anvers) 44.92.45.36. Theatre hall, festive monthly parties. Call.

Le Canotier du Pied de la Butte, 62 Blvd Rochechouart (M: Anvers) 46.06.02.86. Reservations required for performances of nostalgic French songs.

Le Divan du Monde, 75 Rue des Martyrs (M: Pigalle) 42.52.02.46. World music. Cheap drinks. Young crowd.

Moulin Rouge, 82 Blvd du Clichy. 53.09.82.82. The show is great! 9 pm and 11pm. A FAVORITE. We like to go to dinner and get there at 10:30-ish to stand in line for 11p show. Make sure you stop in gift shop for CD and other souvenirs. At end of show, be prepared for everyone trying to hail taxis at the same time.

Theatre de L'Atelier, 1 Pl Charles-Dullin (M: Anvers) 46.06.49.24. Truly Parisian, with red velvet seats. Call Box office Mon. -Sat 11a-7p.

Trianon Théâtre, 80 Blvd Rochechouart (M: Anvers) 44.92.78.03. Theatre and concert hall with red velvet seats. Call for show schedule.

My Special Travel Notes

18

My Special Travel Notes

18

19e. Buttes-Chaumont

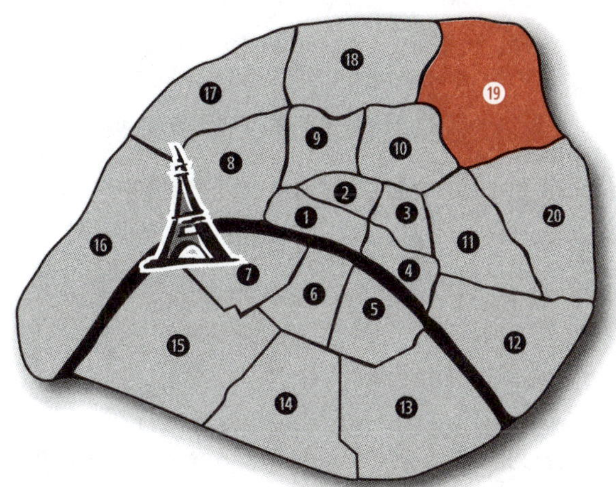

Visit the **Cité de la Musique museum** and you'll see more than 4000 musical instruments. enjoy the café, too.

Children will love the **Cité des Sciences et de l'Industrie** and **La Géode.**

Follow the blue path in **Parc Villette** through ten beautiful gardens.

MAJOR METROS:

- STALINGRAD
- LAUMIERE
- PORTE DE PANTIN
- PORTE DE LA VILLETTE
- BUTTES CHAUMONT
- PORTE DES LILAS

DIVERSIONS:

Canal de l'Ourcq, Amazing gardens in Parc Villette. Follow the blue promenade path through 10 gardens.

Canal St. Martin trips can begin/end at (M: Jaurès)

Cité de la Musique/ Musée de la Musique, 221 Ave Jean-Jaurès (M: Porte de Pantin) 44.84.44.84. See more than 4000 musical instruments. €6.10. Closed Mon.

Parc des Buttes-Chaumont (M: Buttes-Chaumont) Rue Botzaris or Rue Manin (M: Buttes-Chaumont) Example of Hausmann landscaping with grottoes, suspension bridges, waterfalls. Acclaimed to be similar to Central Park, NYC.

Parc de La Villette, 30 Ave Corentin-Cariou. 40.05.81.41. (M: Porte de la Villette) 10a-6p. Tues-Sunday. A FAVORITE. You will find **Cité des Sciences et de l'Industrie** - a vast place filled with exhibits. Good for children, with a multimedia library, planetarium, "inventorium" and **La Géode.** 40.05.80.00. (M: Porte de La Villette).

RESTAURANTS: LES PLATS DU JOUR:

Au Boeuf Couronné, 188 Jean Jaures (M: Porte de Pantin) 42.39.44.44. Classic French cuts of meat served in what was once an old slaughterhouse. A FAVORITE.

Bar Fleuri, 1 Rue du Plateau (M: Buttes Chaumont) 42.08.13.38. Classic. Closed Sunday.

Café de la Musique, Pl Fontaine aux Lions (M: Porte de Pantin) 48.03.15.91. Another restaurant owned by Côstes brothers. Open Sunday.

Chez Vincent, 5 Rue du Tunnel (M: Botzaris) 42.02.22.45. Chef-owner Vincent Cozzoli serves premium-priced pasta, loved by the jet-set.

La Cave Gourmande, 10 Rue du General Brunet (M: Botzaris) 40.40.03.30. Small, cozy. Prix fixe meals only €32. Friendly service. Closed Sat/Sunday.

Lao Siam, 49 Rue de Belleville (M: Belleville) 40.40.09.68. Quality Thai at lower prices. Open Sunday.

BONNEE SOIREE! PARIS AT NIGHT:

Cirque du Grand Céleste, 13 Ave de la Porte des Lilas (M: Porte de Lilas) 53.19.99.13. Here is a special night under the stars. Make reservations for dinner in a garden served to you by the circus performers. After dinner, you move into the "small top" and sit in armchairs, sofas, benches and enjoy circus (sans animals)... followed by joining the performers for salsa dancing after the show. Seasonal.

Zenith concert hall, 211 Ave Jean Jaurès (M: Porte de Pantin) 8. 92.68.36.22. Call for shows.

My Special Travel Notes

My Special Travel Notes

19

20e. Ménilmontant

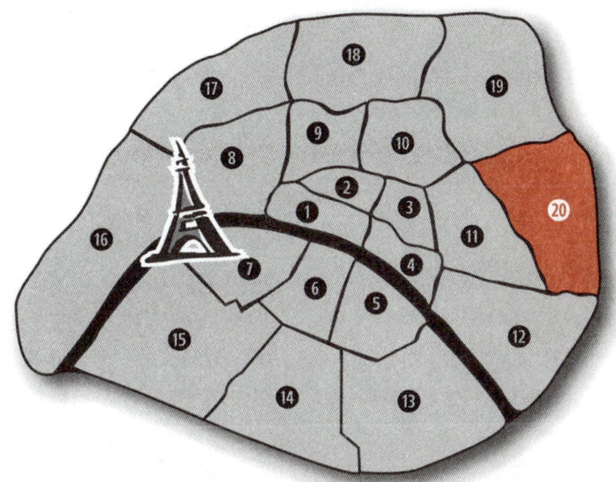

Buy a map of the **Cimetière de Pere Lachaise** to find the graves of Jim Morrison, Edith Piaf, Gertrude Stein, Frederik Chopin, Colette, and Oscar Wilde.

Sing along at **Le Vieux Belleville** after your dinner.

Les Allobroges has a superb prix fixe menu at savory prices. Worth the trip!

MAJOR METROS:
- BELLEVILLE
- PÈRE LACHAISE
- MÉNILMONTANT
- GAMBETTA
- PORTE DE MONTREUIL

20e. Ménilmontant

DIVERSIONS:

Walk around Belleville - a hip, funky neighborhood filled with cafés. Relax in the park. (M: Couronnes). A FAVORITE.

Le Jardin Naturel, natural ecosystem of wild plants and trees indigenous to the city. Enter at 120 Rue de la Réunion. (M: Alexandre Dumas).

Les Lucioles, 102 Blvd de Ménilmontant (M: Ménilmontant) 40.33.10.24. Poetry readings Tuesday evenings. Poets will receive a free drink, if you read a poem.

Cimetière de Père Lâchaise, (M: Père Lachaise) A very famous cemetery - buy map from vendor. Frederic Chopin, Colette, Oscar Wilde, Gertrude Stein, Edith Piaf, Jim Morrison are all buried here. A FAVORITE.

SUPERLATIVES:

Best pâtisserie: Chez Nani, 104 Rue de Belleville (M: Belleville) 47.97.38.05. Scrumptious pastries.

Best sing-along dinner: Le Vieux Belleville, 12 Rue des Envierges (M: Pyrénées) 44.62.92.66. Call to reserve seat at one of the long tables to dine and then sing along to accordion music, organ, or swing. Music begins 9p. Tues-Thurs.

Best Wine bar: Le Baratin. See Restaurants.

Biggest independent bookstore: Le Merle Moqueur. See Shops.

Grand Prix de la Baguette: Eric Sanna's Retro d'Or, 3 Rue du Retrait (M: Gambetta) 47.97.53.04.

SHOPS:

Best Affaires, 94 Rue de Bagnolet (M: Alexandre Dumas) 43.67.10.25. Housewares bazaar not to be missed if you are in area.

Eric Sanna's Retro d'Or, 3 Rue du Retrait (M: Gambetta) 47.97.53.04 Winner of Grand Prix de la Baguette.

Le Merle Monqueur, 51 Rue Bagnolet (M: Alexandre Dumas) 40.09.08.80. Book shop.

RESTAURANTS: LES PLATS DU JOUR:

Brasserie Le Soleil, 136 Blvd de Ménilmontant (M: Ménilmontant) 46.36.47.44. Small brasserie with terrace. Very local.

La Boulangerie, 15 Rue des Panoyaux (M: Ménilmontant) 43.58.45.45. Popular neighborhood restaurant. Original twist on classic French cuisine at reasonable prices. Open Sunday.

La Mère Lachaise, 78 Blvd de Ménilmontant (M: Ménilmontant) 47.97.61.60. Fabulous terrace.

La Renaissance, 28 Blvd Ménilmontant (M: Ménilmontant) 43.71.90.64. Terrace. Good corner. Reliable food.

Le Baratin, 3 Rue Jouye Rouve (M: Pyrénées) 43.49.39.70. Good food and well-stocked wine cellar. Inquire to see the "private reserve" wine list. Reserve ahead. A FAVORITE.

Le Piston Pélican, 15 Rue de Bagnolet (M: Alexander Dumas) 43.70.35.00. Basic café. Lunch for two $19.

Le Vieux Belleville, 12 Rue des Envierges (M: Pyrénées) 44.62.92.66. Reserve a seat at one of the communal tables to dine and sing along to accordion music, organ, or other musical pleasures. Music begins at 9p. Open Tues-Thurs.

Le Zephyr, 1 Rue du Jourdain (M: Jourdain) 46.36.65.81. Art deco setting with good prix fixe menu by chef-owner Enne. Open Sunday.

Les Allobroges, 71 Rue des Grands Champs (M: Maraîchers) 43.73.40.00. Great, classic bistro. Prix fixe savory menu at affordable prices. It's worth the trip. A FAVORITE. Closed Sunday.

BONNE SOIREE! PARIS AT NIGHT:

La Maroquinerie, 23 Rue Boyer (M: Ménilmontant) 40.33.35.06. Theatre, music. Call for schedule.

Studio de l'Ermitage, 8 Rue de l'Ermitage (M: Ménilmontant) 44.62.02.86. Avant-garde scene, young jazz bands.

My Special Travel Notes

20

Photos

4e. Hôtel de Ville

7e. Les Invalides

18e. Mime in Montmartré

5e. Bookinistes along the Seine

8e. Petit Palais

18e. Sacré Coeur

11e. Place de la Bastille

7e. Tour d'Eiffel

7e. Picnic at Champs de Mars

7e. Musée d'Orsay

le. Musée du Louvre from Pont Neuf

7e. Musée Rodin

Index

TIP! Names of restaurants can be a little confusing because of all the le's and la's and sometimes Parisians will drop the prefix when referring to a favorite place. You will often find that the prefix is different in printed directories. We have tried to get it right. When using this Index, check all the varieties if you are not sure. Merci beaucoup!

Index

Index

Index

Index

L'Opportun, 14e
L'Orangerie, 4e
L'Os à Moelle, 15e
L'Osteria, 4e
L'Oulette, 12e
L'Ourcine, 13e
La Bague de Kenza, 11e
La Balade au Couer des Sens, 4e
La Bastide Odeon, 6e
La Belle Ecole, 16e
La Belle Epoque, 2e
La Belle Hortense, 4e
La Biche en Bois, 12e
La Boca, 10e
La Boite à Musique, 7e
La Boulangerie, 20e
La Boutique du Palais Royal, 1e
La Braisière, 17e
La Brasserie Italiana, 6e
La Brouette, 5e
La Bulle Kenzo, 1e
La Butte Chaillot, 16e
La Butte-aux-Cailles, 13e
La Cabane, 17e
La Cagouille, 14e
La Cantine du Faubourg, 8e
La Casbah, 10e
La Castafiore, 4e
La Cave de L'Insolité, 11e
La Cave Gourmande, 19e
La Cerisaie, 14e
La Chaise au Plafond, 4e
La Chaise Lounge, 1e/4e
La Chambre Claire, 6e
La Chapelle Miraculeuse, 7e
La Charrue et les Etioles, 3e
La Cigale Recamier, 7e
La Clo, 7e
La Cloche des Halles, 1e
La Cloche d'Or, 9e
La Closerie de Lilas, 6e
La Contre Allée, 14e
La Corbeille, 3e
La Cordonnerie, 1e
La Cornue, 6e
La Corte, 1e
La Coupole, 14e
La Cour Jardin, 8e
La Cremerie, 6e
La Crémerie Caves Miard, 6e
La Creperie de Josselin, 14e
La Creperie Saint Germain, 6e
La Cuisine, 7e
La Derniere Goûte, 6e
La Dinée, 15e
La Divette du Moulin, 18e
La Droguerie, 1e
La Famille, 18e
La Farnesina, 8e
La Ferme des Mathurins, 8e
La Ferme Saint-Simon, 7e
La Fermette du Sud-Ouest, 1e
La Fermette Marbeuf, 8e
La Ferrandaise, 6e
La Folie en Tete, 13e
La Fontaine, 10e
La Fontaine de Mars, 7e
La Fontaine Gaillon, 2e
La Fourmi Café, 18e
La Fournée d'Augustin, 14e
La Galerie D'Architecture, 4e
La Gare, 16e
La Gazetta, 12e
La Geode, 19e
La Grande Galerie del'Evolution, 5e
La Grand Rue, 15e
La Grande Armée, 16e
La Grande Cascade, 16e
La Grille, 10e
La Grille Montorgueil, 2e
La Guirlande de Julie, 3e
La Licorne, 4e
La Madonnina, 10e
La Main d'Or, 11e
La Main de la Paté, 6e
La Maison Blanche, 8e
La Maison Courtine, 14e
La Maison de L'Aubrac, 8e
La Maison de la Chine, 6e
La Maison des Arts et Metiers, 16e
La Maison des Millesimes, 6e
La Maison des Trois Thés, 5e
La Maison du Chocolate, 8e
La Maison du Haut, 2e
La Maison du Jardin, 6e
La Maison du Miel, 8e
La Maison Rouge, 12e
La Marée Verte, 5e
La Marine, 10e
La Marlotte, 6e
La Maroquinerie, 20e
La Mascotte, 8e
La Maxence, 6e
La Méditerranée, 6e
La Mere Lachaise, 20e
La Methode, 5e
La Moulin de la Galette, 18e
La Mousson, 1e
La Muse Vin, 11e
La Palette, 6e
La Perla Bar, 4e
La Petite Auberge, 15e
La Petite Cour, 6e
La Petite Fabrique, 11e
La Petite Robe Noir, 1e
La Pince à Sucre, 13e
La Poule au Pot, 7e
La Quincaillerie, 5e
La Regalade, 14e
La Renaissance, 20e
La Rhumerie, 6e
La Robe et la Palais, 1e
La Rose de France, 4e
La Rôtisserie d'Armaille, 17e
La Rotisserie D'en Face, 6e
La Rotisserie du Beaujolais, 5e
La Ruccola, 17e
La Ruche, 15e
La Saint Amarante, 12e

Index

Index

Index

Index

My Special Travel Notes

My Special Travel Notes

My Special Travel Notes